A TEXTBOOK OF

PHYSICAL ACTIVITY TRAINER

Subject Code: 845 | Skill Education

Including Part A and Part B

(As per Latest NEP Guidelines)

11
CBSE

Name ....

Class .... Section............ Roll No.............

School ....

Address ....

Phone ....

Dr. Rakesh Bharti

Dr. Mali Ram Yadav

A TEXTBOOK OF
PHYSICAL ACTIVITY TRAINER

Subject Code: 845 | Skill Education

Including Part A and Part B

(As per Latest NEP Guidelines)

CLASS XI

By:

Dr. Rakesh Bharti
Dr. Mali Ram Yadav

S.K. KATARIA & SONS®
Educational Publishers
4885/109, Prakash Mahal, Dr. Subhash Bhargav Lane,
Opposite Delhi Medical Association, Daryaganj, New Delhi-110002 (INDIA)
Phone: +91-11-43551243, *Mobile:* +91-9871775858, 7678425209
e-mail: katariabook@gmail.com, katariabooks@yahoo.com
Website: www.skkatariaandsons.com
(e-books, subscriptions and bulk buying also available on our website)

Published by:

S.K. Kataria & Sons®

4885/109, Prakash Mahal, Dr. Subhash Bhargav Lane,
Opposite Delhi Medical Association, Daryaganj, New Delhi-110002 (INDIA)
Phone: +91-11-43551243, *Mobile:* +91-9871775858, 7678425209
e-mail: katariabook@gmail.com, katariabooks@yahoo.com
Website: www.skkatariaandsons.com

First Edition: 2025-2026 Reprint: 2026-2027

ISBN: 978-93-49499-06-5

Laser Typesetting by : PANWAR COMPUTERS *Printed at :* ATHARV ENTERPRISES

PREFACE

Physical education plays a vital role in the holistic development of individuals, fostering physical fitness, mental well-being, and social skills. This work aims to highlight the importance of physical education in shaping a healthy and active lifestyle, emphasizing its impact on overall growth, discipline, teamwork, and resilience.

Through this study, I explore various aspects of physical education, including its significance in academic settings, the benefits of sports and fitness activities, and the challenges faced in its implementation. By shedding light on these areas, I hope to contribute to a greater appreciation of physical education and its essential role in personal and societal well-being.

Authors

ACKNOWLEDGEMENTS

I extend my sincere gratitude to all those who have contributed to the completion of this work. My heartfelt thanks go to my mentors and teachers for their invaluable guidance, support, and encouragement throughout this journey. Their expertise and insights have been instrumental in shaping this study.

I am also deeply grateful to the physical education instructors, coaches, and students who shared their experiences and knowledge, enriching this research with real-world perspectives. Their dedication to promoting fitness and well-being has been truly inspiring.

Lastly, I express my appreciation to my family and friends for their constant encouragement and belief in my efforts. Their unwavering support has been a source of motivation throughout this endeavor.

Authors

CBSE | DEPARTMENT OF SKILL EDUCATION
CURRICULUM FOR CLASS XI

PHYSICAL ACTIVITY TRAINER

(Subject Code–845)

COURSE OVERVIEW

Physical Education Assistant (Primary Years) works in a primary school, an apartment and clubs to teach basic sports to build sports skills and fitness for children up to the age of 12 years. He/she is involved in conducting play activities, coaching, mentoring and training children at primary level. Physical fitness is considered a measure of the body's ability to function efficiently, effectively and without injury in work and leisure activities. The responsibilities of the individual include the implementation and delivery of an appropriately broad, balanced, relevant and differentiated physical education curriculum for students and preparing and inducting students for competitive sports. S/he needs to ensure that students are physically active within the physical education class.

COURSE OUTCOMES

On completion of the course, students should be able to:

1. Apply effective oral and written communication skills to interact with people and customers;
2. Identify the principal components of a computer system;
3. Demonstrate the basic skills of using computer;
4. Demonstrate self-management skills;
5. Demonstrate the ability to provide a self-analysis in context of entrepreneurial skills and abilities;
6. Demonstrate the knowledge of the importance of physical activity in child development;
7. Demonstrate the knowledge of hygiene and safety;
8. Demonstrate the application of Ms. Excel in maintenance of records;
9. Describe the purpose of emergency management;
10. Follow steps for maintaining health and hygiene in the play area;
11. Demonstrate the knowledge of the importance of green skills in meeting the challenges of sustainable development and environment protection and perform assessment and evaluation of students.

SYLLABUS

CBSE | DEPARTMENT OF SKILL EDUCATION

PHYSICAL ACTIVITY TRAINER

CLASS XI (Session 2026-2027)

(Subject Code–845)

Total Marks: 100 *(Theory-50 + Practical-50)*

<table>
<tr><th></th><th>UNITS</th><th colspan="2">No. of Hours for Theory and Practical</th><th>Max. Marks For Theory and Practical</th></tr>
<tr><td></td><td colspan="4">EMPLOYABILITY SKILLS</td></tr>
<tr><td rowspan="6">PART A</td><td>Unit-1: Communication Skills-III</td><td colspan="2">15</td><td>2</td></tr>
<tr><td>Unit-2: Self-management Skills-III</td><td colspan="2">10</td><td>2</td></tr>
<tr><td>Unit-3: Information and Communication Technology Skills-III</td><td colspan="2">15</td><td>2</td></tr>
<tr><td>Unit-4: Entrepreneurial Skills-III</td><td colspan="2">10</td><td>2</td></tr>
<tr><td>Unit-5: Green Skills-III</td><td colspan="2">10</td><td>2</td></tr>
<tr><td>Total</td><td colspan="2">60</td><td>10</td></tr>
<tr><td rowspan="6">PART B</td><td>SUBJECT-SPECIFIC SKILLS</td><td>Theory</td><td>Practical</td><td>Total</td></tr>
<tr><td>Unit 1: Role of Physical Education in Child Development</td><td>19</td><td>27</td><td>13</td></tr>
<tr><td>Unit 2: Props and Equipment</td><td>9</td><td>18</td><td>6</td></tr>
<tr><td>Unit 3: Hygiene and Safety</td><td>13</td><td>18</td><td>8</td></tr>
<tr><td>Unit 4: Sports and Fitness</td><td>19</td><td>27</td><td>13</td></tr>
<tr><td>Total</td><td>60</td><td>90</td><td>40</td></tr>
<tr><td rowspan="4">PART C</td><td colspan="4">PRACTICAL WORK</td></tr>
<tr><td>Practical Examination</td><td colspan="2"></td><td>15</td></tr>
<tr><td>Written Test</td><td colspan="2"></td><td>10</td></tr>
<tr><td>Viva Voce</td><td colspan="2"></td><td>10</td></tr>
<tr><td></td><td>Total</td><td colspan="2"></td><td>35</td></tr>
<tr><td rowspan="4">PART D</td><td colspan="4">PROJECT WORK/FIELD VISIT</td></tr>
<tr><td>Practical File/Student Portfolio</td><td colspan="2"></td><td>10</td></tr>
<tr><td>Viva Voce</td><td colspan="2"></td><td>05</td></tr>
<tr><td>Total</td><td colspan="2"></td><td>15</td></tr>
<tr><td></td><td>Grand Total</td><td colspan="2">210</td><td>100</td></tr>
</table>

SYLLABUS

DETAILED CURRICULUM/TOPICS FOR CLASS XI
PHYSICAL ACTIVITY TRAINER
(CODE–845)

PART–A: EMPLOYABILITY SKILLS

S.No.	Units	Duration in Hours
1.	Unit-1: Communication Skills-III	13
2.	Unit-2: Self-management Skills-III	07
3.	Unit-3: Information and Communication Technology Skills-III	13
4.	Unit-4: Entrepreneurial Skills-III	10
5.	Unit-5: Green Skills-III	7
	Total	**50**

NOTE: Detailed Curriculum/ Topics to be covered under Part A: Employability Skills can be downloaded from CBSE website.

PART–B: SUBJECT SPECIFIC SKILLS

- Unit-1: Role of Physical Education in Child Development
- Unit-2: Props and Equipment
- Unit-3: Hygiene and Safety
- Unit-4: Sports and Fitness

UNIT-1: 1: ROLE OF PHYSICAL EDUCATION IN CHILD DEVELOPMENT

Learning Outcomes	Theory	Practical
1. Identify the physical and emotional needs of the children	1. Physical and emotional needs of children 2. Health triangle • Physical health • Mental health • Social health	1. Prepare chart on Health triangle
2. Identify factors influencing physical activities	1. Factors affecting physical fitness 2. Influence of sports in well being 3. Influence of society on sports based on • Environment • Economy • Technology • Political	1. Group activity on demonstration of factors influencing physical activities 2. Group discussion on how behavioral factors influence physical activity
3. Create different levels of physical activities planning for children	1. Identifying physical activity sessions 2. Structuring physical activity sessions 3. Macro-planning 4. Meso-planning 5. Micro-planning 6. Weekly planning 7. Yoga and their benefits 8. Lesson plans for various physical activities	1. Prepare flow chart on planning cycle. 2. Preparation of lesson plans for various physical activities

UNIT-2: PROPS AND EQUIPMENT

Learning Outcomes	Theory	Practical
1. Identify the various factors that need to be considered while selecting props and equipment	1. Selection of props and equipment 2. Purpose and importance of props and equipment 3. Factors affecting the selection of props and equipment	1. List down factors affecting selection of props and equipment 2. Preparation of poster of props and equipment 3. Preparation of list of equipment for conducting physical and sports activities.

Learning Outcomes	Theory	Practical
2. Identify the reasons affecting the playground and equipment condition	1. Inspection of Playfields • Low frequency inspections • High frequency inspections 2. Maintenance of sport facilities	1. Prepare a timetable for the inspection of playfield area 2. List down the safety measure to be kept in mind while doing playfield inspection

UNIT-3: HYGIENE AND SAFETY

Learning Outcomes	Theory	Practical
1. Identify the steps required in maintenance of hygiene in play area	1. Maintenance of hygiene in Play Area	1. Identification of cleaning materials for play area 2. List the steps to maintain hygiene at playground.
2. Demonstrate the knowledge of basic First- Aid practices	1. First Aid 2. First Aid - Purpose and basic principle 3. Cuts and bruises 4. Heat exhaustion 5. Breathing difficulties 6. Choking 7. Basic sports injuries • Sprain • Strain 8. First Aid for Sprains 9. Concept of First Aid kit	1. Prepare a poster on First Aid principles 2. Conduct on ground demonstration of first aid
3. Identify sports injuries and its rehabilitation processes	1. Types of sports injuries 2. How do you prevent sports injuries? 3. First Aid – CPR (Cardiopulmonary resuscitation) 4. Rehabilitation of sports injuries 5. Exercise for rehabilitation	1. Preparation of flowchart on the sequential steps of CPR 2. Demonstration of CPR

UNIT-4: SPORTS AND FITNESS

Learning Outcomes	Theory	Practical
1. Describe the criteria for selecting yearly sports activities	1. Health and Physical fitness 2. Benefits of Physical fitness 3. Stages of Team selection 4. Process of Talent Detection, Identification and Development • Football • Basketball • Volleyball	1. Preparation of chart for selection of students for competition 2. Group discussion on importance of resources for conduction of sports competition
2. Identify resources required for organizing sports competition	1. Organizing sports day • Pre Sports Day • Sports Day • Post Sports Day 2. Organizing Tournament • Pre-tournament Day • Tournament Day • Post-tournament Day	1. Preparation of chart for describing the various aspects of organising sports competition 2. Preparation of chart for describing the various aspects of organising tournament
3. Importance of fitness sessions	1. Aerobic capacity 2. Anaerobic capacity 3. Strength 4. Flexibility 5. Warm-up 6. Benefits of Proper Warm-up	1. List down the important point to be kept in mind before beginning any physical activity

WORK DETAIL

S.No.	Chapter Name	Date	Teacher's Signature

MY PERFORMANCE

Date	Text/ Exam	Marks Grade Obtained			Highest Marks/Grade in the class	Teacher's Remarks	Parents Signature
		Theory	Practical	Total			

CONTENTS

PART A

EMPLOYBILITY SKILLS

- **UNIT 1:** Communication Skills-III
- **UNIT 2:** Self-Management Skills-III
- **UNIT 3:** Information and Communication Technology Skills-III
- **UNIT 4:** Entrepreneurial Skills-III
- **UNIT 5:** Green Skills-III

UNIT 1 Communication Skills—III

UNIT OUTLINE

- **Session 1:** Introduction to Communication Skills
- **Session 2:** Verbal Communication
- **Session 3:** Non-Verbal Communication
- **Session 4:** Communication Styles – Assertiveness
- **Session 5:** Writing Skills: Parts of Speech
- **Session 6:** Writing Skills: Sentences

SESSION 1: INTRODUCTION TO COMMUNICATION SKILLS

1.1. Introduction to Communication Skills

"Communication is a skill that you can learn. It's like riding a bicycle or typing. If you're willing to work at it, you can rapidly improve the quality of every part of your life."

–Brian Tracy

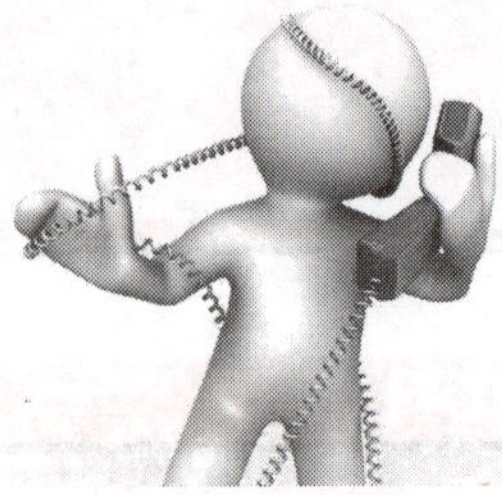

To see **Introduction to Communication Skills** in Action

Scan QR Code

Communication skills are essential for expressing ideas and emotions clearly through speaking or writing. Mastering these skills is the key to becoming an effective communicator. A person who can communicate his thoughts clearly and simply, using vocabulary and content that the audience can understand, can be an effective speaker or writer. Effective communication encompasses not only speaking and writing but also the ability to listen actively and read with understanding

Being multilingual enhances communication. While we are often most comfortable with our mother tongue, English has become a significant language for global conversations. Proficiency in English, combined with strong communication skills, is valuable in any profession.

1.2. Importance of Communication

To see **Importance of Communication** in Action

Scan QR Code

The term 'communication' comes from the Latin word 'communicare', which means 'to share' or 'to participate'. Communication involves sharing information to achieve mutual understanding. Effective communication is vital in all relationships and interactions. It serves various purposes:

(*i*) **Information:** Sharing facts or information, such as informing a friend about a class test.

(*ii*) **Influencing:** Changing someone's opinion or helping them with a problem, like convincing a friend to join a party.

(*iii*) **Expressing Feelings:** Sharing emotions and experiences, such as describing a cricket match to friends.

1.3. Elements of Communication

To see **Elements of Communication** in Action

Scan QR Code

Communication is a two-way exchange that involves both sharing and receiving information. We convey information through speaking or writing, and we receive it by listening or reading.

1.4. Various Perspectives on Communication

A communication perspective focuses on the way of thinking, the manner in which a message transmits information, and how our ideas or messages are evaluated by others. This perspective examines how messages are produced, circulated among groups, and interpreted. For instance, if your mother is very strict, even if she tries to help you or speak softly, you may still feel that she is scolding you or being rude.

Communication always makes a difference. Acquiring a communication perspective involves learning how to make a positive difference in the world using language, symbols, and messages.

1.5. Barriers to Communication

Various barriers or influencing factors can impact our communication skills or shape how we perceive communication.

To see **Barriers to Communication** in Action

Scan QR Code

Communication barriers are obstacles that arise in the communication process. These barriers may occur at any stage of the communication process, i.e., while the message is being transmitted, developed, received, or interpreted. Due to these obstacles, the intended message may not be communicated effectively, and the message is not received in its original form. Communication is successful only if the receiver understands what the sender is trying to convey. If your message is not clearly interpreted or the receiver does not provide the desired feedback, you are facing a communication barrier. To understand these barriers better, let's discuss the process of communication to identify how and where these barriers arise.

1.6. Communication Process

The communication process includes several stages, each with potential barriers:

(i) **Source:** The sender of the communication.

(ii) **Message:** The information being communicated.

(iii) **Encoding:** Translating the message into a suitable format.

(iv) **Channel:** The medium used for communication, such as face-to-face or email.

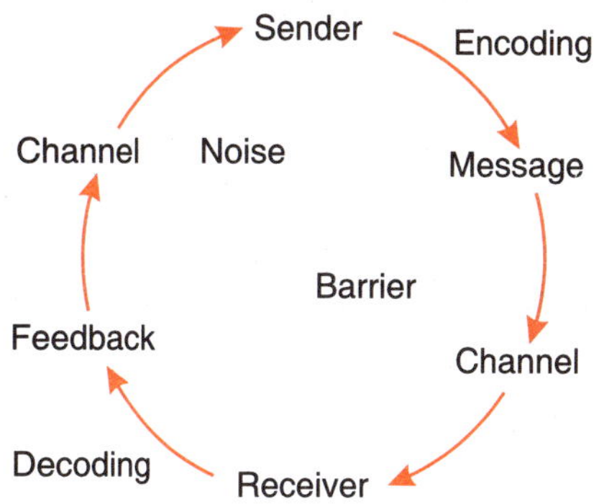

Fig. 1.1 Process of Communication

(v) **Decoding:** Interpreting the received message.

(vi) **Receiver:** The person for whom the message is intended.

(vii) **Feedback:** The response to the message indicates successful communication.

(viii) **Context:** The situation in which communication occurs.

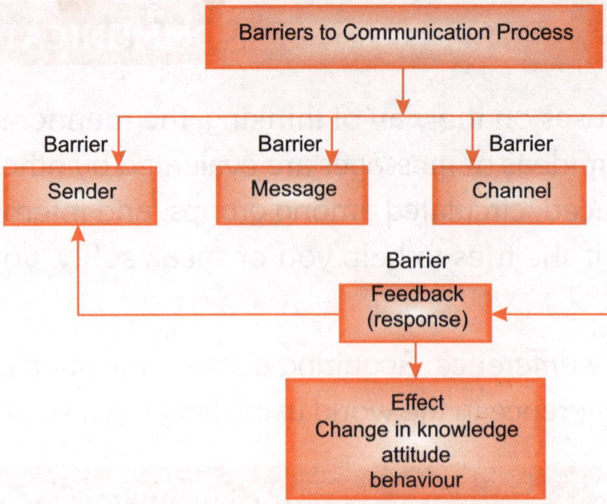

Fig. 1.2 Barriers to Communication Process

1.7. Barriers to Effective Communication

These barriers may arise when the sender encodes the message with the help of a channel, but it does not reach the receiver in its original form due to obstacles in between, such as noise barriers, human noise, traffic noise, or internal thoughts.

1.8. Types of Barriers

Barriers can be classified into two categories: Internal and External.

(*i*) **Internal Barriers:** These are obstacles that originate from within the individual, such as personal biases, emotions, or cognitive limitations.

(*ii*) **External Barriers:** These are external obstacles that stem from the environment, such as physical noise, technical difficulties, or other distractions in the surroundings.

1.9. Definition of Barriers

Definition 1: A barrier is anything that impedes the communication process and prevents the intended meaning of the message from reaching the receiver.

Definition 2: Errors, misunderstandings, and several other factors can prevent us from sharing our ideas meaningfully.

1.9.1 Understanding Communication Barriers

Communication barriers can be broadly categorised into three types: **intrapersonal, interpersonal, and organizational**.

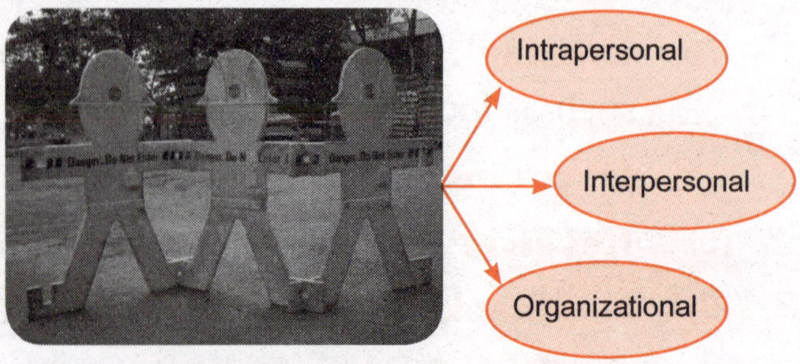

Fig. 1.3 Types of Barriers

(*i*) **Intrapersonal barriers** stem from a person's attitude or habits.

(*ii*) **Interpersonal barriers** arise due to inappropriate exchanges of words between two or more persons because of:

(*i*) Inefficient communication skills

(*ii*) Negative aspects of nurturing in the climate

(*iii*) **Organizational barriers** occur due to a rigid and hierarchical structure.

1.9.2 Intrapersonal and Interpersonal Barriers

Intrapersonal barriers arise from incorrect assumptions, varied perceptions, differing backgrounds, wrong inferences, resistance to change (misoneism), and categorical thinking (pansophism). For instance, miscommunication can occur if a doctor assumes a patient understands medical jargon. Similarly, varied perceptions, such as different interpretations of the same situation, and differing backgrounds, like diverse cultural or educational experiences, can lead to misunderstandings. Wrong inferences — like assuming that some colleagues were laid off when they were actually promoted, highlight the need for fact-based communication. Resistance to new technologies and categorical thinking also hinder effective communication.

Interpersonal barriers include incongruity between verbal and non-verbal messages, selective listening, cultural variations, poor listening skills, and noise in the communication channel. For example, a CEO's inconsistent body language during an introduction can confuse listeners, and selective listening occurs when a receiver only hears parts of a message that interests them. Cultural differences and poor listening skills also impede communication, as do various forms of noise, such as audio or visual disturbances.

Organizational barriers encompass too many transfer stations, fear of superiors, negative tendencies within groups, inappropriate media use, and information overload. Excessive links in a communication chain increase the risk of miscommunication, while rigid hierarchies may prevent honest feedback. Groups formed within Organizational can also create communication barriers if they have negative tendencies. The choice of inappropriate media and the overwhelming volume of information further complicate effective communication. Prioritising quality over quantity in information dissemination is crucial for maintaining clear and efficient communication within organizations.

1.9.3 How to Overcome Communication Barriers

Communication is a vital management function. Success depends largely on effective communication. To overcome barriers, the following measures should be adopted:

- Clear and Brief Messages
- Continuous Process
- Mutual Faith and Trust
- Proper Medium and Transmission Technique
- Use of the Seven C's
- Adequate Facilities
- Appropriate Language
- Emphasising Key Points

- Eliminating Environmental Barriers
- Sensitivity to the Receiver's Point of View
- Using Direct, Simple Language
- Supportive Communication
- Shortening Scalar Chain
- Encouraging Subordinates to Express
- Listening Patiently
- Facilitating Feedback
- Listening to Understand
- Using Proper Channels
- Being Brief
- Keeping an Open Mind
- Paying Complete Attention

1.9.4 Key Takeaways

Communication barriers are obstacles in the communication process.

These barriers can arise at any stage of the communication process: while the message is developed, transmitted, received, or interpreted.

Due to these obstacles, what is intended to be communicated does not get communicated.

The most common reason is that the message is not received in its original form.

To overcome barriers to communication, pay attention to details, strive to understand the target meaning, consider your non-verbal expressions, and review, reflect, and revise.

1.9.5 The 7 C's of Communication

To see **7 C's of Communication** in Action

Scan QR Code

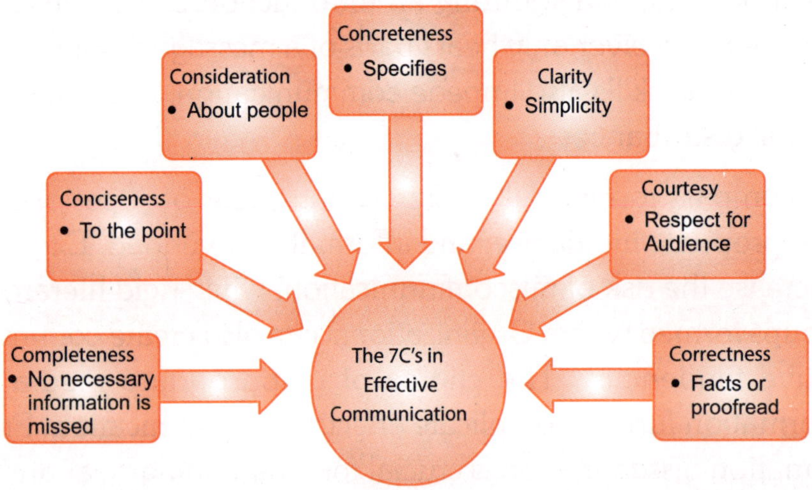

Fig. 1.4 7C's of Communication

The 7 C's of communication act as a helpful checklist to enhance communication skills and ensure the message is understood as intended. Following these seven principles is key to communicating effectively.

1. **Clear:** The message should be clear and effectively convey its intended meaning to the recipient. For this to happen, the sender must first have a clear understanding of the purpose of the communication. The message should focus on one main idea at a time, avoiding the confusion that can come from trying to express too many thoughts in a single sentence.

2. **Correct:** The message should be communicated in the correct language, with no grammatical or spelling mistakes. Additionally, the message should be timely and precise.
3. **Complete:** The message should be complete and include all relevant information for the receiver. Providing complete information helps the receiver make better decisions.
4. **Concrete:** The communication should be concrete, meaning that all facts and figures should be clearly mentioned to clarify the sender's motive.
5. **Concise:** The message should be precise and to the point. The sender should avoid lengthy and roundabout sentences and convey the subject matter in as few words as possible. A brief message helps maintain the receiver's attention.
6. **Consideration:** The sender must consider the receiver's opinions, knowledge, mindset, background, etc., to engage the receiver's interest. The sender should empathise with the receiver for better communication.
7. **Courteous:** The sender must be courteous and respect the feelings and viewpoints of the receiver, ensuring that the receiver remains receptive.

1.9.6 Different Methods of Communication

Communication can be defined as the process of understanding and sharing information. The essence of communication is to understand and be understood. This can be achieved in the following ways:

(*i*) **Verbally:** Orally (face-to-face, on the telephone, or in classroom teaching) or in written form (letters, notes, e-mails, SMS, books, and newspapers).

(*ii*) **Visually:** For example, images, graphs, and maps.

(*iii*) **Non-verbally:** For example, body language, eye contact, and gestures.

1.9.7 Communication Style

Everybody has their own way of communicating their views or thoughts. The main aim of any conversation is to express these thoughts in a congenial manner. There are four basic communication styles: Passive, Aggressive, Passive-Aggressive, and Assertive.

People have different communication styles:

(*i*) **Passive:** Indifferent and not expressing thoughts or opinions.

(*ii*) **Aggressive:** Loud, demanding, and often disrespectful.

(*iii*) **Passive-Aggressive:** Indirectly expressing anger or discontent.

(*iv*) **Assertive:** Politely and clearly expressing thoughts while respecting others.

1.9.8 Passive

The passive communication style is often used by those who are indifferent about the topic. They either keep their views or thoughts to themselves or try to appear as if they support every statement in the discussion. When speaking, passive communicators display insecure non-verbal communication signs, such as avoiding eye contact or having poor body posture.

1.9.9 Aggressive

The aggressive communication style is characterised by speaking in a loud and demanding voice and often expressing one's opinions without hesitation. People using this style frequently make intense eye contact, point fingers, and stand their ground. This style includes expressing viewpoints and opinions in a way that insults others and violates their rights.

1.9.10 Passive-Aggressive

The passive-aggressive communication style combines elements of both passive and aggressive styles, resulting in another form of ineffective communication. This style is used when people speak as if they don't care about anything (passive), but show their frustration in an indirect, angry manner (aggressive).

1.9.11 Passive-Aggressive Phrases

"I do not care, but someone else might."

"We can do this your way, but I do not think it is going to work."

"I think you did a good job, but they might not think so."

Passive-aggressive communicators might whisper comments to themselves in the presence of others as if they don't want others to hear. They often refuse to confront others about something that is bothering them.

1.9.12 Assertive

The assertive communication style is considered the most effective among all communication styles. Assertive communicators reasonably express their thoughts, showing consideration for other people's opinions. They respect all values, thoughts, and ideas, and speak in a calm voice while maintaining normal eye contact.

1.9.13 Assertive Phrases

"What are all the options we have here?"

"I think we should go with this method."

"Even though we do not agree, I respect your opinion."

EXERCISE

A. Multiple Choice Questions with Answers

Read the questions carefully and encircle the letters (a), (b), (c), or (d) that best answer the question.

1. **What is the purpose of communication?**
   (a) Inform (tell someone about something)
   (b) Influence (get someone to do something you want)
   (c) Share thoughts, ideas, feelings
   (d) All of the above
2. **Which of the following methods is used to receive information from the sender through a letter?**
   (a) Listening (b) Speaking
   (c) Reading (d) Writing
3. **How do you receive information on the phone?**
   (a) Listening (b) Speaking
   (c) Reading (d) Writing
4. **Communication is an exchange of:**
   (a) Facts (b) Ideas
   (c) Opinions (d) All of these
5. **Feedback is an essential aspect of:**
   (a) Ideas (b) Information
   (c) Communication (d) None of these
6. **Which one is not a part of the communication process:**
   (a) Channel (b) Feedback
   (c) Noise (d) Receiver
7. **Encoding refers to:**
   (a) Converting message into idea (b) Transferring message
   (c) Converting an idea into a message (d) Both a and b
8. **Decoding refers to:**
   (a) Converting an idea into a message
   (b) Transferring message
   (c) Understanding the message
   (d) Both a and b

9. Which communication style is characterised by indifference and not expressing thoughts or opinions?

(a) Passive (b) Aggressive

(c) Passive-Aggressive (d) Assertive

10. Rich communication style involves being loud, demanding, and often disrespectful?

(a) Passive (b) Aggressive

(c) Passive-Aggressive (d) Assertive

11. How does a person with a passive-aggressive communication style typically express their anger or discontent?

(a) Loudly and directly (b) Indirectly

(c) By not expressing any thoughts (d) Assertively

12. Which communication style is not mentioned in the given list of styles?

(a) Passive (b) Assertive

(c) Collaborative (d) Passive-Aggressive

13. Which communication style is often seen as most effective for expressing thoughts in a congenial manner?

(a) Passive (b) Aggressive

(c) Passive-Aggressive (d) Assertive

14. An assertive communicator is most likely to:

(a) Avoid sharing their true feelings

(b) Dominate the conversation

(c) Use indirect methods to express anger

(d) Express their thoughts and feelings clearly and respectfully

15. Which of the following is a potential disadvantage of an aggressive communication style?

(a) Builds strong relationships

(b) Respect others' opinions

(c) Often leads to conflicts and resentment

(d) Ensures clear communication

16. Which of the following is NOT one of the 7 C's of Effective Communication?

(a) Clarity (b) Confidence

(c) Conciseness (d) Concreteness

17. What is the origin of the term "communication"?

(a) Greek word 'koinonia'
(b) Latin word 'communicare'
(c) French word 'communiquer'
(d) German word 'kommunizieren'

18. What does the Latin word 'communicare' mean?

(a) To understand
(b) To write
(c) To share or to participate
(d) To speak

19. Which of the following best describes the purpose of communication?

(a) To impose one's ideas
(b) To share information to achieve mutual understanding
(c) To entertain
(d) To confuse others

20. Which of the following is NOT a purpose of communication?

(a) To inform
(b) To mislead
(c) To persuade
(d) To entertain

ANSWERS

1. (d)	**2.** (c)	**3.** (a)	**4.** (d)	**5.** (c)	**6.** (c)	**7.** (c)	**8.** (c)
9. (a)	**10.** (b)	**11.** (b)	**12.** (c)	**13.** (d)	**14.** (d)	**15.** (c)	**16.** (b)
17. (b)	**18.** (c)	**19.** (b)	**20.** (b)				

B. Match the Columns

Column A: Communication Barriers	Column B: Examples
1. Language	A. Trying to read a book while someone else is watching TV in the same room.
2. Emotional	B. In some cultures, wearing shoes and walking inside the kitchen is considered disrespectful.
3. Environmental	C. Speaking in Hindi when others only understand Tamil.
4. Cultural	D. The parent is not speaking to the child.

ANSWERS

1. C. **2.** D. **3.** A. **4.** B.

C. Short Answer Questions

1. Write down the seven factors affecting perspectives in communication.

Ans. Seven Factors Affecting Perspectives in Communication:

1. Cultural Background
2. Experience and Knowledge
3. Emotions and Moods
4. Language and Semantics
5. Context and Environment
6. Perceptions and Stereotypes
7. Personal Beliefs and Values

2. Give an example of each of the following:

(a) Clear communication (b) Complete communication

Ans. Examples of Communication:

Clear Communication: "Please submit your homework by 5.00 pm tomorrow."

Complete Communication: "The meeting will be held on Monday at 10.00 am in Room 202. Please bring your project reports."

3. What are the elements of communication? Also, draw a communication cycle showing all the elements of communication

Ans. Elements of Communication:

1. **Sender:** The person who starts the communication.
2. **Message:** What is being communicated?
3. **Medium:** How the message is sent (e.g., speech, text).
4. **Receiver:** The person who gets the message.
5. **Feedback:** The receiver's response to the message.
6. **Context:** The situation in which communication takes place.
7. **Noise:** Anything that disturbs the communication.

4. Mention the 7 C's of effective communication.

Ans. The 7 C's of Effective Communication:

- **Clarity:** Make your message easy to understand.
- **Conciseness:** Keep your message short and to the point.
- **Concreteness:** Be specific and clear.
- **Correctness:** Use correct grammar and facts.
- **Completeness:** Provide all necessary information.
- **Courtesy:** Be polite and respectful.
- **Consideration:** Understand the receiver's perspective.

SESSION 2: VERBAL COMMUNICATION

2.1. Verbal Communication

When we communicate with the help of words, it is called verbal communication. This form of communication is the expression or exchange of information or messages through written or oral words.

Oral Communication:

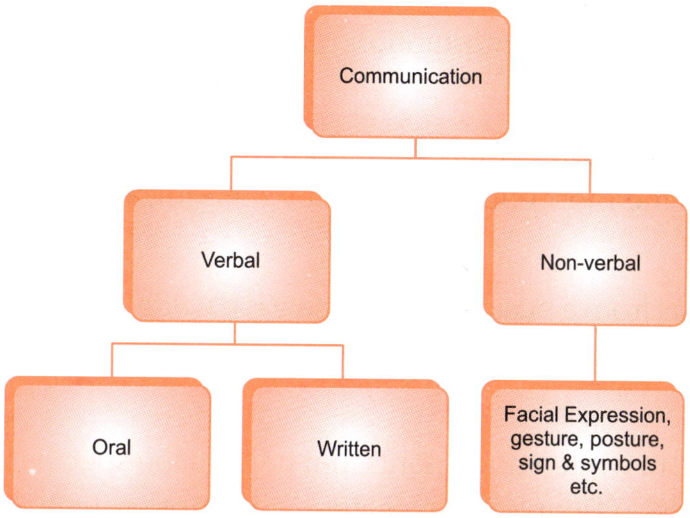

Fig. 2.1 Types of Communication

Oral communication is the process in which messages or information are exchanged or communicated between the sender and receiver or a mass audience through word of mouth.

It can be divided into two ways: (a) Speaking and (b) Listening.

Various forms of oral communication are described below:

(*i*) **Face-to-face conversation:** Oral communication is most effective when done face-to-face. This form of communication ensures that there is no miscommunication or misunderstanding. There is an immediate response from the listener.

(*ii*) **Telephone:** Communication through the telephone is a type of oral communication that depends entirely on the voice without any physical presence. One has to have clarity in their voice and speech to ensure passing the correct information. This type of communication has more chances of miscommunication due to connection issues.

(*iii*) **Presentation:** A presentation is a formal type of face-to-face oral communication.

(*iv*) **Public speech:** A public speech is an oral communication that can be formal or informal. In a public speech, the speaker addresses the audience. It may be for entertainment, sharing ideas, inspiring, or encouraging people.

(*v*) **Interview:**

(a) An interview is a formal means of oral communication that takes place for recruitment.

(vi) Meeting:

(a) A meeting involves more than two people and has a head who presides over it. It is held for a purpose to address an issue or pass on some crucial piece of information. It is a type of formal oral communication that is always backed by a written form of communication.

2.2. Written Communication

Written communication is a type of verbal communication that involves written words. It involves the passing of messages, information, or data in a written form.

(i) E-mails:

- In an organisation, e-mail is the most common means of written communication. E-mail is the most effective way of communicating with clients or partners.

(ii) Proposals:

- A proposal from a business perspective is a written document draft for an upcoming project or for a client to obtain a specific job.

(iii) Reports:

- Reports are written documents that narrate the specific function or performance of business or employee activities. It is another type of written form of formal communication.

(iv) Brochures:

- Brochures are written documents used for promotional purposes to inform the customer about the company or its products.

2.3. Advantages of Oral Communication

(i) **Immediate Feedback:** It enables immediate clarification, helping to reduce misunderstandings—particularly during face-to-face conversations, phone calls, and meetings.

(ii) **Personal Touch:** Adds emotional depth through tone, facial expressions, and body language, making interactions more engaging.

(iii) **Efficiency:** Facilitates quick information exchange, crucial for immediate decision-making and actions.

(iv) **Clarity and Understanding:** Enables real-time explanation and adjustment based on listener reactions, ensuring better comprehension.

(v) **Relationship Building:** Strengthens rapport and trust through direct interaction, enhancing teamwork and stakeholder relations.

(vi) **Flexibility:** Adaptable to different contexts and audiences, allowing for effective and impactful communication.

(vii) **Convenience:** Accessible in various settings like meetings, phone calls, and video conferences, requiring less preparation than written communication.

(viii) **Conflict Resolution:** Effective for resolving disputes through open dialogue, active listening, and immediate feedback.

(ix) **Motivation and Persuasion:** Powerful for inspiring and influencing others with voice, gestures, and expressions.

(x) **Versatility:** Suitable for both informal and formal settings, from casual conversations to structured presentations and meetings.

2.4. Disadvantages/Limitations of Oral Communication

(*i*) **Lack of Record:** Oral communication does not provide a permanent record, making it difficult to refer back to the details later.

(*ii*) **Misunderstanding:** There is a higher chance of misinterpretation or misunderstanding, especially if the message is complex or if there are language barriers.

(*iii*) **Limited Reach:** Oral communication is often limited to small groups or one-on-one interactions, making it less effective for reaching a larger audience.

(*iv*) **Time Consuming:** Engaging in detailed conversations or meetings can be time-consuming, particularly if there are multiple participants or topics to cover.

(*v*) **No Legal Validity:** Oral agreements or communications generally lack legal validity unless backed up by written documentation.

(*vi*) **Dependence on the Speaker:** The effectiveness of oral communication heavily depends on the speaker's skills, including their clarity, articulation, and ability to engage the audience.

(*vii*) **Difficult to Disseminate:** Oral messages are harder to distribute widely compared to written communication, especially across different locations and time zones.

(*viii*) **Interruptions and Distractions:** Oral communication is susceptible to interruptions and distractions, which can disrupt the flow and clarity of the message.

(*ix*) **Memory Constraints:** Both the sender and receiver may forget parts of the message over time, leading to incomplete or inaccurate recollection.

(*x*) **Emotional Influence:** Emotions can affect how messages are delivered and received, potentially distorting the intended meaning.

2.5. Advantages of Written Communication

(*i*) **Permanent Record:** Keeps a lasting copy for future reference and accountability.

(ii) **Clarity:** Allows careful wording to avoid misunderstandings.

(iii) **Wider Reach:** Easily shared with many people, locally or globally.

(iv) **Legal Validity:** Often used for contracts and formal agreements.

(v) **Detailed:** Includes specific information and instructions.

(vi) **Consistency:** Delivers the same message to everyone.

(vii) **Editing:** This lets you review and improve the message before sending it.

(viii) **Convenience:** Recipients can read and reply at their own pace.

2.6. Disadvantages of Written Communication

(i) **Lack of Immediate Feedback:** Delays in response can hinder quick clarification and decision-making.

(ii) **Misinterpretation:** Without non-verbal cues, the message may be misunderstood.

(iii) **Time-consuming:** Requires time to draft, edit, and proofread before sending.

(iv) **Less Personal:** Lacks the personal touch and emotional connection of face-to-face communication.

(v) **Potential for Misplacement:** Documents can be lost or misplaced, leading to potential communication breakdowns.

(vi) **Formality Required:** Often needs a formal tone and structure, which may not suit all situations.

(vii) **Cost:** Printing and distributing physical documents can be expensive.

(viii) **Limited Immediate Interaction:** This does not allow for real-time discussions or immediate problem-solving.

PRACTICE TEST

Activity 1: "The Elevator Pitch Challenge"

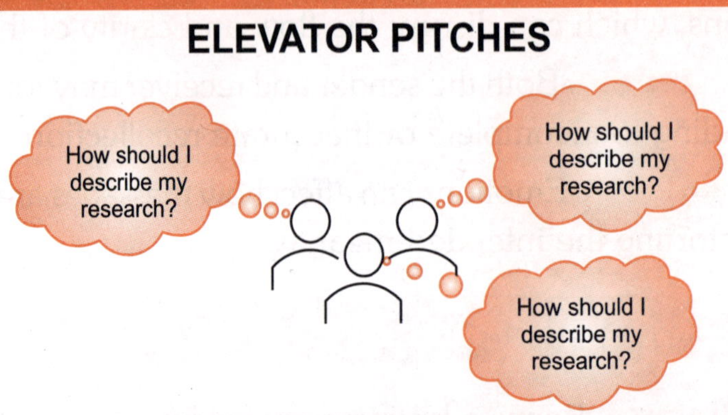

Fig. 2.2 Elevator Pitch

Objective: To practice delivering concise and impactful speeches in a short amount of time.

Materials Needed:

- Timer or stopwatch
- Pen and paper or digital devices for note-taking
- Optional: Index cards or slips of paper with various topics

Duration: 45-60 minutes

Instructions:

1. **Introduction (5 minutes):** Explain the concept of an elevator pitch: a brief, persuasive speech that you can deliver in the time it takes for an elevator ride (usually 30-60 seconds).
   - Discuss the importance of clarity, conciseness, and engaging content in a short speech.
2. **Preparation (10 minutes):**
   - Have each student choose or be assigned a topic. Topics can range from "the benefits of a healthy lifestyle" to "why technology is important for education."
   - Students write a brief outline for their pitch, focusing on key points they want to include in their 30-60-second speech.
3. **Practice (15 minutes):**
   - Students practice their elevator pitches in pairs or small groups. Each student delivers their pitch while their partner(s) provide constructive feedback on clarity, engagement, and effectiveness.
   - Encourage students to make adjustments based on the feedback they receive.
4. **Performance (15-20 minutes):**
   - Select a few students to deliver their elevator pitches to the entire class.
   - After each pitch, provide positive feedback and highlight what worked well. Offer suggestions for improvement if necessary.
5. **Reflection (5 minutes):**
   - Conclude the activity by discussing what students learned about public speaking, the challenges they faced, and how they can apply these lessons in future presentations.

Additional Tips:

- Encourage students to focus on their body language and vocal tone during their practice.
- Remind them to keep their content engaging and relevant to the audience.

This activity helps students practice speaking clearly and confidently in a short time frame, which is a valuable skill for effective public speaking.

Activity 2: 3Ps Method Prepare, Practice, Perform.

Objective: Enhance public speaking skills by practicing concise and impactful speeches using the 3Ps method: Prepare, Practice, Perform.

Fig. 2.3

Materials Needed:

- Timer or stopwatch
- Pen and paper or digital devices for notes
- Optional: Index cards with various topics

Duration: 45-60 minutes

Instructions:

1. **Form Groups (5 minutes):**
   - Divide the class into groups of three students each.
2. **Choose a Topic (5 minutes):**
   - Within each group, select a topic for a very short speech. Topics can be assigned or chosen based on current interests or classroom discussions.
3. **Prepare (10 minutes):**
   - Each student prepares a brief speech outline on the chosen topic, focusing on clarity and impact.
4. **Practice (15 minutes):**
   - Each student takes turns delivering their speech to the group.
   - The other group members provide constructive feedback on clarity, engagement, and effectiveness.
5. **Perform (15 minutes):**
   - One student from each group volunteers to deliver their speech in front of the entire class.
   - After each speech, offer positive feedback and discuss what was effective and what could be improved.
6. **Reflection (5 minutes):**
   - Conclude with a class discussion on what students learned from the activity, the challenges they faced, and how they can apply these skills in future public speaking scenarios.

This structured approach provides students with opportunities to practice in a supportive environment while receiving constructive feedback to help them improve their public speaking skills.

Activity 3: Public Speaking Practice

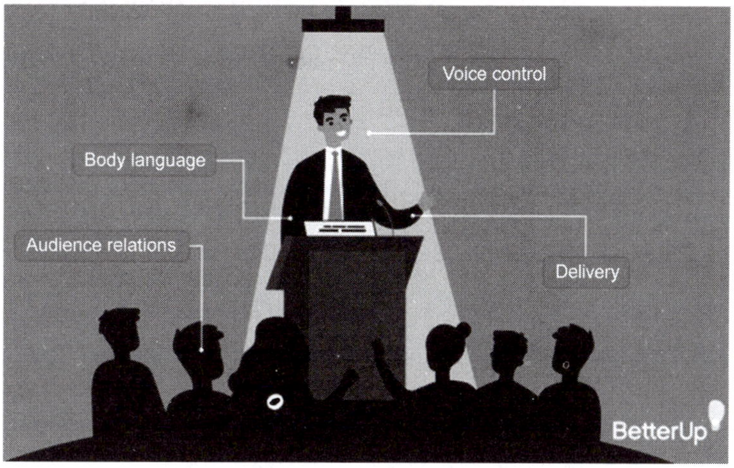

Fig. 2.4 Public Speaking Skills

Objective: Improve your public speaking skills by preparing, practicing, and performing a short speech on a given topic.

Instructions:

1. **Form Groups:** Divide the class into groups of three students each.
2. **Choose a Topic:** Each group selects one topic from the list below for their speeches.
3. **Prepare and Practice:**
    - **Prepare:** Each student prepares a brief speech (2-3 minutes) on the chosen topic using the 3Ps method: Prepare, Practice, and Perform.
    - **Practice:** Within the group, each student delivers their speech to the other two members.
    - **Feedback:** After each speech, group members provide constructive feedback. Discuss whether the speaker effectively communicated their message and offered suggestions for improvement.
4. **Perform:** One student from each group volunteers to deliver their speech in front of the entire class.

Topics to Choose From:

- My promise to myself
- Any good thing about Delhi
- My favorite historical place and why
- Is my country changing?

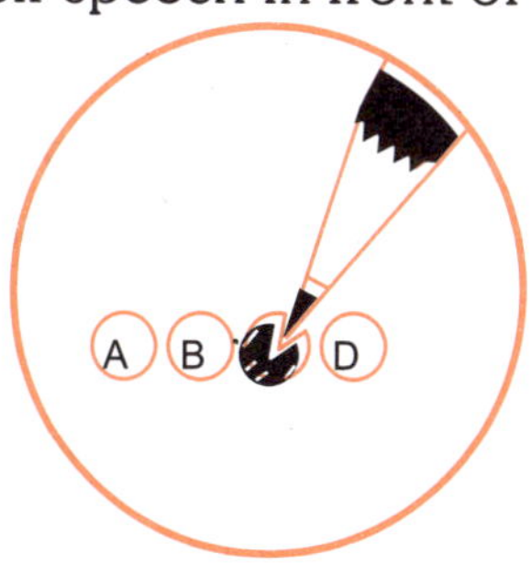

Fig. 2.5

- My plan for 2025
- Do I respect myself?
- Am I a self-confident person?

Tips for Success:

- **Be Clear and Concise:** Keep your speech focused and to the point.
- **Engage Your Audience:** Use eye contact and a confident tone.
- **Practice Regularly:** Rehearse your speech to gain confidence and improve delivery.
- **Goal:** By the end of this activity, you will have enhanced your public speaking skills and gained valuable feedback to continue improving.

EXERCISE

A. Multiple Choice Questions with Answers

Read the questions carefully and encircle the letters (a), (b), (c), or (d) that best answer the question.

1. Choose the correct example of oral communication.

(a) Reports (b) Newspapers
(c) Face-to-face conversation (d) Notes

2. When we communicate verbally, we should use—

(a) Difficult words (b) Simple words
(c) Confusing words (d) Abbreviations

3. Why do we send e-mails?

(a) To reach on time (b) To share documents and files
(c) To talk to each other (d) To meet each other

4. Which of the following is an advantage of written communication?

(a) Immediate feedback (b) Personal touch
(c) Permanent record (d) Flexibility

5. What is a key disadvantage of oral communication?

(a) Provides a permanent record (b) Limited by immediate feedback
(c) Requires time for editing (d) Can be distributed widely

6. Which technique is useful for improving public speaking skills?

(a) Avoiding eye contact (b) Using complex language
(c) Practicing regularly (d) Speaking quickly

7. **What is the main purpose of non-verbal communication?**
   (a) To replace written documents
   (b) To add emphasis and meaning to spoken words
   (c) To exchange emails
   (d) To create permanent records
8. **Which factor contributes to effective public speaking?**
   (a) Ignoring audience feedback
   (b) Using monotonous tone
   (c) Engaging with the audience
   (d) Reading directly from notes
9. **What is the benefit of using simple words in verbal communication?**
   (a) It makes the message harder to understand
   (b) It ensures clarity and reduces misunderstandings
   (c) It increases the complexity of the message
   (d) It lengthens the communication process
10. **What should you focus on to build confidence in public speaking?**
   (a) Worrying about mistakes
   (b) The audience's needs and problems
   (c) Speaking without preparation
   (d) Avoiding eye contact

ANSWERS

1. (c) **2.** (b) **3.** (b) **4.** (c) **5.** (b) **6.** (c) **7.** (b) **8.** (c) **9.** (b) **10.** (b)

B. Very Short Answer Questions

1. **What does Kinesics stand for?**

Ans. Kinesics refers to the study of body language, including gestures, facial expressions, posture, and movements, as a form of nonverbal communication.

2. **What are the two kinds of communication?**

Ans. The two kinds of communication are:
1. **Verbal Communication** (spoken or written words)
2. **Non-verbal Communication** (body language, facial expressions, tone, etc.)

3. **Give the name of 7C's to communication.**

Ans. The 7C's of communication are:
1. Clarity
2. Conciseness
3. Concreteness
4. Correctness
5. Consideration
6. Completeness
7. Courtesy

4. Name five oral communication situations.

Ans. 1. Face-to-face conversations 2. Telephone calls 3. Group discussions
4. Public speeches 5. Interviews

5. Define communication.

Ans. Communication is the process of sharing information, ideas, emotions, and messages between individuals or groups through verbal, nonverbal, or written means to achieve mutual understanding.

C. Short Answer Questions

1. What are the various types of verbal communication, provide an example for each?

Ans. The two main types of verbal communication are:

1. **Oral Communication**
   - **Definition:** Spoken words exchanged in real-time.
   - **Examples:** Conversations, speeches, phone calls, presentations.
2. **Written Communication**
   - **Definition:** Messages conveyed through written or typed text.
   - **Examples:** Emails, letters, reports, books, and text messages.

2. How can we speak confidently in public using the 3Ps method?

Ans. The 3Ps method stands for Preparation, Practice, and Presentation:

1. **Preparation:**
   - Research the topic thoroughly and outline your speech.
   - Anticipate questions or challenges from the audience.
2. **Practice:**
   - Rehearse the speech multiple times, focusing on timing and clarity.
   - Practice in front of a mirror, record yourself, or rehearse with friends.
3. **Presentation:**
   - Deliver the speech with confidence, maintaining eye contact and using appropriate gestures.
   - Speak clearly, emphasise key points, and engage with the audience.

3. Explain the verbal method of communication.

Ans. **Verbal communication** is the process of sharing information through spoken or written words.

Key Features:

- Involves the use of language, tone, and clarity to express ideas.

- Can be synchronous (real-time, like conversations) or asynchronous (delayed, like emails).
- Enhances understanding through direct expression and the ability to clarify.

Examples:

- **Oral:** Lectures, discussions, debates.
- **Written:** Emails, memos, academic essays.

SESSION 3: NON-VERBAL COMMUNICATION

3.1. Non-verbal Communication

Introduction to Non-verbal Communication

To see **Introduction to Non-Verbal Communication** in Action

Scan QR Code

Fig. 3.1 Gestures to understand Body Language

Non-verbal communication is the exchange of information or messages between two or more persons through gestures, facial expressions, eye contact, proximity, touch, and other forms of body language, without using any spoken or written words. This type of communication is spontaneous, often occurring naturally without prior planning or rehearsal. It happens almost instantaneously, conveying feelings and emotions through facial expressions, gestures, body movements, and eye usage.

Facial expressions, for instance, can reveal a person's emotions, whether they are happy, sad, angry, or surprised. Gestures, such as a wave, a thumbs-up, or a nod, can convey messages of greeting, approval, or agreement. The way you use your eyes—whether you maintain eye contact, look away, or blink frequently—can also communicate a wide range of emotions and intentions.

Unlike other modes of communication, non-verbal communication does not follow any set rules, formality, or structure. People often engage in non-verbal communication unknowingly and habitually, as movements of various body parts naturally express thoughts and feelings. This form of communication is a powerful and integral part of human interaction, adding depth and nuance to the words we speak.

3.2. The Importance of Non-verbal Communication

To see **The Importance of Non-verbal Communication** in Action

Scan QR Code

Non-verbal communication plays a crucial role in expressing emotions such as happiness, anger, sadness, interest, curiosity, annoyance, anxiety, embarrassment, pleasure, hope, and many others. Often, people unconsciously convey these emotions through their body language, facial expressions, and gestures.

When you communicate, it's essential to complement your words with appropriate non-verbal cues. Your gestures and body language should align with your spoken message to create a cohesive and authentic expression. This harmony between verbal and non-verbal communication enhances understanding, reinforces your message, and helps build trust and rapport with others.

Non-verbal communication adds depth to your interactions, allowing you to express complex emotions and subtle nuances that words alone cannot capture. It is a powerful tool that, when used effectively, can significantly improve the quality and impact of your communication.

3.3. Advantages and Disadvantages of Non-verbal Communication

Advantages	Disadvantages
Conveys Emotions Non-verbal communication effectively expresses emotions such as happiness, sadness, anger, and surprise, often more vividly than words. **Example:** A smile or a frown can instantly convey feelings of joy or displeasure.	**Ambiguity** Non-verbal communication can be ambiguous and open to interpretation, leading to misunderstandings. **Example:** A crossed arm can be seen as defensiveness or simply a comfortable position.
Enhances Understanding It complements verbal communication, adding depth and clarity to the message. **Example:** Nodding while saying 'yes' reinforces agreement.	**Cultural Differences** Non-verbal cues can vary widely between cultures potentially causing miscommunication. **Example:** Direct eye contact is considered respectful in some cultures but rude in others.
Universal Language Certain non-verbal cues, such as facial expressions, can be universally understood across different cultures. **Example:** A thumbs-up is widely recognised as a sign of approval.	**Lack of Precision** It can be less precise than verbal communication, making it difficult to convey specific details. **Example:** Pointing in a general direction lacks the specificity of verbal instructions.

Builds Relationships	Unconscious Cues
Effective use of non-verbal communication, like maintaining eye contact and appropriate touch, can build trust and rapport. **Example:** A warm handshake can create a positive first impression.	People often send non-verbal signals unconsciously, which may not align with their intended message. **Example:** Nervous fidgeting can be interpreted as dishonesty, even if the person is truthful.
Quick and Efficient	**Limited in Complexity**
Non-verbal signals can convey messages quickly without the need for words. **Example:** Raising a hand can signal a need to speak in a meeting.	Complex ideas and detailed information are challenging to convey non-verbally. **Example:** Explaining technical concepts or detailed instructions requires verbal explanation.
Understanding both the advantages and disadvantages of non-verbal communication helps individuals use it more effectively and avoid potential pitfalls.	

3.4. Key Takeaways: Advantages of Non-verbal Communication

- **Clear Expression:** Conveys emotions effectively, often more vividly than words.
- **Accessible:** Facilitates communication with deaf and mute individuals.
- **Emotional Exchange:** Helps share feelings and emotions easily.
- **Time-Saving:** Communicates messages quickly without words.
- **Complementary:** Enhances and reinforces verbal communication.
- **Inclusivity:** Assists in communicating with illiterate individuals.

3.5. Disadvantages of Non-verbal Communication

- **Feedback Issues:** Hard to provide immediate feedback.
- **Incomplete:** This can leave messages unclear or partial.
- **Inflexible:** Difficult to adapt or modify.
- **Misinterpretation:** Encoding and decoding can be problematic.
- **No Record:** Lacks a permanent record for future reference.
- **Cultural Differences:** Varies across cultures, leading to misunderstandings.

3.6. Comparison Between Verbal and Non-verbal Communication

Basis	Verbal Communication	Non-verbal Communication
Use of Words	Verbal Communication: Uses spoken or written words.	Non-verbal Communication: Does not use spoken or written words.
Types	Verbal Communication: Two types - Oral and written.	Non-verbal Communication: Various types - visual, audio, audio-visual, silent, etc.
Comprehensibility	Verbal Communication: Easy to understand.	Non-verbal Communication: Difficult to understand.
Structure	Verbal Communication: Highly structured.	Non-verbal Communication: Lacks formal structure.
Distortion of Information	Verbal Communication: Less possibility of distortion.	Non-verbal Communication: High possibility of distortion.
Continuity	Verbal Communication: Begins and ends with words.	Non-verbal communication: Continues until the purpose is achieved.
Feedback	Verbal Communication: Limited and delayed feedback.	Non-verbal Communication: Provides a lot of immediate feedback.

3.7. Key Takeaways: Verbal vs. Non-verbal Communication

Verbal communication uses spoken or written words, making it easy to understand and highly structured, with less possibility of information distortion. It can be divided into oral and written types and typically begins and ends with words, offering limited and delayed feedback. In contrast, non-verbal communication does not use words and includes various types such as visual, audio, audio-visual, and silent. It is often more difficult to understand and lacks formal structure, leading to a higher possibility of information distortion. Non-verbal communication continues until its purpose is achieved and provides a lot of immediate feedback.

3.8. Visual Communication

To see **Visual Communication** in Action

Scan QR Code

Visual communication is the exchange of information through images and pictures. It includes graphic design, illustration, animation, books, magazines, print media, screen-based media, interactive web design, short films, advertising designs, promotion, corporate identity, packaging, and more. Visual presentation has a significant impact on our daily lives and can effectively convey information. For example, a red sign indicates danger and an image of a crossed-out cigarette indicates no smoking.

Types of visual communication aids include:

- PowerPoint Presentations (PPT)
- Pictures

- Charts/Graphs
- Maps
- Films/Videos
- Objects

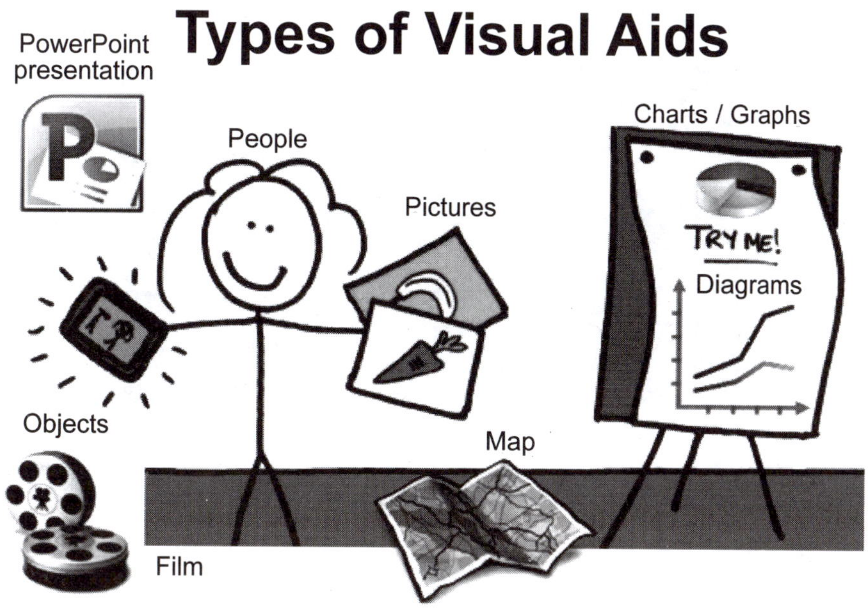

Fig. 3.2 Types of Visual Aids

3.9. Advantages of Visual Communication

1. **No Language Barrier:** Effective for illiterate people who can easily understand visual information.
2. **Simple Presentation:** Complex information can be presented simply using graphs, pictures, and diagrams.
3. **Instant Communication:** Visual techniques save time and can reach many people simultaneously.
4. **Quick Decisions:** Helps in making quick decisions, which is why management often prefers visual communication.
5. **Universality:** Popular and consistent across different places, as diagrams and charts do not need to change.

3.10. Disadvantages of Visual Communication

1. **Costly:** Visual methods can be more expensive than other communication methods. Creating maps, charts, and diagrams can be costly, making this technique more suitable for large companies or organisations.
2. **Complexity:** Sometimes, visual presentations can be complex, and receivers may struggle to understand the information.

PRACTICE TEST

Fig. 3.3 Steps Towards Success

Activity 1: "Communication in Action"

Objective: To understand and differentiate between visual and non-verbal types of communication.

Instructions:

1. **Group Formation:**
   - Divide the class into groups of five students. Each group will be assigned a specific task related to different types of communication.
2. **Task Assignment:**
   - **Group 1:** Prepare Flashcards with Visual Communication
     - Create a set of flashcards that represent different forms of visual communication. This might include images, symbols, charts, or graphs.
   - **Group 2:** Prepare Examples of Non-verbal Communication
     - Develop a list or a series of scenarios that depict non-verbal communication. This can include body language, facial expressions, gestures, and other forms of non-verbal cues.
3. **Presentation:**
   - Each group will present their prepared materials to the class. Group 1 will showcase their flashcards, while Group 2 will demonstrate their non-verbal communication examples.
4. **Identification and Discussion:**
   - After each presentation, discuss with the class how the types of communication presented by each group are used in real-life scenarios.

- Identify and analyse how visual and non-verbal communication are applied and how they differ from one another.

5. **Reflection:**
   - Conclude the activity by reflecting on how understanding different types of communication can enhance public speaking skills. Discuss the importance of visual and non-verbal cues in effective communication.

EXERCISE

A. Multiple Choice Questions with Answers

Read the questions carefully and encircle the letters (a), (b), (c), or (d) that best answer the question.

1. **Which of these is a positive facial expression?**
   (a) Staring hard
   (b) Nodding while listening
   (c) Wrinkled forehead
   (d) Looking away from the speaker
2. **What does an upright body posture convey?**
   (a) Shyness
   (b) Fear
   (c) Confidence
   (d) Intelligence
3. **Which of these is not appropriate for non-verbal communication at work?**
   (a) Putting your arm around a co-worker's shoulder
   (b) Shaking hands firmly
   (c) Looking at the speaker with a smile
   (d) Standing with an upright posture
4. **When preparing for a presentation, you should:**
   (a) Focus on the objectives of the presentation
   (b) Practice your speech in front of a mirror or a friend
   (c) Rehearse to time your presentation slides
   (d) All of the above
5. **What does maintaining eye contact with your audience typically show?**
   (a) Disinterest
   (b) Nervousness
   (c) Engagement
   (d) Confusion

6. **How can you use gestures effectively during a presentation?**

(a) By keeping them minimal and subtle

(b) By using them only when you forget your speech

(c) By making them exaggerated and frequent

(d) By avoiding them altogether

7. **Which of these is a sign of active listening?**

(a) Interrupting the speaker

(b) Checking your phone frequently

(c) Nodding and making verbal acknowledgments

(d) Looking around the room

8. **What should you do if you don't understand something during a presentation?**

(a) Ignore it and move on

(b) Ask questions for clarification

(c) Pretend you understand

(d) Leave the room

ANSWERS

1. (b) **2.** (c) **3.** (a) **4.** (d) **5.** (c) **6.** (a) **7.** (c) **8.** (b)

B. Put a × mark against the actions below that are incorrect for demonstrating non-verbal communication:

- Laughing during formal communication
- Scratching your head
- Smiling when speaking to a friend
- Nodding when you agree with something
- Standing straight
- Yawning while listening
- Sitting straight
- Maintaining eye contact while speaking
- Biting your nails
- Firm handshake
- Clenching your jaws
- Looking away when someone is speaking to you
- Intense staring

Here is the answer key for the exercise, marking the actions that are incorrect for demonstrating non-verbal communication:

- Laughing during formal communication ×
- Scratching your head ×
- Yawning while listening ×
- Biting your nails ×
- Clenching your jaws ×
- Looking away when someone is speaking to you ×
- Intense staring ×

C. Short Answer Questions

1. **What is visual communication?**

Ans. **Visual communication** is the process of conveying information or ideas through visual elements such as images, symbols, charts, graphs, videos, or illustrations. It enhances understanding by making complex information more accessible and engaging.

2. **Give an example of a visual communication tool.**

Ans. An example of a visual communication tool is **PowerPoint presentations**, which use slides with text, images, graphs, and videos to convey information effectively.

3. **How can visual communication enhance a presentation?**

Ans. Visual communication enhances a presentation by:

1. **Simplifying Complex Information:** Charts, graphs, and infographics make data easier to understand.
2. **Capturing Attention:** Visuals make presentations more engaging and appealing.
3. **Improving Retention:** People tend to remember visual content better than text alone.
4. **Supporting Verbal Communication:** Visuals reinforce spoken messages, making them clearer and more impactful.

4. **Name three types of non-verbal communication.**

Ans.
1. **Kinesics:** Body language, including gestures, posture, and facial expressions.
2. **Proxemics:** Use of personal space and physical distance in interactions.
3. **Paralinguistics:** Tone, pitch, and volume of voice (vocal elements that accompany speech).

5. Why is non-verbal communication important in conveying messages?

Ans. Non-verbal communication is important because:

1. **Expresses Emotions:** It conveys feelings like happiness, anger, or confusion more effectively than words.
2. **Reinforces Verbal Communication:** Gestures and tone add depth and meaning to spoken words.
3. **Builds Trust:** Consistent non-verbal cues create credibility and authenticity.
4. **Universal Understanding:** Facial expressions and gestures are often understood across cultures.
5. **Clarifies Intentions:** It helps in understanding the speaker's true intentions and attitudes.

SESSION 4: COMMUNICATION STYLES – ASSERTIVENESS

4.1. Communication Styles – Assertiveness

Introduction

To see **Communication Styles – Assertiveness** in Action

Scan QR Code

In the previous session, we explored various methods of communication. While these different types are crucial for effective interactions, the style of communication itself is equally important. Communication style refers to how we convey information to others, whether through language or other media. Also known as conversational style, it significantly impacts how well the sender and receiver understand each other. The more effective our communication style, the clearer and more meaningful the exchange becomes.

4.2. Important Communication Styles

Our mood often reflects the quality of our conversations. When our communication is positive, we feel happy, but if it's not, our mood can be negatively affected. This is largely due to our communication style. In real life, there are several communication styles used to express emotions and ideas. Four common types of communication styles are:

1. Aggressive
2. Assertive
3. Passive
4. Passive-Aggressive

4.3. Communication Styles Overview

	Aggressive	**Passive**	**Passive-Aggressive**	**Assertive**
Verbal Communication Aspects	Demanding and threatening Voice is loud	Apologetic Finding it difficult to take responsibility	Sarcastic Indirectly aggressive Unreliable	Medium pitch, speed, and volume in voice Emotionally expressive
Non-verbal Communication Aspects	Big and fast gestures 'Bigger than' others posture	No eye contact Tends to fidget	Insincere smile Pretends to be friendly	Open body posture Appropriate eye contact

Source: O'Toole (2016a)

In addition to these four styles, there is another less common style known as the manipulative style. This style is used by individuals skilled at influencing or controlling others for their own advantage.

4.4. Detailed Explanation of Communication Styles

(*i*) **Aggressive:** An aggressive communication style disregards others' opinions and feelings, focusing solely on winning arguments. This style often involves ignoring or insulting others and using strong, harsh language. For example, saying "You are a stupid person, I just hate you" reflects aggression.

(*ii*) **Assertive:** An assertive communication style involves respecting both oneself and others. It balances expressing one's views while also listening to others. Assertive communicators can disagree or refuse requests without being hurtful. For instance, saying "When can I talk to you?" demonstrates assertiveness.

(*iii*) **Passive/Submissive:** A passive or submissive communication style involves avoiding conflict and accepting incorrect remarks. This style often avoids confrontation and may lead to unnecessary apologies. An example of passive communication is saying "I just don't care, do as you like."

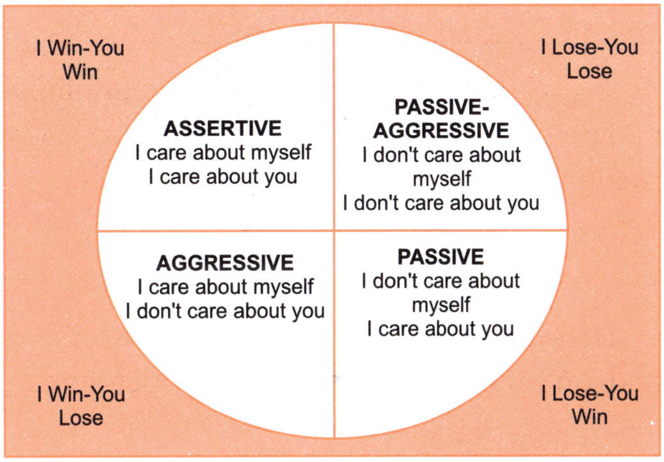

Fig. 4.1 Communication Styles

(*iv*) **Passive-Aggressive:** A passive-aggressive communication style seeks to get one's way without taking responsibility or facing conflict directly. This style can hurt both others and oneself. An example of passive-aggressive communication is saying "It is your fault." From the above explanations, it is clear that the most effective communication style is assertiveness.

4.5. Assertive Communication

Assertive communication is a healthy and respectful style that shows regard for both your own and others' opinions. It aims to balance your needs with those of others, leading to clearer and more effective communication. Assertive communication fosters a positive environment and demonstrates self-respect by standing up for your interests and expressing your thoughts and feelings.

4.6. Advantages of Assertive Communication

Being assertive has several benefits:

- Enhances self-confidence and self-esteem
- Helps in understanding and recognising your feelings
- Earns respect from others
- Improves communication
- Creates win-win situations
- Enhances decision-making skills
- Builds honest relationships
- Increases job satisfaction

4.7. Principles of Assertive Communication

To practice assertive communication effectively, consider the following principles:

(*i*) **Speak Slowly and Clearly:** Speaking quickly can hinder communication. If the other person is aggressive, remain calm and respond slowly and clearly after they have finished speaking.

(*ii*) **Be Confident:** Confidence attracts attention and can be reflected through your body language. It conveys positivity and leaves a good impression.

(*iii*) **Dress Smartly:** Dressing neatly and smartly creates a positive impression. People often judge based on attire, so dressing appropriately can enhance how you are perceived.

(*iv*) **Avoid Aggression:** Aggression, including shouting and using inappropriate language, should be avoided. It is important to remain composed and respectful.

(*v*) **Be Honest:** Honesty builds trust and supports open communication. Express your views truthfully.

(*vi*) **Express Yourself:** Clearly articulate your opinions and thoughts without prejudging others' views. It is crucial to express yourself openly.

(*vii*) **Learn to Say 'No':** If something is unacceptable, clearly state 'no' without hesitation. Being firm about your boundaries is important and justified when necessary.

SESSION 5: WRITING SKILLS: PARTS OF SPEECH

5.1. Writing Skills: Parts of Speech

Introduction

We use sentences to express our thoughts. A sentence is made up of a group of words that communicates a complete idea. Sentences are important because they can communicate a person's views or thoughts. A sentence starts with a capital letter and ends with a period, question mark, or exclamation mark. If a group of words is incomplete, it is known as a phrase.

Examples of full sentences are:

1. I have done my work.
2. What are you doing?
3. You have done a great job!

5.2. Using Capitals

We start our sentences with capital letters. There are specific rules for using capital letters in a sentence. The main rule to remember is MINTS:

- **M:** Months
- **I:** I (when referring to yourself)
- **N:** Names
- **T:** Titles
- **S:** Start of sentences

To see **Using Capital Letters: MINTS Rule** in Action

Scan QR Code

These rules help us use capital letters correctly in our writing.

5.3. Using Capital Letters: MINTS Rule:

Alphabet	Meaning/Rule	Example
M	Names of months, days, and holidays must begin with a capital letter.	My birthday is in October.
I	Always capitalise the letter 'I' when referring to yourself.	I played hockey every day.
N	Names of people and places should start with a capital letter.	Mr. Narendra Modi is our prime minister.
T	Capitalise titles of books, movies, and titles used before people's names.	Dr. Naresh Trehan is a famous heart specialist.
S	Always start the first letter of a sentence with a capital letter.	The dog is a very faithful animal.

This chart helps you remember when to use capital letters in your writing.

5.4. Punctuation Marks

Punctuation marks are symbols that help us organise and structure sentences. The term "punctuation" comes from the Latin word "punctum," which means the correct use of punctuation marks like periods or commas in writing. Punctuation marks help us separate parts of a sentence, such as phrases and clauses, and clarify its meaning.

Punctuation Name	Sign	Use	Examples
Full Stop	.	Shows the end of the sentence	He is a good doctor.
Comma	,	Shows a pause in the sentence	I like apples, oranges and mangoes.
Question mark	?	Shows end of the question	What are you doing ?
Exclamation mark	!	Used at the end of a sentence or a word to show strong feeling like anger, shock, etc	Excellent ! Keep it up.
Apostrophe	‘	To show that something belongs to someone	Robert's books keep lying scattered

5.5. Parts of Speech

Parts of speech are categories that describe how words are used in sentences to make them meaningful and grammatically correct. Each part of speech serves a different function, and an individual word can act as more than one part of speech depending on how it is used in a sentence.

To see **Parts of Speech** in Action

Scan QR Code

There are eight main parts of speech in English:

(i) **Noun:** A word that names a person, place, thing, or idea.
- Example: *dog, school, happiness*

(ii) **Pronoun:** A word that takes the place of a noun.
- Example: *he, she, it*

(iii) **Verb:** A word that expresses an action or state of being.
- Example: *run, is, seem*

(iv) **Adjective:** A word that describes a noun or pronoun.
- Example: *happy, blue, tall*

(v) **Adverb:** A word that describes a verb, adjective, or another adverb.
- Example: *quickly, very, well*

(vi) **Preposition:** A word that shows the relationship between a noun (or pronoun) and other words in a sentence.
- Example: *in, on, under*

(vii) **Conjunction:** A word that connects words, phrases, or clauses.
- Example: *and, but, or*

(viii) **Interjection:** A word or phrase that expresses strong emotion or reaction.
- Example: *wow, ouch, hey*

In modern usage, articles are also included as a fundamental part of speech. They help define nouns and indicate whether the noun is specific or general. Articles are:

- Definite Article: *the*
- Indefinite Articles: *a, an*

So, the basic list of parts of speech expands to nine:

1. Noun	2. Pronoun	3. Verb
4. Adjective	5. Adverb	6. Preposition
7. Conjunction	8. Interjection	9. Article

Understanding these parts of speech helps you use words correctly and construct sentences that are clear and grammatically accurate.

(i) **Noun:** A noun is a word that names a person, place, thing, or idea. Nouns are often used with articles (the, a, an), but not always. Proper nouns always start with a capital letter, while common nouns do not. Nouns can be singular or plural, concrete or abstract.

Example: *Ram brought apples.* (Both *Ram* and *apples* are nouns.)

(ii) **Pronoun:** A pronoun is a word used in place of a noun. Pronouns can function as subjects, objects, or complements in a sentence.

Example: *She is Meena's mother.* (*She* is a pronoun.)

Parts of speech	Definition	Examples	Use in a sentence
Nouns	people, places, things (and animals)	dog, cat, garden, work, music, town, Manila, teacher. Bob	the sun shines Anna goes to school
Pronouns	replace nouns	he. I. its. me. my, she, that, this, those, us, who, whom, you.	John is hungry. He wants to eat.
Verbs	show action or state of being	run, go, have, invite, laughed, listen, playing, singing, walk	The dog and cat are running
Adjectives	describe nouns	angry, brave, healthy, little, old, red, smart, two, some, good. big. interesting	Brown dog. Fat Cat. Big garden
Adverbs	describe verbs, adjectives or other adverbs	badly, fully, hardly, nearly never, quickly, silently, well, very, almost	Runs quickly, Eats very slowly
Articles	signals that a noun is going to follow	the, a, an	The dog, The cat
Prepositions	show relationship between words in a sentence	above, before, except, from, in, near, of, since, between, upon, with to. al after, on	I am going to my garden.
Conjunctions	connect words, phrases, clauses or sentences	and, or. but, so, after, before, unless, either, neither, because, since	I was tired so 1 went to sleep.
Interjections	exclamations that express strong feelings	aha!, gosh!, great!, hey!, hil, hooray!, oh!, oops!, phew!, oh!, ouch!, well!	Oops! I spilled the milk.

(iii) **Verb:** A verb in a sentence expresses action or being. There is a main verb and, sometimes, one or more helping verbs. Verbs also change form to indicate tense.

Example: *She can sing.* (*Sing* is the main verb; *can* is the helping verb.)

(iv) **Adjective:** An adjective is a word used to modify or describe a noun or pronoun. It usually answers the questions of which one, what kind, or how many.

Example: *The cat is black.* (Here, *black* is an adjective that describes the noun *cat*.)

(v) **Adverb:** An adverb describes or modifies a verb, an adjective, or another adverb, but never a noun. It usually answers questions about when, where, how, why, under what conditions, or to what degree. Many adverbs end in *–ly*.

Example: *Tom moves quickly.* (Here, *quickly* is an adverb.)

(*vi*) **Preposition:** A preposition is a word placed before a noun or pronoun to form a phrase that modifies another word in the sentence. Therefore, a preposition is always part of a prepositional phrase.

Example: *The cat is on the roof.* (Here, *on* is a preposition.)

(*vii*) **Conjunction:** A conjunction joins words, phrases, or clauses and indicates the relationship between the elements joined. Coordinating conjunctions connect grammatically equal elements: *and, but, or, nor, for, so, yet*. Subordinating conjunctions connect clauses that are not equal: *because, although, while, since*, etc.

Example: *Do you want to buy apples or oranges?* (Here, *or* is a conjunction.)

(*viii*) **Interjection:** An interjection is a word used to express emotions. It is often followed by an exclamation mark.

Example: *Wow! What nice weather!* (Here, *Wow!* is an interjection.)

(*ix*) **Articles:** Articles help determine whether you are referring to something specific (with definite articles) or something general (with indefinite articles). There are three articles in the English language: *the, a, an*.

Example: *An apple a day keeps the doctor away.* (*a*, *an*, and *the* are articles.)

5.6. Persuasion Skills

Persuasion is the ability to convince others to understand or follow your point of view. This can lead them to agree to a commitment, purchase a product or service, or take a desired action. Strong persuasion skills are important both in oral and written communication, especially in the workplace.

To see **Persuasion Skills** in Action

Scan QR Code

In Business:

(*i*) **Advertising:** Advertising is a common form of persuasion. It aims to influence customers to visit a store or use a product or service. Effective advertisements convince people of the benefits and value of what is being offered.

(*ii*) **Negotiation:** Persuasion is crucial in negotiations. Business people use persuasion to convince vendors to offer better prices or services. It helps in reaching agreements that benefit all parties involved.

(*iii*) **Motivating Employees:** Persuasion can also be used to motivate staff. By persuading employees to increase their effort, take on new tasks, or adapt to changes, you can enhance productivity and adapt to evolving workplace demands.

Understanding and mastering persuasion skills can help you effectively communicate your ideas, influence decisions, and achieve your goals in various professional settings.

Activity 1: Identifying and Correcting Parts of Speech

Read aloud the paragraph given below. "On Sunday, I have an appointment to meet Dr. Patel in Delhi. my house is near Mr. Patel's shop I went to his shop on Friday to buy vegetables I bought potatoes onions carrots and a cabbage Mr. Patel is a friendly man have you met him"

1. This paragraph contains examples of the parts of speech you learnt about in this lesson.
2. Identify as many of these parts of speech as you can and mark them.
3. Write the paragraph with proper punctuation and capitalisation.

EXERCISE

A. Parts of Speech

1. **Today was a very ___ day.**
   (a) colder (b) cold (c) coldly
2. **We'll have to ___ if we want to catch that bus.**
   (a) running (b) run (c) ran
3. **It's OK to use that phone, it's ___.**
   (a) me (b) mine (c) my
4. **___ was that man you were talking to?**
   (a) why (b) what (c) who
5. **I forgot my umbrella ___ I got wet.**
   (a) so (b) because (c) although
6. **The resort opens ___ spring.**
   (a) on (b) in (c) at
7. **___ is a global problem.**
   (a) Poor (b) Poorly (c) Poverty
8. **You speak English very ___.**
   (a) good (b) beautiful (c) well
9. **When was the last time you ___?**
   (a) cried (b) crying (c) cry
10. **She ___ made her presentation to the class.**
   (a) confident (b) confidently (c) confidence

ANSWERS

1. (b) 2. (b) 3. (b) 4. (c) 5. (a) 6. (b) 7. (c) 8. (c)
9. (a) 10. (b)

B. Multiple Choice Questions with Answers

Instruction: Read the questions carefully and encircle the letters (a), (b), (c), or (d) that best answer the question.

1. **What is a sentence?**
   (a) A group of ideas that form a complete paragraph
   (b) A group of words that communicate a complete thought
   (c) A set of rules that we must follow to write correctly
   (d) A set of words that contains all the basic punctuation marks
2. **Which of these sentences uses upper case letters correctly?**
   (a) I am Hungry. (b) Divya and Seema are reading.
   (c) The bucket is full of water. (d) She lives in Delhi.
3. **Which of these sentences is punctuated correctly?**
   (a) Where are you going?
   (b) I have a pen a notebook and a pencil.
   (c) I am so happy to see you!
   (d) This is Abdul's house.
4. **Underline the noun, pronoun, adjective, verb, and adverb in these sentences.**
   (a) Sanjay plays football everyday.
   (b) Divya gave him new books.
   (c) I opened the red box carefully.
5. **Which word is a preposition in the following sentence?**
   "*The cat is under the table.*"
   (a) cat (b) under
   (c) table (d) is
6. **Which sentence uses a conjunction correctly?**
   (a) I want ice cream and cake. (b) I want ice cream, but cake.
   (c) I want ice cream cake. (d) Ice cream I want cake.
7. **What is the role of an interjection in a sentence?**
   (a) To modify a noun (b) To express emotions
   (c) To connect clauses (d) To describe an action

8. In which sentence is "I" used as a pronoun?

(a) I will go to the store. (b) I love the book.

(c) The store is near me. (d) John said I can go.

ANSWERS

1. (b) **2.** (d) **3.** (c) **4.** (a) **5.** (b) **6.** (a) **7.** (b) **8.** (a)

C. Fill in the Blanks

Use correct nouns and verbs from the box to fill in the blanks given below.

girl, girls, boy, man, dog, skipping, riding, running, studying, drinking, barking, singing

(a) The ________ is ________ a song.

(b) The ________ is ________ a rope.

(c) The ________ is ________ milk.

(d) The ________ are ________ .

(e) Raju is ________

(f) A ________ is ________ bicycle.

Ans. (a) The **girl** is **singing** a song. (b) The **girl** is **skipping** a rope.

(c) The **man** is **drinking** milk. (d) The **girls** are **studying**.

(e) Raju is **running**. (f) A **boy** is **riding** a bicycle.

D. Short Answer Questions

1. Identify the conjunctions and prepositions (Remember, conjunctions join two sentences while prepositions help answer the words 'where', 'when' ,and 'how'.). Choose the conjunctions and prepositions from the box given below and list them in the correct box.

Ans. **Under, And, In, At, Or, Up**

Conjunction	Preposition
• And	• Under
• Or	• In
	• At
	• Up

SESSION 6: WRITING SKILLS: SENTENCES

6.1. Writing: Expressing Thoughts and Ideas

Writing is a form of communication used to express views and thoughts. People often write to convey their beliefs and form convincing arguments.

To see
Writing: Expressing Thoughts and Ideas
in Action

Scan QR Code

6.2. Types of Sentences

There are four types of sentences in the English language:

(*i*) **Simple Sentence:** Contains one independent clause.

Example: *Ram is a singer.*

(*ii*) **Compound Sentence:** Contains at least two independent clauses.

Example: *Ram is a singer, and Shyam is a painter.*

(*iii*) **Complex Sentence:** Contains one independent clause and at least one dependent clause.

Example: *She returned the computer after she noticed it was damaged.*

Independent clause: *She returned the computer*

Dependent clause: *after she noticed it was damaged*

(*iv*) **Compound-complex sentence:** Contains two or more independent clauses and at least one dependent clause.

Example: *The team captain jumped with joy, and the fans cheered because they won the state championship.*

Independent clauses: *The team captain jumped with joy,* and *the fans cheered*

Dependent clause: *because they won the state championship*

6.3. Phrases

A phrase is a group of words that does not form a complete sentence. It lacks a subject and a predicate. Examples include:

- in the air
- along the road
- beside the bed
- to live and breathe

6.4. Types of Phrases

(i) Noun Phrase: Consists of a noun and its modifiers.

Examples: *The flu clinic has seen many cases of infectious disease.*

It was a story as old as time.

(ii) Verb Phrase: Consists of a verb and its modifiers.

Examples: *He was waiting for the rain to stop.*

You have been sleeping for a long time.

(iii) Prepositional Phrase: Begins with a preposition and can act as a noun, adjective, or adverb.

Examples: *The book was on the table.*

We stood by the river bank.

(iv) Verbal Phrase: Includes gerunds, infinitives, and participles.

- **Gerund Phrase:** Functions as a noun.

  Examples: *Jumping is fun.*

  He liked skiing.

- **Infinitive Phrase:** The base form of a verb with "to".

  Examples: *To jump is fun.*

  I like to ski.

- **Participle Phrase:** Acts as an adjective.

  Examples: *The dancing parrots entertained the crowd.*

  The wrecked sailboat washed up on the shore.

- **Appositive Phrase:** Gives more information about a noun.

  Examples: *The puppy, a great warrior, is my newest pet.*

  Venus, the evening star, shines brightly in the sky.

- **Absolute Phrase:** Has a subject but no finite verb.

  Examples: *Being a doctor, you should know it.*

  The exams were over, the friends were ready to hang out.

6.5. Parts of a Sentence

A sentence consists of a subject, verb, and object. The subject performs the action, the verb describes the action, and the object receives the action.

Examples:

- *The woman [subject] built [verb] a strong stone wall [object].*
- *The children [subject] eat [verb] buns, cakes, and biscuits [object].*
- *The professor [subject] threw [verb] a chalk [object].*

6.6. Types of Objects

- **Direct Object:** Receives the verb's action.

  Example: *Seema saw a peacock.*

  - **Direct object:** *peacock*
- **Indirect Object:** Receives the direct object.

  Example: *Seema gave a book to her father.*

  - **Direct object:** book
  - **Indirect object:** her father

6.7. Active and Passive Voice

- **Active Voice:** The subject acts

  Example: *I ate the strawberry cake.*
- **Passive Voice:** The subject receives the action.

  Example: *The strawberry cake was eaten by me.*

6.8. Types of Sentences (According to Purpose)

1. **Declarative Sentences:** Provide information.

   Example: *I like eating mangoes.*
2. **Interrogative Sentences:** Ask questions.

   Example: *How is the weather in Delhi?*
3. **Imperative Sentences:** Give instructions, requests, or commands.

   Example: *Please don't give the sweet to the dog.*

4. **Exclamatory Sentences:** Express strong feelings.

Example: *Excellent! You broke all the records.*

6.9. Paragraphs

A paragraph is a group of sentences supporting one main idea. The key to writing a good paragraph is to focus on one idea and organise sentences logically.

Example of a paragraph:

My School is located in a beautiful part of town. It has a large campus with modern infrastructure. Founded in 1995, it has a rich history of academic excellence. I love the supportive and friendly environment.

ACTIVITIES

Activity 1: Making Sentences

1. Write three sentences with direct objects.
2. Write three sentences with both direct and indirect objects.
3. Use different colors to mark the subject, verb, and object in each sentence.

Activity 2: Writing a Paragraph

1. Write a paragraph on any topic.
2. Include at least two sentences in the active voice and two sentences in the passive voice.

EXERCISE

A. Multiple Choice Questions with Answers

1. Identify the subject in the sentence, "The children played football."

(a) The children (b) Children played

(c) Played (d) Football

Ans. (a) The children

Explanation: The subject is the doer of the action, in this case, "The children."

2. Identify the object in the sentence, "The children played football."

(a) The children (b) Children played

(c) Played (d) Football

Ans. (d) Football

Explanation: The object is what the action is being done to, in this case, "football."

3. Which of these sentences has both indirect and direct objects?

(a) I am watching TV. (b) She bought a blue pen.

(c) The girls played cricket. (d) He wrote his sister a letter.

Ans. (d) He wrote his sister a letter.

Explanation: This sentence has both a direct object ("a letter") and an indirect object ("his sister").

4. Which of these sentences is in passive voice?

(a) They are watching a movie. (b) The clock was repaired by Raju.

(c) He is sleeping in the room. (d) My pet dog bit the postman.

Ans. (b) The clock was repaired by Raju.

Explanation: This sentence is in passive voice, as the action is being done to the subject ("The clock").

B. Short Answer Questions

1. Write one sentence of each type: statement, question, exclamatory, and command.

Ans. Sentences of Each Type:

- **Statement:** I enjoy reading books in my free time.
- **Question:** What time does the movie start?
- **Exclamatory:** Wow! That was an amazing performance!
- **Command:** Please close the door quietly.

2. Write two paragraphs about your favorite festival, with at least four sentences each. Use proper sentence structure and paragraph organisation.

Ans. Paragraph 1: My favourite festival is Diwali, the Festival of Lights, celebrated with great enthusiasm in India. It marks the victory of light over darkness and good over evil. People decorate their homes with colourful rangolis, light oil lamps, and burst fireworks to celebrate this joyous occasion. The atmosphere is filled with happiness and togetherness as families come together to celebrate.

Paragraph 2: During Diwali, people also exchange gifts and sweets with friends and family. It is a time of renewal, as many clean and redecorate their homes to welcome prosperity and good fortune. The streets are adorned with beautiful lights, creating a magical ambiance that makes the festival even more special. Diwali brings everyone closer, fostering a sense of unity and warmth.

❑❑❑

UNIT 2

Self-Management Skills—III

UNIT OUTLINE

- **Session 1:** Strength and Weakness Analysis
- **Session 2:** Grooming
- **Session 3:** Personal Hygiene
- **Session 4:** Teamwork
- **Session 5:** Networking Skills
- **Session 6:** Self-Motivation
- **Session 7:** Goal Setting
- **Session 8:** Time Management

SESSION 1: STRENGTH AND WEAKNESS ANALYSIS

1.1. Strength and Weakness Analysis

When you understand "Who am I?", it means that you actually want to know your strengths, abilities, skills, hidden talents, and weaknesses. It's important to recognise not only your positive traits but also the areas where you can grow. Your obstacles and issues that might hinder your progress are discussed as well. A strengths and weaknesses analysis can also be called a personal SWOT analysis (Strength, Weaknesses, Opportunities, and Threat Analysis).

To see **Strength And Weakness Analysis** in Action

Scan QR Code

Evaluating Student Performance and Development Needs

1. Your strengths refer to those areas where you excel or where you can perform well according to your abilities. Each one of us has some strengths.
2. Your weaknesses refer to those areas where you need to improve yourself since you lack abilities in those areas. Each one of us has some weaknesses as well.

1.2. Identifying Strengths

To identify your strengths, you need to:

- Take time to analyse what you are good at.
- Think of those areas where you excel.
- Recall what others appreciate in you.

1.3. Identifying Weaknesses

To identify your weaknesses, you should:

1. Write down the areas where you face problems while performing.
2. Carefully read the feedback given to you by others.
3. Take your feedback as a motivating factor instead of criticism.

Let us see which questions can help us find our strengths and weaknesses:

- Which quality makes me a team leader?
- What do other people like about me?
- What can I do best?
- Why do I worry?

- Why and where do others perform better than me?
- How am I different from others?
- What should I do to increase my performance?

Understanding "Who am I?" involves recognising both your strengths and weaknesses. This self-awareness encompasses your abilities, skills, hidden talents, and personal obstacles that might hinder your progress. This process is often referred to as a personal SWOT analysis (Strengths, Weaknesses, Opportunities, and Threats).

1.4. Strengths

Strengths are areas where you excel and can perform well. Everyone possesses unique strengths. To identify them:

1. Analyse what you are good at.
2. Reflect on areas where you excel.
3. Recall what others appreciate about you.

To see **Strengths and Challanges** in Action

Scan QR Code

1.5. Weaknesses

Weaknesses are areas where you need improvement. Everyone has weaknesses too. To identify them:

1. Note areas where you struggle.
2. Carefully consider feedback from others.
3. Use feedback as a motivation for improvement, not criticism.

Q. What is the full form of SWOT?	(a) Strength, Wealth, Opportunities ,and Timeliness analysis (b) Success, Wealth, Optimism, and Timeliness Analysis (c) Strength, Weakness, opportunities and threat analysis

Finding Strengths and Weaknesses

List of Strengths and Weaknesses	
Strengths	**Weakness**
1. Creativity	1. Self-criticism
2. Versatility	2. Insecurity
3. Flexibility	3. Too detail-oriented
4. Being of focused	4. Public speaking fright
5. Taking initiative	5. Poor presentation skills

1.6. Difference between Interests and Abilities

Interests are activities you enjoy, capture your attention, and satisfy your curiosity. **Abilities** are your natural strengths or talents—things that come to you with ease. Sometimes, your interests might not align with your abilities. In such cases, you can choose to develop your skills or shift your focus to a related area of interest." For example, if you love music but can't sing, you might learn to play an instrument instead.

Questions to Identify Strengths and Weaknesses:

1. What quality makes me a good team leader?
2. What do others like about me?
3. What can I do best?
4. What worries me?
5. Why and where do others perform better than me?
6. How am I different from others?
7. What should I do to improve my performance?

1.6.1 Interests vs. Abilities

(i) Interests

- Activities you enjoy and are curious about.
- Capture your attention and fulfill your need to accomplish things.

(ii) Abilities

- Natural strengths or acquired positive traits.
- Sometimes interests do not match abilities; you can either improve your ability or align with your interests.
- Write any two differences between interest and abilities.

Questions

1. Write any two difference between interest abilities.

1.6.2 Self-exploration Techniques

Self-exploration helps you understand your true self, capabilities, and goals, leading to personal growth and fulfillment. Here are some techniques:

(i) **Learning:** Engage in formal, informal, or self-directed learning to acquire skills and adapt to changing requirements.

(ii) **Career Counseling:** Utilise career counseling and computerised systems for information on courses and career paths.

(iii) **Self-Reflection:** Reflect on past experiences and behaviors to discover your interests and strengths.

(*iv*) **Feedback:** Seek feedback from family, friends, and mentors to identify hidden talents and strengths.

Self-exploration is a journey that enhances clarity, happiness, and success in life.

PRACTICAL ACTIVITY: SELF-EXPLORATION

This activity will help you explore your personal beliefs, strengths, goals, and aspirations.

INSTRUCTIONS:

Fill in the table below with your responses. Be honest and reflective to gain the most from this activity:

List what you believe as a person by starting the sentences with 'I am' (I am a sensitive person).	
List all tasks you can do well by starting the sentences with 'I can' (I can identify safety aspects and seek support when witnessing or experiencing violence and abuse).	
List what you plan to do by starting the sentences with 'I will' (I will train myself in yoga).	
State your aim in life. Start the sentence with 'My aim is' (My aim is to become an accomplished sportsperson).	

1. Fill in the table given below which can help you in preparing an action plan to overcome your weaknesses. Identify and list the activities that you would like to undertake to improve upon your weaknesses and continue to build on strengths.

S.No.	Strengths	Weaknesses	Action plan to overcome your weaknesses
	For example,	For example,	
1.	I can speak many languages	I do not understand computers	Improve computer skills by attending extra classes after school.
2.			
3.			
4.			
5.			

2. What is the difference between interest and abilities?
3. How are strengths different from weaknesses?

SESSION 2: GROOMING

2.1. Grooming

Grooming and Dressing

Grooming refers to making your appearance clean and neat. This includes activities such as brushing your hair and wearing clean, ironed clothes to look neat and tidy.

Dressing is a part of grooming. It means putting on clothes in a proper way to present yourself well.

What is grooming?

When you are well groomed, you ensure that:
Your hair and finger nails are clean;
Your face, body and teeth are clean;

2.2. Importance of Grooming

Grooming helps us in many ways:

Importance of Grooming

"A picture is worth a thousand words." Your appearance speaks volumes and greatly influences others' opinions about you.

Studies have shown that most people form an impression within the first seven seconds of seeing someone. When you are well-groomed, you feel good about yourself, naturally conveying confidence and a positive attitude.

When you are well-groomed, you look smart and polished. This boosts your confidence and leaves a lasting, positive impression on others. Furthermore, it fosters a sense of positive thinking and self-assurance.

2.3. Guidelines for Dressing Up and Grooming

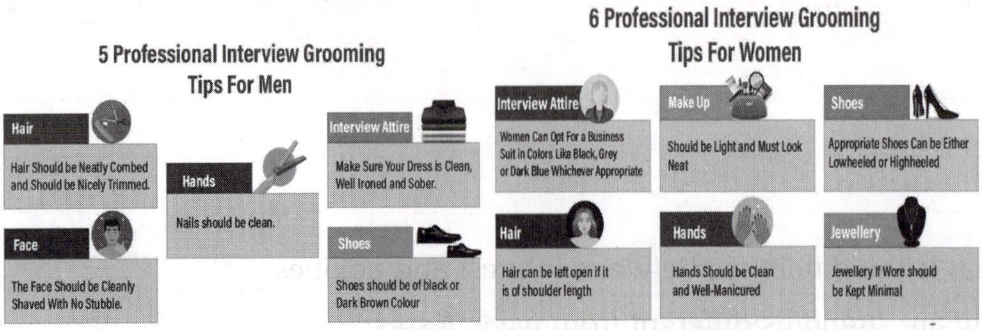

Fig. 2.1 Dressing & Grooming Essentials

2.4. Clothes and Shoes

- Wear neat, clean, and ironed clothes: Ensure your attire is well-maintained and presentable.
- Shoes should be clean and polished: Maintain a polished look for your footwear.
- Wear clean socks: Fresh, clean socks complete your outfit.
- Avoid visible tattoos: It is preferred to keep tattoos covered.

(*i*) Hair

- Keep hair clean and properly combed: Maintain a neat appearance with regular washing and combing.
- Opt for a simple hairstyle: Choose a style that is easy to manage and suits your face shape.
- Regular care: Frequent washing, brushing, and combing are essential to keep your hair and scalp healthy and lice-free.

(*ii*) Face

- Men should be properly shaved: Ensure a clean shave and well-trimmed mustache.
- Brush and clean teeth: Maintain oral hygiene with regular brushing.
- Avoid consuming 'paan': Prevent any stains or odors by avoiding this habit.

Adhering to these guidelines helps you present yourself in the best possible light, contributing to a confident and polished appearance.

2.5. Impressive Appearance and Grooming

"The first impression is the last impression." This saying underscores the crucial role of our appearance in shaping how others perceive us. An impressive appearance and well-groomed behavior make a significant impact, reflecting our personality and attention to detail. In any setting, especially the workplace, the way you dress and present yourself matters. Clean, ironed clothes and positive body language—marked by respectful, decent, and appropriate gestures—enhance your overall impression.

Why Dressing Appropriately and Positive Body Language Matter:

(a) **Promotes Self-Respect:** Shows that you value yourself and others.

(b) **Enhances Self-Confidence:** Boosts your self-assurance and how others perceive you.

(c) **Encourages Improvement:** Reflects your attention to detail and commitment to personal growth.

(d) **Highlights Observational Skills:** Demonstrates that you notice and care about the details.

(e) **Leaves a Lasting Impression:** Every expression and gesture counts.

(f) **Precedes Your Words:** Your appearance often speaks before you do.

(g) **Attracts Attention:** Conveys the right message and draws positive interest.

2.6. Personal Grooming Checklist

Maintain high standards of personal hygiene and grooming with this checklist:

- **See a Doctor Regularly:** Maintain a disease-free lifestyle.
- **Eat a Balanced Diet:** Support overall health and well-being.
- **Use Good Posture:** Communicate effectively with your body language.
- **Bath time:** Shower or bathe daily.
- **Clean Hair:** Wash and maintain your hair regularly.
- **Trim Nails:** Keep fingernails and toenails neat.
- **Style Hair Appropriately:** Choose a hairstyle that suits you.
- **Brush Teeth Twice Daily:** Ensure oral hygiene.
- **Wear Properly Fitting Clothes:** Choose attire that fits well and looks tidy.
- **Dress in Clean, Ironed Clothes:** Maintain a polished appearance.
- **Change Socks Daily:** Prevent foot odor by changing socks and stockings regularly.
- **Avoid Jewelry or Perfume with Uniforms:** Keep accessories minimal.
- **Cover Your Mouth when Sneezing or Coughing:** Use a tissue to maintain hygiene.

Following these guidelines ensures a polished, professional, and respectful appearance, contributing to a positive impression wherever you go.

Answer the statements with a **'Yes'** or a **'No'**. If your answer is 'Yes,' then you are already following the desired norms of grooming. If your answer is 'No,' then you need to start working on various aspects of personal grooming.

Statements	yes/no	My plan for improvement
Wear proper clothes that fit you		
Make sure your clothes are neat and ironed		
Your hair is clean and always combed		
Teeth are always clean and brushed every day		
Wear shoes that are clean and polished		

Write your plan to improve for the 'No' answers in space provided.

EXERCISE

A. Multiple Choice Questions with Answers

Read the questions carefully and circle the letter (a), (b), (c) or (d) that best answers the question.

1. **Dressing up smartly and grooming are important because they help us to look.**
   (a) smart (b) untidy
   (c) shabby (d) All of the above

2. **The following image is an example of shirt.**
   (a) informal (b) formal
   (c) Both of the above (d) None of the above
3. **The following image is an example of T-shirt.**
   (a) informal (b) formal
   (c) Both of the above (d) None of the above

4. **Which of the following is an example of good personal grooming?**
   (a) Wearing wrinkled clothes (b) Having clean, combed hair
   (c) Skipping daily showers (d) None of the above
5. **Why is it important to maintain clean and polished shoes?**
   (a) To impress others (b) To show personal hygiene
   (c) To avoid foot color (d) All of the above
6. **Which statement about personal grooming is true?**
   (a) Personal grooming is only important for formal occasions.
   (b) Good grooming includes regularly cleaning and trimming nails.
   (c) Personal grooming is not necessary for daily activities.
   (d) None of the above
7. **What should you avoid when dressing in a professional setting?**
   (a) Wearing clean, ironed clothes
   (b) Wearing casual or informal attire
   (c) Keeping hair neatly styled
   (d) None of the above
8. **How often should you brush your teeth to maintain good oral hygiene?**
   (a) Once a day (b) Twice a day
   (c) Three times a day (d) Whenever you feel like it

9. **What is a key benefit of positive body language?**
   - (a) It helps you hide your feelings.
   - (b) It makes you appear uninterested.
   - (c) It enhances how others perceive you
   - (d) None of the above

10. **What is the primary purpose of wearing clean and properly fitting clothes?**
   - (a) To follow trends
   - (b) To feel comfortable only
   - (c) To ensure a polished and professional appearance
   - (d) None of the above

ANSWERS

1. (a)	**2.** (b)	**3.** (a)	**4.** (b)	**5.** (d)	**6.** (b)	**7.** (b)	**8.** (b)
9. (c)	**10.** (c)						

B. Short Answer Questions

1. **Write the benefits of personal grooming**

Ans.
- Boosts self-confidence and self-esteem.
- Helps make a positive impression on others.
- Improves personal hygiene and overall health.
- Promotes a polished, professional appearance.
- Increases social acceptance and improves relationships.
- Reflects a sense of discipline and responsibility.

2. **What are some of the important tips regarding dressing up and grooming?**

Ans.
- Always wear clean, well-maintained clothes.
- Choose outfits appropriate for the occasion.
- Keep your hair clean, styled, and trimmed.
- Practice good personal hygiene (e.g., regular showers, oral hygiene).
- Wear accessories that complement your outfit, but avoid overdoing it.
- Ensure your clothes fit properly and are ironed.
- Pay attention to the condition of your shoes and other accessories.

3. **How can proper grooming contribute to your self-confidence?**

Ans.
- It helps you feel more comfortable and positive about your appearance.
- It ensures that you are ready for social interactions, reducing anxiety.

- Being well-groomed makes you feel in control and prepared for any situation.
- Positive feedback from others can reinforce your self-assurance.
- Grooming signals that you respect yourself, which in turn boosts your confidence.

4. Explain why maintaining a positive body language is important in social interactions.

Ans.
- Positive body language enhances how others perceive you, making you appear approachable and friendly.
- It helps establish rapport and trust in personal and professional relationships.
- It conveys confidence, even when you're feeling nervous or unsure.
- Good body language can support effective communication and prevent misunderstandings.
- It allows you to manage social situations better by showing attentiveness and interest.

5. What should you consider when choosing attire for a formal event?

Ans.
- Ensure your outfit is appropriate for the type of event (e.g., wedding, corporate gathering).
- Choose classic and timeless styles rather than overly trendy ones.
- Pay attention to the colour, ensuring it's suitable for the occasion and setting.
- Make sure your clothes are clean, well-fitted, and in good condition.
- Avoid casual clothing like jeans or T-shirts unless explicitly allowed.
- Complement your attire with subtle accessories to avoid distraction.

SESSION 3: PERSONAL HYGIENE

3.1. Personal Hygiene

Personal hygiene means keeping yourself clean to stay healthy. It involves regular practices like washing your body, hands, hair, brushing and flossing your teeth, and caring for your gums. Good hygiene helps prevent illness, reduces the spread of germs, and makes you feel good about yourself. It's essential for staying fit and healthy.

To see **Personal Hygiene** in Action

Scan QR Code

3.2. Importance of Personal Hygiene

Personal hygiene is crucial for our well-being because it helps us:

- Stay healthy
- Create a positive image
- Build our personality
- Look and feel better

PRACTICAL ACTIVITY

1. Answer the statements with a **'Yes'** or a **'No'**. If your answer is **'Yes'**, you are already following personal hygiene standards. If your answer is 'No', then you have to start following the personal hygiene standard immediately.

Statements	yes/no	My plan for improvement
I wash my hands with soap every time I use the toilet.		
I do not bite my nails. They are always clean and clipped.		
I cover my mouth every time I cough or sneeze in public places.		
I regularly take baths to avoid body odor.		
I do not have dandruff or dirt in my hair.		
I never wear dirty clothes.		
My feet are smooth and not dry.		
My hair is clean, non-greasy/not oily and it smells fresh all the time.		

Write your plan to improve for the entire No' answers, in the space provided.

EXERCISE

A. Multiple Choice Questions with Answers

Read the questions carefully and circle the letter (a), (b), (c), or (d) that best answers the question.

1. **Do you think people living on hill stations can skip taking baths for many days?**
   (a) No, irrespective of the climate, one should take a bath regularly.
   (b) Yes, not taking a bath for many days is acceptable for people living in cold climates.
   (c) Yes, if they wipe themselves with a wet cloth, then it is fine.
   (d) None of the above
2. **Radha wants to grow her hair long and she applies a lot of hair oil. She does not wash her hair for days and sometimes it smells too bad. What would be your suggestion to her?**
   (a) She can leave the oil in her hair; after all, it helps her hair to grow.

(b) She can leave it on at night and wash her hair every day before leaving for work.

(c) She should not apply the oil at all.

(d) She can apply the oil and pour a little water on her hair before leaving for work to reduce the smell.

3. How often should you change your toothbrush to maintain good oral hygiene?

(a) Every 3-4 months (b) Once a year

(c) Every 6 months (d) Whenever it looks worn out

4. What is the main benefit of washing your hands before meals?

(a) It keeps your hands clean and free from germs.

(b) It makes your hands smell good.

(c) It helps in warming up your hands.

(d) None of the above

5. Why is it important to trim your nails regularly?

(a) To keep them looking nice

(b) To prevent the accumulation of dirt and bacteria

(c) To improve nail growth

(d) To match fashion trends

ANSWERS

1. (a) **2.** (b) **3.** (a) **4.** (a) **5.** (b)

B. Short Answer Questions

1. List three things that are required for personal grooming in each category of care, wash and avoid keeping clean.

Ans. **1. Care:**

- Hair care (using shampoo and conditioner).
- Skin care (moisturising and protecting from sun).
- Nail care (trimming and cleaning regularly).

2. Wash:

- Showering daily to remove dirt and sweat.
- Washing hands before meals.
- Cleaning face regularly to prevent acne.

3. Avoid Keeping Clean:

- Avoid wearing dirty clothes.

- Avoid using unclean towels.
- Avoid leaving food residue on your hands or face.

2. Mention the benefits of maintaining personal hygiene.

Ans. Benefits of maintaining personal hygiene:

- Prevents the spread of infections and diseases.
- Boosts self-confidence and social interactions.
- Improves physical and mental well-being.

3. What are the benefits of maintaining good personal hygiene?

Ans. Benefits of maintaining good personal hygiene:

- Reduces the risk of illnesses and infections.
- Enhances physical appearance and attractiveness.
- Promotes better overall health and well-being.

4. Why is it important to change your toothbrush regularly?

Ans. Importance of changing your toothbrush regularly:

- Prevents the buildup of bacteria.
- Ensures more effective cleaning of teeth and gums.
- Avoids worn-out bristles that can damage teeth and gums.

5. How does regular hand washing contribute to personal health?

Ans.
- Prevents the spread of germs and infections.
- Reduces the risk of illnesses like cold, flu, and stomach infections.
- Promotes a healthier immune system.

6. What are some effective ways to keep your hair clean and healthy?

Ans.
- Wash hair regularly with a mild shampoo.
- Use conditioner to keep hair hydrated.
- Avoid excessive heat styling and protect hair from sun damage.

7. Why should you avoid wearing unwashed socks?

Ans.
- Prevents the buildup of bacteria and fungi.
- Reduces the risk of foot infections and odor.
- Helps maintain good foot hygiene and comfort.

8. How often should you wash your hair to maintain good hygiene?

Ans.
- It depends on hair type, but generally 2-3 times a week.
- Oily hair may require washing more frequently, while dry hair can go longer between washes.

SESSION 4: TEAMWORK

4.1. Teamwork

Teamwork is very important for solving problems efficiently. By working together and sharing ideas, we can discover the best solutions. Collaboration helps us meet deadlines, maintain high-quality work, and boost team morale. Working as a team creates a strong sense of belonging and commitment towards a common goal.

A team is a group of people who unite to achieve a shared objective. By working together, team members experience the true essence of teamwork.

4.2. Benefits of Teamwork

Teamwork is crucial for the success of any big task. Here's why:

- **Shared Responsibility:** Success depends on the whole team, not just one person.
- **Support System:** Team members help each other fix mistakes.
- **Confidence Boost:** Achieving success as a team builds your confidence.
- **Faster Completion:** Dividing tasks speeds up the work.
- **Better Problem-Solving:** Teams resolve problems more effectively.
- **Knowledge Sharing:** Teams share knowledge and help each other learn new skills.
- **Understanding Sharing:** Teamwork teaches us how to share and collaborate.

Together
Everyone
Achieves
More

EXAMPLE

Imagine a school science fair where two teams, Team A and Team B, are competing.

Team A is made up of three students: Priya, Arjun, and Ravi. Priya is responsible for designing the experiment, Arjun handles the data collection, and Ravi presents the results. Each member knows their role and works together, helping each other when needed. Priya designs a fantastic experiment, Arjun collects accurate data, and Ravi presents it. Because they work well together, Team A wins first place, and everyone feels proud of their collective achievement.

Team B consists of four students: Sara, Raj, Neha, and Amit. Sara thinks she's the only one who can design the experiment perfectly, so she doesn't let others contribute to the planning. Raj, Neha, and Amit try to help but feel sidelined. Their lack of collaboration leads to confusion and errors in the experiment. As a result, Team B's project doesn't meet the judges' expectations, and they don't place in the competition.

This example shows that teamwork, where everyone collaborates and supports each other, leads to success, while a lack of teamwork can cause failure.

4.3. Skills in Teamwork

Teamwork leads to higher productivity, especially for tasks that are complex, interconnected, or too large for one person.

Here are some important factors that influence team building and teamwork:

4.4. Factors Influencing Team Building

- **Work Team Structure:** Includes goals, objectives, guidelines, performance measures, and role specifications.
- **Work Team Process:** Competitiveness and cooperative behavior are key.
- **Diversity:** Gender, background, and skill diversity enhance team effectiveness and creativity.
- Factors Influencing Teamwork
- **Team Rules:** Standards governing group performance, decided either in writing or verbally.
- **Team Unity:** Bonding happens when members realise their contribution to a larger goal.
- **Social Loafing:** Occurs when individuals exert less effort in a group. Mitigated by recognising individual contributions.
- **Loss of Individuality:** Members lose self-awareness and responsibility, focusing on team performance rather than individual.
- These points highlight the essentials of building and maintaining effective teamwork.

PRACTICAL QUESTIONS

1. What are the stages of team development?

Ans. Stages of team development:

- **Forming:** Team members get acquainted.
- **Storming:** Conflicts arise as roles and expectations are clarified.
- **Norming:** Team members establish norms and work collaboratively.
- **Performing:** Team functions efficiently toward achieving goals.
- **Adjourning:** Team disbands after completing its objectives.

2. How can communication be improved within a team?

Ans.
- Foster open and honest conversations.
- Use clear and concise language.
- Encourage active listening and feedback.
- Utilise digital tools for quick updates and collaboration.

3. What are the best practices for setting team goals and objectives?

Ans.
- Ensure goals are **SMART** (Specific, Measurable, Achievable, Relevant, Time-bound).
- Align objectives with the team's overall mission.
- Involve all team members in the goal-setting process.
- Break down larger goals into manageable tasks.

4. How can trust be built and maintained among team members?

Ans.
- Be transparent and honest in all interactions.
- Follow through on commitments and responsibilities.
- Show respect for each other's ideas and contributions.
- Promote a supportive environment where everyone's input is valued.

SESSION 5: NETWORKING SKILLS

5.1. Networking Skills

Networking is about getting to know people, staying in touch, and using each other's knowledge and skills for mutual benefit. Effective networking involves two key skills: **listening sincerely** and **asking thoughtful questions**.

- **Listening sincerely** shows respect and value for the other person's words.
- **Asking thoughtful questions** shows interest and helps build trust.

5.2. Example of Networking Skills

Tarun and Neeraj, both B.Tech graduates, were looking for jobs. Tarun used LinkedIn to find opportunities and secured a job quickly, while Neeraj relied on newspapers and struggled longer. Tarun's networking skills made the difference.

5.3. Benefits of Networking Skills

Networking helps you build dependable and trusted relationships where you can:

- **Share expertise and skills:** Ask friends or neighbors for help in preparing for an interview.

- **Seek and provide support:** Get help from friends when you're late or need assistance with projects.
- **Inform and be informed about opportunities:** Use connections to find part-time jobs or other opportunities.

5.4. How to Build Networking Skills

(i) Practice Good Communication Habits:

- Maintain eye contact.
- Nod in understanding or agreement.
- Use simple, straightforward language.
- Ask questions and invite opinions.
- Pay attention to body language to ensure understanding.

(ii) Ask for Constructive Feedback:

- Ask friends how you come across in conversations.
- Use their feedback to improve your communication style.

(iii) Attend Networking Events:

- Practice your skills by attending events.
- Focus on building meaningful connections.
- Show interest by asking questions and listening closely.
- Prioritise the quality of relationships over the quantity.

(iv) Practice Active Listening:

- Listen more than you speak.
- Maintain eye contact and positive body language.
- Formulate your response after the other person finishes speaking.

(v) Ask Good Questions:

- Build trust by asking positive and relevant questions.
- Keep your questions focused on the topic at hand.

(vi) Read Body Language:

- Observe the body language of others.
- Be mindful of the signals you're sending with your body language.

These steps will help you develop strong networking skills, which are essential for building valuable relationships in both personal and professional settings.

PRACTICAL ACTIVITIES

1. How can networking skills lead to unexpected opportunities? Write a story illustrating this.
2. Your brother has opened a grocery shop, but his sales are low. What networking strategies can he use to attract more customers and increase sales?
3. What role do networking skills play in personal and professional growth? Why are they essential in real life?

SESSION 6: SELF-MOTIVATION

6.1. Self-Motivation

Self-motivation is the inner drive that pushes you to achieve your goals, work hard, and improve yourself. It helps you attain happiness and a better quality of life without needing external influence. Different people are motivated by different things at various times in their lives.

6.2. Types of Motivation

(*i*) Internal/Intrinsic Motivation:

Definition: Motivation that comes from within, driven by personal satisfaction or desire.

Examples:

- Starting your own business.
- Participating in a competition.
- Winning a trophy by working hard.
    - **Benefits:** Makes you happy, and healthy, and boosts self-respect.

(*ii*) External/Extrinsic Motivation:

Definition: Motivation that comes from external rewards or recognition.

Examples:

- Money.
- Prizes.
- Encouragement.
    - **Benefits:** Provides respect, recognition, and appreciation.

6.3. Qualities of Self-Motivated People

Elattuvalapil Sreedharan, known as the 'Metro Man', is a great example of a self-motivated person. He successfully led the construction of the Konkan Railway and the Delhi Metro, demonstrating unwavering dedication and inspiring his team to achieve outstanding results.

Building Self-Motivation

Follow these steps to build self-motivation:

(*i*) **Find Your Strengths:** Identify your positive qualities.

(*ii*) **Set and Focus on Your Goals:** Define clear goals and concentrate on them.

(*iii*) **Develop a Plan:** Create a roadmap to reach your goals.

(*iv*) **Stay Loyal to Your Goals:** Be dedicated and persistent in achieving your goals.

PRACTICAL ACTIVITIES

1. **Are You Self-Motivated?**
    - Discuss with friends how you can make yourself more internally motivated.
    - Make a list of these points.
2. **Famous Personalities**
    1. Write a brief life sketch of a famous person who achieved success through self-motivation.

    Self-motivation is the key to achieving personal goals and improving your life. By understanding and harnessing both internal and external motivators, you can stay driven and focused on your path to success.

SESSION 7: GOAL SETTING

7.1. Goal Setting

Goal Setting is a process that helps you think about your ideal future and motivates you to turn your aspirations into reality. By setting goals, you can focus your efforts on what you want to achieve in life.

7.2. Goals and Setting SMART Goals

Goals: These are your dreams with a deadline. For example, saving pocket money to buy a favorite mobile phone by a certain date.

Goal Setting: It involves identifying your goals and planning how to achieve them. Goals help you prioritise what's important and focus on the end result, leading to success in both your career and personal life.

7.3. How to Set Goals

Use the SMART model to set your goals. SMART stands for:

(i) **Specific:** Clearly define your goal.

- **Questions to answer:**
  - Who is involved?
  - What do I want to achieve?
  - Where will it happen?
  - When will it start and finish?
  - Which resources are needed?
  - Why is this goal important?
- **Example:**
  - Not specific: "I want to learn to play the guitar."
  - Specific: "I want to learn to play the guitar from a teacher to participate in the inter-school competition next year."

(ii) **Measurable:** Determine how you will measure your progress.

- **Questions to answer:**
  - How much or how many?
  - How will I know when it's achieved?
- **Example:**
  - Not measurable: "I want to be rich."
  - Measurable: "I want to have five times more money than I currently have."

(iii) **Achievable:** Break down big goals into smaller, manageable parts.

- **Example:**
  - Not clear: "I want to become a teacher in a reputed school."

Achievable steps:

1. Complete higher secondary education.
2. Complete graduation.
4. Complete B.Ed.
5. Apply for teaching jobs.

(iv) **Realistic:** Ensure your goal is practical and possible.

- **Example:**
  - Unrealistic: "I will prepare for exams in three hours."
  - Realistic: "I will spend three hours every day preparing for my exams."

(v) **Time-bound:** Set a deadline for your goal.

- **Example:**
  - Not time-bound: "I want to lose 20 kg."
  - Time-bound: "I want to lose 20 kg in the next six months."

PRACTICAL ACTIVITIES

1. Discuss with friends how to control your emotions and make a list of these points.
2. Write a brief life sketch of a famous person who achieved their goal using the SMART model.

Goal setting helps you focus on your aspirations and provides a clear path to achieve them. By using the SMART model, you can set specific, measurable, achievable, realistic, and time-bound goals, ensuring a higher chance of success.

SESSION 8: TIME MANAGEMENT

8.1. Time Management

Time management is the process of planning and controlling how much time to spend on specific activities. Good time management helps you achieve more in less time reduces stress, and leads to success in your career and personal life.

8.2. Importance of Time Management

- Helps you complete tasks on time
- Allows you to make a daily timetable
- Helps you estimate how long tasks will take
- Ensures you submit homework and assignments on time
- Prevents wasting time during the day

8.3. Tips for Effective Time Management

- Avoid delaying or postponing activities
- Organise your room and study area
- Create a 'No Disturbance Zone' for important tasks
- Use waiting time productively
- Prepare a 'To-do' list
- Prioritise tasks
- Replace unproductive activities with productive ones

8.4. Time Management Strategies and Techniques

Time management involves planning and managing your time to increase efficiency and effectiveness. Here are some important points for effective time management:

(*i*) **Setting and Prioritising Goals:**

- Take charge of your life by setting goals.
- Prioritise daily activities to align with your goals.
- Focus on constructive use of your time.

(*ii*) **Creating a Schedule:**

- Make a schedule to live a disciplined and punctual life.
- Ensure effective use of your time.

(*iii*) **Making Lists of Tasks:**

- Create a daily list of tasks.
- Prioritise the tasks to make your day worthwhile.

(*iv*) **Balancing Work and Leisure:**

- Balance work with leisure activities.
- Leisure helps you relax and recharge.

(*v*) **Breaking Large Tasks into Smaller Tasks:**

- Break large tasks into smaller, manageable ones.
- Completing smaller tasks motivates you to tackle more.

PRACTICAL ACTIVITIES

1. Group Discussion on Time Management:

- Form groups of 5 students each and appoint a group monitor.
- Discuss the importance of time management.
- List down the key points from the discussion.

2. Planning Study Time:

- Have you created a timetable before exams for studying?
- If yes, how do you plan your time? Write down the points briefly.

Time management is essential for achieving success in both personal and professional life. By setting goals, creating schedules, making task lists, balancing work and leisure, and breaking large tasks into smaller ones, you can manage your time effectively and increase your productivity.

PRACTICE SESSION

1. How can effective time management contribute to achieving your academic goals?
2. Describe a situation where teamwork helped you accomplish a challenging task. What strategies did you use to work effectively as a team?
3. List three personal goals you want to achieve this year and explain how you plan to achieve them using the SMART model.
4. Explain the importance of setting realistic goals and provide an example of how setting an unrealistic goal could lead to failure.
5. Discuss how self-motivation can impact your daily routine and provide an example of a time when self-motivation helped you succeed in a task.

❑❑❑

Unit 3
Information and Communication Technology Skills-III

UNIT OUTLINE

SESSION 1: INFORMATION AND COMMUNICATION TECHNOLOGY SKILLS-III

1.1. Information and Communication Technology Skills-III

INTRODUCTION TO ICT

To see **Introduction to ICT** in Action

Scan QR Code

ICT stands for "Information and Communication Technologies." These technologies provide access to information through telecommunication. This includes Information Technology (IT) with a focus on communication technologies such as the Internet, wireless networks, cell phones, and other communication media.

In recent times, ICT has introduced many new communication skills and devices. For example, people can communicate instantly with others in different countries using technologies like instant messaging, voice-over IP (VoIP), and video conferencing. Social networking websites like Facebook and Instagram allow users worldwide to stay in contact and communicate regularly.

In digital technology, information is translated into a binary format, while in analog technology, it is translated into electric pulses of different amplitudes.

People use technology daily at home and work. Various ICT tools are used to work on the Internet. For example, you can find job-related information and apply for jobs online by posting your resume or even having interviews via phone or email.

Through ICT skills, you can communicate with friends and family, use them for business or job-related work, and stay updated on the latest trends.

1.2. Using a Word Processor

To see **Using a Word Processor** in Action

Scan QR Code

To write a letter or make a report, we can use a word processor instead of pen and paper. A word processor is a software application that helps us create documents by typing text, making corrections (editing), arranging it neatly (formatting), and printing it.

1.3. Advantages of Using a Word Processor

There are many advantages to using a word processor:

- If you need to add or remove text after getting your report checked, you can easily do it in a Word document.

- When making a resume, it is important not to have any spelling mistakes. A word processor helps check spelling and grammar.
- If you are writing a long report and need to work on it for several days, you can save the report and return to it whenever required. You can also print the document if you need to send a hard copy.
- You can make the document attractive by adding different colors, text styles, and text sizes. For example, you can write the title in a special style or highlight an important date.
- You can create posters by inserting pictures, bulleted lists, tables, shapes, and charts.

1.4. Common Word Processors

Some common word- processing applications are Microsoft Word, WordPerfect, Softword, OpenOffice Writer, and LibreOffice Writer. Most functions of all word processors are the same. Here, we will use OpenOffice Writer to understand how a word processor works.

1.5. Getting Started with OpenOffice Writer

Apache OpenOffice is free and open-source software developed by the Apache Software Foundation. It can be downloaded for free from **OpenOffice.org**. It is available in many languages and can read/write files created in other Office software packages.

The Apache OpenOffice package contains:

- OpenOffice Writer (Word processor)
- OpenOffice Calc (Spreadsheet)
- OpenOffice Impress (Presentation)
- OpenOffice Base (Database Management System)
- OpenOffice Draw (Graphics)
- OpenOffice Math (Equation Editor)

The new version of Apache OpenOffice shows a sidebar on the interface of Writer, Impress, and Calc, similar to the ribbon in Microsoft Office.

Creating a New Document

To create a new document in OpenOffice Writer, follow these steps:

1. Click the File menu.
2. Click the New option.
3. Click Text Document.

OR

1. Click the New option icon drop-down arrow from the toolbar.

2. Click Text Document.

OR

Press Ctrl + N on the keyboard.

A blank document will open. You can start typing the text. Click on the File menu and save the file using the Save As option.

Activities

1. Open the OpenOffice Writer application. Create a new document and type some text. Explore the various options available in OpenOffice Writer and save the file. Write down the steps you followed.
2. Open the OpenOffice Writer application and explore the toolbar options. Make a list of all the toolbar names and their options.
3. **Multiple Choice Questions:**

(i) Using a word processor, you can create resumes and posters. State whether this is true or false.

(i) True *(ii)* False

(ii) Which of the following options are word processors? Select all the correct options.

(i) OpenOffice Writer

(ii) LibreOffice Writer

(iii) Microsoft Word *(iv)* All of the above

(iii) Which shortcut key is used to create a new document?

(i) Ctrl + C *(ii)* Ctrl + N

(iii) Ctrl + M *(iv)* Ctrl + D

4. List the advantages of using a word processor to write a letter.

SESSION 2: BASIC INTERFACE OF OPENOFFICE WRITER

2.1. Basic Interface of OpenOffice Writer

When you open a document in OpenOffice Writer, the document window appears along with the application window. The document window is where you can start writing your text. It has several components like the title bar, toolbar, menu bar, document area, and status bar.

To see **Basic Interface of OpenOffice Writer** in Action

Scan QR Code

2.2. Major Components of OpenOffice Writer

(i) **Title Bar:** The topmost bar that shows the name of the application (OpenOffice Writer) and the document (usually 'untitled1' by default).

(ii) **Menu Bar:** Below the title bar, it has options like File, Edit, View, etc., which help you perform various functions. For example, three dots (...) after a submenu indicate a dialog box will open, and an arrow (→) means another submenu will open.

(iii) **Toolbar:** Below the menu bar, it has icons for shortcuts to common commands.

- **Standard Toolbar:** Icons for common commands like creating or opening documents.
- **Formatting Toolbar:** Icons for formatting text like changing font type, size, and alignment. For example, to make the text bold, click the Bold icon.

(iv) **Ruler Bar:** Below the formatting toolbar, it helps adjust margins, indentation, and tab stops.

(v) **Status Bar:** At the bottom of the document, it shows page numbers, word count, and other details. It also has a zoom bar to change the text size for viewing without changing the font size.

(vi) **Scroll Bar:** Helps move through the document up/down and left/right.

(vii) **Work Area:** The area in the document window where you enter text.

(viii) **Zoom:** Allows changing the scale of text and pictures for viewing.

(ix) **Sidebar:** On the right side of the Writer window, it has five sections by default: Properties, Page, Styles, Gallery, and Navigator. Click on the icons to open each section.

2.3. Various Menu Options

- **File:** Commands like New, Open, Close, Save, Print.
- **Edit:** Commands like Undo, Cut, Copy, Paste, Find and Replace.
- **View:** Commands to change the document display, like Zoom in/out, Web, Status Bar, and Ruler.
- **Insert:** Commands to add objects like images, shapes, charts, headers, footers, and page numbers.
- **Format:** Commands to change text appearance, like bold, alignment, and paragraph settings.
- **Table:** Commands to insert or delete tables and format them.
- **Tools:** Functions like Spelling and Grammar check, Mail merge, Macros.
- **Window:** Shows all OpenOffice Writer windows and lets you switch between them.
- **Help:** Options to open the Writer's built-in help or go to online help.

2.4. Context Menu

Right-click on any word, paragraph, image, or object to see a context menu with options specific to the selected item.

2.5. Multiple Ways to Perform Functions

You can perform most tasks in several ways. For example, to save a file:

1. Click the File menu, then click Save.
2. Press Ctrl + S on the keyboard.
3. Click the Save icon on the standard toolbar.

To make text bold, select the text and:

1. Click the Character option from the Format menu and choose Bold.
2. Click the Bold icon in the Formatting toolbar.
3. Right-click the text, select Style, then choose Bold.
4. Press Ctrl + B on the keyboard.

Activities

1. Open OpenOffice Writer, create a new document, type some text, explore options, and save the file. Write down the steps you followed.
2. Explore the toolbar options in OpenOffice Writer and list their names and options.

EXERCISE

A. Multiple Choice Questions with Answers

1. Undo, Cut, Copy, and Paste are commands found in which menu?

(a) View (b) Edit
(c) Styles (d) File

2. Which option changes the page magnification?

(a) Page indicator (b) Proofing level
(c) Zoom bar (d) Help

3. Where can you see the page number and word count in OpenOffice?

(a) Right (b) Centre
(c) Left (d) Middle

4. **Which menu option has the commands Save, Print, and Close?**

(a) Insert
(b) File
(c) Tools
(d) Format

ANSWERS

1. (b) 2. (c) 3. (a) 4. (b)

B. Subjective Questions

1. **List different ways to format text (bold, underlined, font size).**

Ans. Different ways to format text:

- Bold, Italics, Underlined
- Change Font Size
- Change Font Style
- Text Colour
- Highlight Text

2. **Explain the basic user interface of OpenOffice Writer.**

Ans. Basic user interface of OpenOffice Writer:

- The interface includes a Menu Bar, Toolbar, Ruler, Workspace (where you type), and Status Bar (showing information like page number and word count).

3. **List the various menu options available in OpenOffice Writer.**

Ans. Various menu options in OpenOffice Writer:

- File, Edit, View, Insert, Format, Tools, Table, Window, Help

4. **Identify basic icons in the toolbar.**

Ans. Basic icons in the toolbar:

- Save, Undo, Redo, Bold, Italics, Underline, Font Color, Align Left, Center, Align Right, Print, Cut, Copy, Paste

5. **Use OpenOffice Help to explore how to perform various functions.**

Ans. Using OpenOffice Help:

- Press F1 or go to the Help menu to search for topics. You can explore how to use functions like formatting, inserting objects, or customising settings.

SESSION 3: SAVE, CLOSE, OPEN, AND PRINT DOCUMENTS

3.1. Save, Close, Open, and Print Documents

After creating a document in OpenOffice Writer, you need to save it to use later for viewing or printing. When you save a file in OpenOffice, it gets a default extension of .odt, indicating it's an OpenOffice Writer document. You can also save it in different formats like .doc, .txt, and .rtf.

3.2. Creating a New Document

To create a new text document in OpenOffice Writer:

1. **Using the File Menu:**
    1. Select the File menu.
    2. Choose New and then Text Document.
2. **Using the Toolbar:**
    1. Click the New button on the Standard toolbar.
    2. Select the desired option to create a new text document.
3. **Using Keyboard Shortcut:**
    - Press Ctrl + N to create a new document.

3.3. Saving a Document

To save a document, follow these steps:

1. **Using the File Menu:**
    - Click the File menu.
    - Select Save As.
2. **Using the Toolbar:**
    - Click the Save button on the Standard toolbar.
3. **Using Keyboard Shortcut:**
    - Press Ctrl + Shift + S to open the Save As dialog box.

Then:

1. The Save As dialog box appears.
2. Select the location where you want to save the document.
3. Type the file name and click the Save button.

3.4. Opening a Document

To open an already saved document in OpenOffice Writer:

1. **Using the File Menu:**
    - Click the Open option from the File menu.
2. **Using the Toolbar:**
    - Click the Open button on the Standard toolbar.
3. **Using Keyboard Shortcut:**
    - Press Ctrl + O to open a document.

3.5. Closing a Document

To close an open document:

1. **Using the File Menu:**
   - Click the File menu.
   - Select Close.

3.6. Printing a Document

To print a document in OpenOffice Writer:

1. **Using the File Menu:**
   - Click the File menu.
   - Select Print.
2. **Using Keyboard Shortcut:**
   - Press Ctrl + P to open the print dialog.

EXERCISE

A. Multiple Choice Questions with Answers

1. **What is the shortcut to save changes to an existing file?**
   (a) File > Save (b) Insert > Save (c) Home > Save
2. **What is the shortcut to close a document?**
   (a) File > Save (b) File > Close (c) File > Exit
3. **What is the shortcut to print a document?**
   (a) File > Export (b) File > Send (c) File > Print

ANSWERS

1. (a) **2.** (b) **3.** (c)

B. Subjective Questions

1. **Describe the steps to save a new document in OpenOffice Writer.**

Ans. Steps to save a new document in OpenOffice Writer:

- Click on File in the top menu.
- Select Save or Save As.
- If it's the first time saving, choose a location on your computer where you want to save the file.
- Type a name for the document.
- Click Save.

2. Explain how to print a document in OpenOffice Writer.

Ans.
- Click on File in the top menu.
- Select Print.
- Choose your printer from the list.
- Click OK to start printing.

SESSION 4: EDITING IN OPENOFFICE WRITER

4.1. Editing In OpenOffice Writer

Editing a document involves making changes like correcting spelling, deleting text, copying text, and moving text. To edit or format text, you must first select it. Selected text in OpenOffice Writer gets highlighted in blue.

4.2. Selecting Consecutive Text

Using the Mouse:

1. Place the cursor at the beginning of the text.
2. Press and hold the left mouse button.
3. Drag the mouse to the end of the selection.
4. Release the mouse button.

Using the Keyboard:

1. Place the cursor at the beginning of the text.
2. Use the navigation keys with special keys (Shift + Arrow keys) to select the text.

4.3. Selecting Non-Consecutive Text

To select text in different parts of the document:

1. Select the first piece of text.
2. Hold down the Ctrl key.
3. Select the next piece of text.
4. Repeat steps 2 and 3 for additional text selections.

4.4. Inserting and Overtyping Text

In Insert mode, new text is added without deleting existing text. In Overtype mode, new text replaces existing text. Toggle between these modes using the Insert key.

STATUS BAR INDICATORS:

- **INSERT:** Insert mode
- **OVER:** Overtype mode

INSERTING A BLANK LINE

1. Place the cursor at the end of the line.
2. Press Enter to insert a blank line below.

4.5. Deleting Text

To Delete a Character:

1. Position the cursor to the left of the character.
2. Press DELETE. -or-
3. Position the cursor to the right of the character.
4. Press BACKSPACE.

To Delete a Word:

1. Position the cursor to the left of the word.
2. Press Ctrl + Delete. -or-
3. Position the cursor to the right of the word.
4. Press Ctrl + Backspace.

To Delete a Block of Text:

1. Select the text.
2. Press DELETE or BACKSPACE.

4.6. Undo and Redo Commands

- **Undo:** Reverses the last action. Click Edit > Undo or click the Undo button on the Standard toolbar.
- **Redo:** Reverses the last Undo action. Click Edit > Redo or click the Redo button on the Standard toolbar.

4.7. Copying Text

1. Select the text to copy.
2. Click Edit > Copy or click the Copy button on the Standard toolbar.
3. Place the cursor where you want to paste.
4. Click Edit > Paste or click the Paste button on the Standard toolbar.

4.8. Moving Text

1. Select the text to move.
2. Click Edit > Cut or click the Cut button on the Standard toolbar.
3. Place the cursor where you want to paste.
4. Click Edit > Paste or click the Paste button on the Standard toolbar.

EXERCISE

A. Multiple Choice Questions with Answers

1. What is the shortcut to save changes to an existing file?

(a) File > Save (b) Insert > Save

(c) Home > Save

2. What is the shortcut to close a document?

(a) File > Save (b) File > Close

(c) File > Exit

3. What is the shortcut to print a document?

(a) File > Export (b) File > Send

(c) File > Print

ANSWERS

1. (a) **2.** (b) **3.** (c)

B. Subjective Questions

1. Describe the steps to save a new document in OpenOffice Writer.

Ans. To save a new document in OpenOffice Writer, follow these steps:

- Click on File in the top menu.
- Select Save As from the dropdown menu.
- In the Save As dialog box, choose the location where you want to save the document.
- Enter a name for the file in the File Name field.
- Choose the desired file format from the Save as Type dropdown menu (e.g., OpenDocument Text (.odt), Microsoft Word (.docx)).
- Click Save to store the document.

2. Explain how to print a document in OpenOffice Writer.

Ans. To print a document in OpenOffice Writer:

- Open the document you want to print.
- Click on File in the top menu.
- Select Print from the dropdown menu. Alternatively, use the shortcut Ctrl + P.
- In the Print dialog box, select the printer and configure print settings (such as the number of copies, page range, etc.).
- Click OK to send the document to the printer.

3. Write the keyboard shortcuts for the following commands:

(a) Copy (b) Cut

(c) Paste (d) Undo

Ans. (a) Ctrl + C (b) Ctrl + X

(c) Ctrl + V (d) Ctrl + Z

SESSION 5: FORMATTING TEXT IN OPENOFFICE WRITER

5.1. Formatting Text in OpenOffice Writer

Formatting text means changing its appearance to make it more attractive or readable. You can make text bold, underlined, change its color, and more. This can be done using the Format menu or the Formatting toolbar.

To see **Formatting Text in OpenOffice Writer** in Action

Scan QR Code

5.2. Wrapping Text

Word wrap automatically moves text to the next line when it reaches the right margin. It also adjusts text to fit around images or text boxes.

To wrap text around an image:

1. Select the image.
2. Go to the Format menu and select Wrap.
3. Choose the desired wrap option.

5.3. Setting Alignment

Alignment determines how text is positioned within the page margins. The steps to change text alignment are:

1. Select the text.

2. Go to the Format menu and select Paragraph.
3. In the Paragraph dialog box, choose the desired alignment.
4. Click OK.
   - Or - Use the alignment buttons on the Formatting toolbar.

5.4. Font Size, Type, and Face

Font formatting changes the appearance of text, including its type, size, and style. The default font in OpenOffice Writer is Times New Roman, size 12. Font size is measured in points (pt), with 72 points equal to one inch.

Font Style: Refers to bold, italics, underlined, or normal text.

Typeface: The design of the lettering, like Times New Roman.

Font: A specific size and style of a typeface, like "12pt Times New Roman Bold."

5.5. Text Formatting Using the Format Menu

1. Select the text.
2. Go to the Format menu and choose Character.
3. Use the Font tab to change the font, size, and typeface.
4. Use the Font Effects tab to change the color and apply styles like underlining.
5. Use the Position tab to change text position (e.g., superscript, subscript).
6. Click OK after making your selections.

5.6. Text Formatting Using the Formatting Bar

The Formatting bar provides buttons for quick text formatting.

CHANGE CASE

You can change text case without retyping. Steps to change case:

1. Select the text.
2. Go to the Format menu and choose Change Case.
3. Choose the desired option:
   - Sentence case
   - UPPERCASE
   - tOGGLE cASE
   - lowercase
   - Capitalize Every Word

5.7. Header and Footer

Headers appear at the top of each page; footers appear at the bottom. To add a header or footer:

1. Go to the Insert menu and choose Header or Footer, then select Default.
2. Type the text in the header or footer area.
3. For additional options, go to the Format menu and select Page, then choose the Header or Footer tab.

To remove a header or footer:

1. Go to the Insert menu and choose Header or Footer, then select Default.
2. Confirm the deletion when prompted.

5.8. Finding and Replacing Text

To Find Text:

1. Go to the Edit menu and select Find & Replace.
2. In the dialog box, type the word in the Search for box.
3. Click Find to locate the word or Find All to highlight all instances.

To Replace Text:

1. Go to the Edit menu and select Find & Replace.
2. In the dialog box, type the word in the Search for box and the replacement word in the Replace with box.
3. Click Replace to replace one instance or Replace All to replace all instances.

5.9. Page Numbering

To add page numbers:

1. Click in the header or footer area.
2. Go to the Insert menu and choose Fields, then select Page Number.

5.10. Format Painter

The Format Painter copies formatting from one text selection to another.

1. Select the text with the desired formatting.
2. Click the Format Painter button on the toolbar (it looks like a paintbrush).
3. Click on the text where you want to apply the formatting.

5.11. Show/Hide Button

Non-printing characters, like spaces and tabs, can be shown or hidden:

1. Click the Show/Hide button on the Standard toolbar (it looks like a paragraph symbol).

5.12. Printing a Document

1. Go to the File menu and select Print.
2. In the Print dialog box, select the printer, specify the page range and number of copies, then click Print.

5.13. Saving a Document in Different Formats

To save a document in a different format:

1. Go to the File menu and select Save As.
2. In the Save As dialog box, choose the file type from the Save as type drop-down list.
3. Type the file name and click Save.

PRACTICAL QUESTIONS

1. **Vedika wants to make important words darker than normal text.** She should use the **Bold** command. The keyboard shortcut is **Ctrl + B**.
2. **Sukrit wants to make the entire text bold.** He can select all text using the keyboard shortcut **Ctrl + A**.
3. **The command to reverse the last action is** the **Undo** command.
4. **The menu to change text color and size is** the **Format menu**.

Keyboard Shortcuts

1. **Copy:** Ctrl + C 2. **Cut:** Ctrl + X 3. **Paste:** Ctrl + V 4. **Undo:** Ctrl + Z

SESSION 6: AUTOCORRECT AND SPELL CHECK IN OPENOFFICE WRITER

6.1. Autocorrect and Spell Check in OpenOffice Writer

Introduction to Spelling and Grammar Checking

OpenOffice Writer offers powerful tools for spelling and grammar checking, ensuring your documents are error-free. These tools help you easily correct spelling and grammatical mistakes while typing.

When typing in OpenOffice Writer, red or blue wavy lines may appear under your text:

- **Red wavy line:** Indicates a misspelled word.
- **Blue wavy line:** Indicates a grammatical mistake.

OpenOffice Writer provides two main ways to check spelling and grammar:

1. Using Auto-Spell check
2. Using the Spelling and Grammar option

6.2. Using Auto-Spell Check

Auto-Spell check automatically checks your spelling as you type. Follow these steps to use Auto-Spell check:

1. **Enable Auto-Spell check:**
    - Click the **Auto-Spell check** button on the Standard bar.
    - Misspelled words will be underlined in red.
2. **Correct Misspelled Words:**
    - Right-click on the misspelled word (underlined in red).
    - Choose a correct word from the suggested list.
    - If you select a word from the AutoCorrect submenu, the misspelled word and its replacement will be added to the AutoCorrect list for the current language.

Using the Spelling and Grammar Option

The Spelling and Grammar option allows for a more thorough check of your document. Follow these steps:

(*i*) **Open Spelling and Grammar Tool:**

- Go to the **Tools menu** and select **Spelling and Grammar**.
- Or, click the **Spelling and Grammar** button on the Standard bar.
- Or, press **F7**.

(*ii*) **Spelling Dialog Box:**

- The Spelling dialog box appears, showing the first misspelled word in the "Not in Dictionary" text box.
- Suggested corrections are displayed in the Suggestions box.

(*iii*) **Correcting Errors:**

- Click on a suggested word to correct the misspelled word.
- You can choose to:
    - **Ignore Once:** Skip the current misspelled word.

- **Ignore All:** Skip all instances of the misspelled word.
- **Add:** Add the word to the dictionary.
- **Change:** Correct the current instance with the selected suggestion.
- **Change All:** Correct all instances of the misspelled word with the selected suggestion.
- **AutoCorrect:** Automatically corrects the word and adds it to the AutoCorrect list.

(iv) Completing the Spell Check:

- Repeat the correction steps until the message box says, "The spell check is complete."
- Click OK to finish.

PRACTICAL EXERCISE

1. Enabling Auto-Spell check:

- Go to the Standard bar and click the Auto-Spell check button.
- Type a sentence with a misspelled word and observe the red wavy line under it.
- Right-click on the misspelled word and choose a correction from the list.

2. Checking Spelling Errors:

- Open a document with multiple pages.
- Go to the **Tools menu** and select **Spelling and Grammar**.
- Follow the prompts in the Spelling dialog box to correct each misspelled word.

Using Auto-Spell check and the Spelling and Grammar tools in OpenOffice Writer ensures your documents are free of spelling and grammatical errors. These features make it easy to create polished, professional documents.

SESSION 7: INSERTING LISTS AND TABLES IN OPENOFFICE WRITER

7.1. Inserting Lists and Tables in OpenOffice Writer

Introduction

OpenOffice Writer allows you to organise your document effectively using lists and tables. In this session, you'll learn how to insert bulleted and numbered lists and how to create and manipulate tables. This knowledge will help you present information clearly and efficiently.

To see **Inserting Lists and Tables in OpenOffice Writer** in Action

Scan QR Code

7.2. Inserting Lists Using Bullets and Numbering

Lists help organise items sequentially, highlighting key points or showing priority. OpenOffice Writer offers two types of lists:

- **Numbered Lists (Ordered Lists):** Used when the order of items is important, such as ranking students.
- **Bulleted Lists (Unordered Lists):** Used when the order of items is not important, such as a shopping list.

7.3. Steps to Create a Bulleted or Numbered List

1. **Place the Cursor:**
   - Position the cursor where you want the list to start.
2. **Open Bullets and Numbering Dialog:**
   - Select **Bullets and Numbering** from the **Format menu**.
   - The **Bullets and Numbering** dialog box will appear.
3. **Choose List Type:**
   - Click the **Bullets** tab to create a bulleted list or the **Numbering Type** tab to create a numbered list.
4. **Select Style and Confirm:**
   - Choose the desired style and click OK.
5. **Type List Items:**
   - Type each item and press Enter after each one.

Alternatively, you can use the **Bulleted list button** or the **Numbered list button** on the Formatting bar to quickly create lists.

7.4. Inserting Tables

Tables display information in rows and columns, making it easy to read and present data. Here's how to create and manipulate tables in OpenOffice Writer.

Creating a Table Using the Table Button

1. **Open Table Grid:**
   - Click the drop-down arrow of the **Table button** on the Standard bar.
2. **Select Rows and Columns:**
   - Move the mouse pointer to highlight the number of rows and columns needed.
   - A table will be inserted at the cursor's position.

Creating a Table Using the Table Menu

1. **Open Insert Table Dialog:**
   - Click the **Table menu** and choose **Insert Table**.
   - Alternatively, press **Ctrl + F12** or click the **Table icon** on the Standard toolbar.
2. **Specify Table Dimensions:**
   - In the **Insert Table** dialog box, specify the number of columns and rows.
   - Click **OK**.

Entering Data in a Table

- **Click inside a cell** to start typing.
- **Select a row or column** by clicking and dragging the mouse over the cells.

7.5. Modifying Tables

7.5.1 Inserting Rows:

(*i*) Position the cursor in the cell where you want to insert a new row.

(*ii*) Click the **Table menu**, choose **Insert**, and select **Rows**.

(*iii*) In the **Insert Rows** dialog box, specify the number of rows and their position (Before/After).

(*iv*) Click **OK**.

7.5.2 Inserting Columns:

(*i*) Position the cursor in the cell where you want to insert a new column.

(*ii*) Click the **Table menu**, choose **Insert**, and select **Columns**.

(*iii*) In the **Insert Columns** dialog box, specify the number of columns and their position (Before/After).

(*iv*) Click **OK**.

7.5.3 Deleting Rows and Columns:

(*i*) Select the rows or columns to delete.

(*ii*) Click the **Table menu**, choose **Delete**, and select **Rows** or **Columns**.

7.5.4 Merging Cells:

(*i*) Select the cells to merge.

(*ii*) Click the **Table menu** and choose **Merge**.

7.5.5 Splitting Cells:

(i) Click in the cell to split.

(ii) Click the **Table menu** and choose **Split**.

(iii) In the **Split Cells** dialog box, specify the number of parts and direction (Horizontally/ Vertically).

(iv) Click **OK**.

7.5.6 Applying Borders and Background:

(i) Select the table or specific cells.

(ii) Click the **Table menu** and choose **Table Properties**.

(iii) In the **Table Format** dialog box, use the **Borders** tab to select line style and color, and the **Background** tab to choose a background color.

(iv) Click **OK**.

PRACTICAL EXERCISE

1. **Creating a Student Information Table:**

Steps to create the following table and enter values:

2. The teacher wants to enter the information of the students in the following table format. Write the steps to create the table given below and enter the values.

Roll No.	Name of the Student	Mark Sheet						
		Eng	Maths	Hindi	Science	S.St	Csc	Total

3. Write the steps to create the following list:

(a) Vegetables

1. Potato 2. Tomato

(b) Fruits

(i) Orange (ii) Mango (iii) Banana

SUM-UP:

Understanding how to insert and manipulate lists and tables in OpenOffice Writer enhances your ability to organise and present information effectively. Practice these skills to create well-structured documents.

SESSION 8: TRACK CHANGES IN OPENOFFICE WRITER

8.1. TRACK CHANGES IN OPENOFFICE WRITER

TRACK CHANGES IN A DOCUMENT

To see **Track Changes in OpenOffice Writer** in Action

Scan QR Code

Tracking changes in a Word document means keeping a record of modifications made by different users. For example, if a student writes a report and gives it to a teacher for review, the teacher can use the Track Changes feature to highlight corrections, making it easier for the student to see and correct mistakes.

8.2. STARTING AND STOPPING TRACK CHANGES

To start tracking changes in OpenOffice Writer:

1. Click Edit in the menu.
2. Select Track Changes, then click Record.

To stop tracking changes, click Record again.

8.3. TRACK OPTIONS

When Track Changes is on:

- All changes are shown in different colors.
- Deleted text appears as strikethrough.

The Track Changes sub-menu provides several options:

- **Next and Previous:** Navigate through changes.
- **Accept and Reject:** Approve or discard selected changes.
- **Accept All:** Approve all changes.
- **Reject All:** Discard all changes.
- **Show:** Preview the document with all changes accepted.
- **Protect:** Add a password to prevent unauthorised changes.

8.4. Accept or Reject Dialog

The Accept or Reject option opens a dialog box showing all changes in a list. You can:

- Select and accept/reject individual changes.
- Click Accept All or Reject All for bulk actions.

8.5. Compare Documents

To compare documents:

1. Click Edit.
2. Select Compare Document.
3. Open another file to compare with the current one.

This will list all differences between the files, allowing you to accept or reject them.

PRACTICAL ACTIVITIES

1. How will you keep a record of corrections done in the document by a different user?

- Use the Track Changes feature to record all modifications made by different users.

2. Write the steps to accept and delete the changes made in the document using the track changes feature.

- Navigate through changes using the Next and Previous options.
- Select a change and click Accept to keep it or Reject to remove it.

Unsolved Questions/Activities

1. The area in the document window where you can enter text is known as the ....
   (a) window (b) word wrap
   (c) formatting (d) work area
2. The shortcut key to exit from OpenOffice Writer is ....
3. A word processor is a package that has .... features.
   (a) Formatting (b) Editing
   (c) Typing (d) All of the above
4. Seema has contacted to a software consultant to find which word processor to purchase. The consultant recommended OpenOffice. List its important features.
5. Manisha is facing a problem where the previous text gets overwritten when inserting a new word. Explain why this occurs and how to fix it.

6. What are the header and footer? How can you set them in OpenOffice Writer?
7. What is the difference between insert mode and overtype mode?
8. Write steps to find and replace a word in OpenOffice Writer.
9. What is a format painter? How can you use it?
10. Write steps to display non-printing characters in a document.
11. How can you set table properties? Write the steps for applying table properties to a table showing the names and ages of your friends.
12. Rehan wants to remove the header and footer from his file. Write the steps to do this.
13. Shyra wants to check the spelling in her document. How will she use the auto-spellcheck option?
14. Roshni wants to create a bulleted list inside a numbered list. Explain how to do this.
15. What is the difference between toggle case and sentence case in the change case option?

NOTE: E-Learning lessons by cbse are available at http://www.psscive.ac.in/Employability_Skills.html.

❑❑❑

UNIT 4

ENTREPRENEURIAL SKILLS—III

UNIT OUTLINE

SESSION 1: INTRODUCTION TO ENTREPRENEURSHIP

1.1. Introduction to Entrepreneurship

Business is an economic activity that involves the production and distribution of goods and services. Businesses can be either profit-oriented or non-profit organisations. The individuals who plan, take risks, and manage innovative projects are known as entrepreneurs. Entrepreneurship is the process of creating and developing a business by turning innovative ideas into solutions that meet customer needs, with the goal of launching, managing, and growing the venture for profit.

To see **Introduction to Entrepreneurship** in Action

Scan QR Code

The term 'entrepreneur' comes from the French word meaning 'to undertake' or 'to begin something'. Entrepreneurship is the ability to turn ideas into action. It includes creativity, innovation, risk-taking, and the ability to plan and manage projects to achieve predefined objectives. It is essential for promoting innovation, competitiveness, and economic growth.

Fig. 1.1 Entrepreneurship: Turning Ideas into Impact

1.2. What is an Entrepreneur?

An entrepreneur is an individual who creates a new business, bearing most of the risks and enjoying most of the rewards. Entrepreneurs are often seen as innovators who bring new ideas, goods, services, and business procedures to the market. Famous economists like Joseph Schumpeter, Frank Knight, and Israel Kirzner have variously described entrepreneurs as creators of new things, bearers of uncertainty, and agents of discoveries.

1.3. Characteristics of an Entrepreneur

- **Risk-Taker:** Entrepreneurs take risks to bring their ideas to life.
- **Innovative:** They introduce new ideas and concepts to the market.
- **Resourceful:** They combine resources such as capital, land, and labor to create goods or provide services.
- **Resilient:** Entrepreneurs overcome obstacles like bureaucracy, talent hunting, and financing challenges.

To see **Characteristics of an Entrepreneur** in Action

Scan QR Code

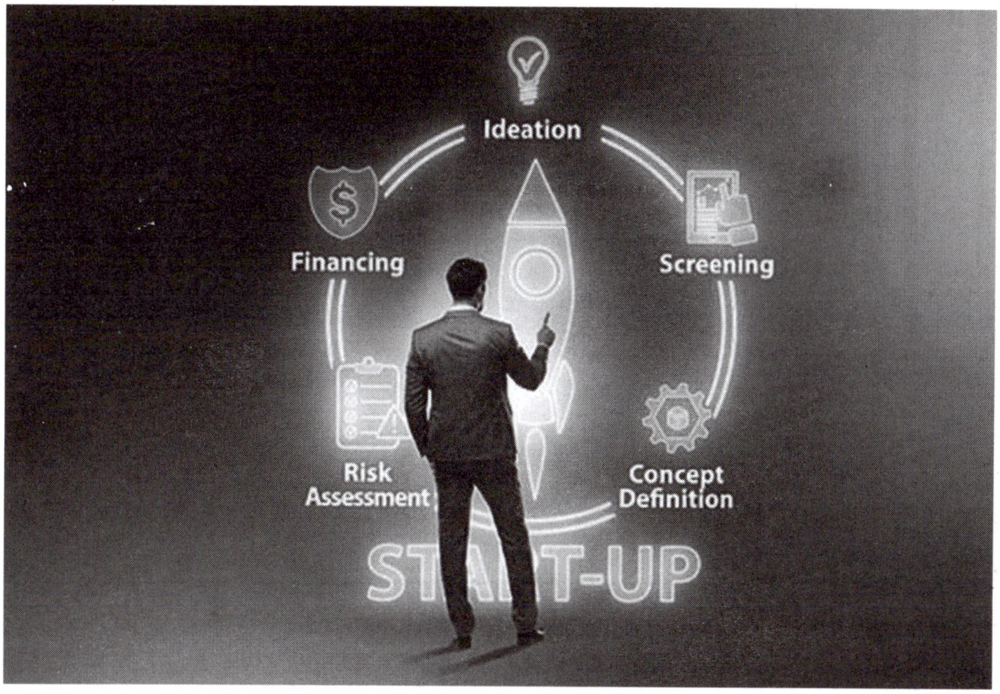

Fig. 1.2 Driven. Daring. Determined – The Mark of an Entrepreneur

Enterprise

An enterprise is a bold project or undertaking that aims to fulfill societal needs through new ventures.

1.4. The Story of Prem Ganapathy — An Entrepreneurial Journey

"Prem Ganapathy's journey is a remarkable testament to resilience and entrepreneurial spirit. After being abandoned at Bandra station in Mumbai, he chose to stay and work despite not knowing the local language. Starting out as a dishwasher, he gradually saved enough to open a small tea stall. Through determination and innovative thinking, he went on to establish Dosa Plaza — a thriving brand with multiple outlets and impressive turnover. His story underscores the power of perseverance and the ability to recognise opportunity in the face of adversity."

1.5. Types of Business Activities

1. **Manufacturing Business:** Converts raw materials into finished products as per customer demand. Example: A furniture maker.
2. **Trading Business:** Sells finished goods from manufacturers to consumers. Example: A music instrument store.
3. **Service Business:** Provides services instead of products. Example: A car driving school.

PRACTICAL ACTIVITIES

1. **Business Ideas Poster:** List business ideas categorized as Product, Service, or Hybrid. Create a poster with drawings or newspaper cut-outs.
2. **Fill in the Blanks:** Identify the type of business for the following:
    1. Ice-cream seller: ____
    2. Restaurant/Cafeteria owner: ____
    3. Car-driving school owner: ____
    4. Sports trainer: ____

Short Answer Questions

1. What are the key differences between product- and service-based businesses?
2. If you could start your own business, what would it be and why?
3. What is the meaning of manufacturing?

Understanding entrepreneurship and the different types of business activities helps students appreciate the importance of innovation, risk-taking, and resource management in creating successful enterprises. Entrepreneurs like Prem Ganapathy demonstrate that with perseverance and a keen eye for opportunity, anyone can overcome challenges and achieve success.

SESSION 2: VALUES OF AN ENTREPRENEUR

2.1. Values of an Entrepreneur

Story of Ramya

During a visit to her grandparents, Ramya noticed they had little to do throughout the day. She also observed that many elderly people in the village were idle and in need of income. When she saw her grandmother skillfully making cotton wicks for pooja (prayer rituals), Ramya was inspired to involve the village elders in making these wicks, turning a simple activity into a meaningful and empowering opportunity.

2.2. Understanding Values

Values are qualities and principles that guide a person's actions. They are beliefs that indicate wishful targets and the ways to achieve them. Values go beyond specific behaviors and situations, serving as standards that guide behavior and decision-making.

2.3. Types of Values

(*i*) **Personal Values:** Attributes such as honesty, passion, determination, and confidence.

(*ii*) **Professional Values:** Attitudes in the business environment like leadership, efficiency, and ethical practice.

(*iii*) **Social Values:** Looking beyond business to support society, like creating beneficial products or engaging in corporate social responsibility.

2.4. Core Values of an Entrepreneur

Personality Factors

Internal factors essential to your personality, such as imagination, optimism, self-confidence, and honesty.

To see **Core Values of an Entrepreneur** in Action

Scan QR Code

2.5. Environmental Factors

External factors around you, such as local market contacts, technical manpower, universities, and favorable government policies.

2.6. Entrepreneurial Values

- **Independence:** Ability to work alone and make decisions.
- **Respect for Work:** Valuing the work done.
- **Respect for Others:** Appreciating others' efforts.
- **Trust:** Building trust with customers and employees.
- **Honesty:** Being truthful in financial matters and business practices.
- **Vision:** Seeing beyond the current position and resources.
- **Outstanding Performance:** Setting high standards and overcoming challenges.
- **Initiative and Ownership:** Taking control and feeling proud of one's work.

- **Creativity and Innovation:** Constantly creating new ideas and improving existing ones.
- **Confidence:** Believing in oneself and one's approach.
- **Perseverance:** Not giving up even in difficult circumstances.
- **Open-mindedness:** Being open to new ideas and feedback.

Case Study: Sonakshi, the Basket Maker

Sonakshi makes bamboo baskets in Assam with the help of local women. Initially, she sold them in nearby cities, but sales were low, and travel was costly. She then registered her business on an online shopping website. Now, she sells more than 500 baskets a month, compared to the 50 she used to sell.

Fig. 2.1 Basket maker

OBSERVATIONS AND ACTIVITIES

1. Observation Task

1. List the people you see on your way to school and their activities.
2. Make two lists: one for people working for themselves and one for those working for others.
3. List different kinds of businesses around you.
4. Identify items that are not available in your neighborhood.
5. Think of a business idea to fill this gap creatively.

2. Multiple Choice Questions

(a) Business is a (an) .... activity.

(*i*) Social (*ii*) Economic

(*iii*) Hazardous (*iv*) Selling

(b) What is the aim of entrepreneurship?

(i) Earn a profit

(ii) Solve customers' needs innovatively

(iii) Both of the above

(iv) None of the above

3. Business Observation

1. List three businesses around you.
2. Share details about what these businesses do and how they are run.

4. Inspiration from Sonakshi

1. Reflect on how Sonakshi's persistence and adaptability led to her success.

Entrepreneurial Evaluation

1. Determine whether the following statements describe an entrepreneur:
2. Ramesh made tea for his friends in the office. Everyone liked it and praised him for his tea-making skills.
3. Sonia, a housewife, needed extra money for her kids' tuition. She sold refreshing Neembu Pani and samosas to college students.
4. Tarun loves dogs and started a dog hotel, taking care of dogs when their owners travel.
5. Monica took care of her neighbor's baby when they went to work, and they rewarded her with chocolates.

Answer **"Yes" or "No"** for each statement to identify if the person is an entrepreneur.

SESSION 3: THE ATTITUDE OF AN ENTREPRENEUR

3.1. The Attitude of an Entrepreneur

INTRODUCTION

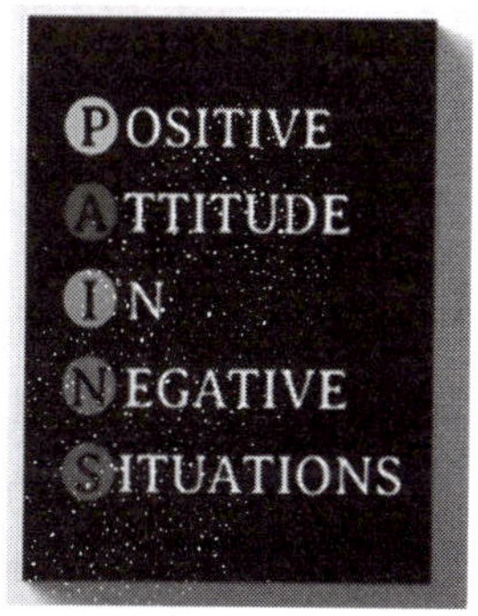

Real entrepreneurs change the way we work or live. For example, Thomas Edison was a true entrepreneur because he invented items like the light bulb and the phonograph that revolutionised our daily lives. The key to being a successful entrepreneur is having the right attitude. In this session, we will learn about how the attitude of an entrepreneur differs from that of a salaried employee.

3.2. Understanding Attitude

Attitude is defined as a set of beliefs, emotions, and behaviors towards a particular place, object, person, situation, event, idea, or thing. An entrepreneur's attitude is critical not only for their success but also for the success of their employees. An employee is someone who works for a salary or wages under the direction of an entrepreneur.

Differences in Attitudes

An individual's experiences and circumstances shape their attitude toward different things. Social psychologists have found that attitudes and actual behavior are not always perfectly aligned. People tend to behave according to their attitudes under certain conditions.

Attitudes and beliefs are influenced by both external forces and internal controls. Attitude is our evaluation of a person, an idea, or an object. We have attitudes towards many things, ranging from products we might select in a supermarket to people around the world to political policies. Attitudes comprise beliefs, feelings, and action tendencies of individuals towards objects, ideas, and people. For example, a high level of productivity leads to a more positive attitude towards work.

3.3. Entrepreneurial Attitudes

To see **Entrepreneurial Attitudes** in Action

Scan QR Code

Entrepreneurs often exhibit certain attitudes that set them apart from others. Some key attributes related to an entrepreneur's attitude include:

- **Ambitious:** Entrepreneurs are competitive and have a strong desire for achievement.
- **Independent:** They are self-starters who prefer to lead rather than follow.
- **Self-confident:** They understand the challenges of starting and running a business and are confident in their problem-solving abilities.
- **Risk-takers:** Successful entrepreneurs favor opportunities with moderate risks where they can control the outcome.
- **Visionary:** They can spot future trends and act on them.
- **Creative:** Entrepreneurs need creative product designs, strong marketing strategies, and innovative solutions to compete.
- **Energetic:** Running a business requires long hours, and many entrepreneurs start their companies while employed full-time elsewhere.
- **Passionate:** Entrepreneurs love their work.
- **Committed:** They are willing to make personal sacrifices to achieve their goals.
- **Persistent:** Entrepreneurs see failures as opportunities to learn and grow, continuing to work towards their goals.

- **Accepting of Criticism:** Constructive feedback is valuable, and entrepreneurs should take it positively.
- **Humble:** Ego should be kept in check, especially when managing employees and building partnerships.
- **Strong Work Ethic:** A set of moral principles helps build trust and a healthy work environment.
- **Trust and Honesty:** Trust is essential in various relationships, and honesty is crucial in financial and asset management.

3.4. Differences between the Attitudes of Entrepreneurs and Employees

The attitudes of entrepreneurs and employees differ significantly in terms of risk tolerance, independence, innovation, goal orientation, motivation, responsibility, work ethic, and approach to learning. Entrepreneurs tend to embrace uncertainty, seek autonomy, and drive innovation with a long-term vision, whereas employees often prefer stability, work within established structures, and focus on short-term goals and extrinsic rewards. Understanding these differences can help in recognising what drives entrepreneurial success and how it contrasts with the mindset of a salaried worker.

To see **Differences between the Attitudes of Entrepreneurs and Employees** in Action

Scan QR Code

Understanding the differences in attitudes between entrepreneurs and employees can provide insights into what drives entrepreneurial success and how it contrasts with the mindset of a salaried worker.

(*i*) Risk Tolerance

Entrepreneurs:

- Willing to take significant risks for potential high rewards.
- View failure as a learning opportunity and are comfortable with uncertainty.

Employees:

- Prefer stability and job security, often avoiding risks.
- Tend to have a lower tolerance for uncertainty and prefer predictable outcomes.

(*ii*) Independence

Entrepreneurs:

- Value autonomy and prefer to be their bosses.
- Enjoy making decisions and taking the initiative without needing approval from others.

Employees:

- Often work within established structures and hierarchies.
- May prefer clear guidance and direction from supervisors.

(iii) Innovation and Creativity

Entrepreneurs:

- Continuously seek innovative solutions and new ways to improve their products or services.
- Think outside the box and are often driven by a desire to disrupt the status quo.

Employees:

- May focus more on executing tasks and following procedures.
- Innovation may be less of a priority unless specifically encouraged by their role.

(iv) Goal Orientation

Entrepreneurs:

- Set long-term visionary goals and are driven by a broader mission.
- Focus on building and growing their businesses, often with a larger purpose in mind.

Employees:

- Tend to have short-term, task-oriented goals aligned with their job responsibilities.
- Focus on achieving targets set by the organisation or their supervisors.

(v) Motivation

Entrepreneurs:

- Motivated by personal passion, purpose, and the desire to make an impacts.
- Often driven by intrinsic rewards such as personal satisfaction and the achievement of personal goals.

Employees:

- Motivated by extrinsic rewards such as salary, benefits, and promotions.
- May also seek job satisfaction and a positive work environment but within the framework of their employment.

(vi) Responsibility and Accountability

Entrepreneurs:

- Take full responsibility for the success or failure of their ventures.
- Accountability is personal, as they often invest their own time, money, and resources.

Employees:

- Responsible for their specific roles and tasks within the organisation.
- Accountability is typically shared with colleagues and the organisation as a whole.

(vii) Work Ethics and Hours

Entrepreneurs:

- Often work long hours and are deeply committed to their ventures.
- Their work-life balance may be skewed towards work, especially during the early stages of their business.

Employees:

- Work regular hours as defined by their employment contracts.
- Aim to maintain a balance between work and personal life, with defined boundaries for work hours.

(viii) Learning and Development

Entrepreneurs:

- Continuously seek to learn and grow, often through self-directed learning and experience.
- Embrace lifelong learning as a necessity for business growth and adaptation.

Employees:

- May rely on organizational training and development programs.
- Learning and development can be more structured and formalized within their job roles.

PRACTICAL ACTIVITIES

1. Which attitudes are most important for an entrepreneur's success?
2. Discuss the statement "Ego must be kept under control" in the context of entrepreneurial attitude.
3. Explain why trust and honesty are important for an entrepreneur's success.

SESSION 4: THINKING LIKE AN ENTREPRENEUR

4.1. Thinking Like an Entrepreneur

This session will help us understand the mindset of entrepreneurs and the challenges they face when starting a business. Entrepreneurs encounter various problems from planning to implementing their ideas daily .

To see **Thinking Like an Entrepreneur** in Action

Scan QR Code

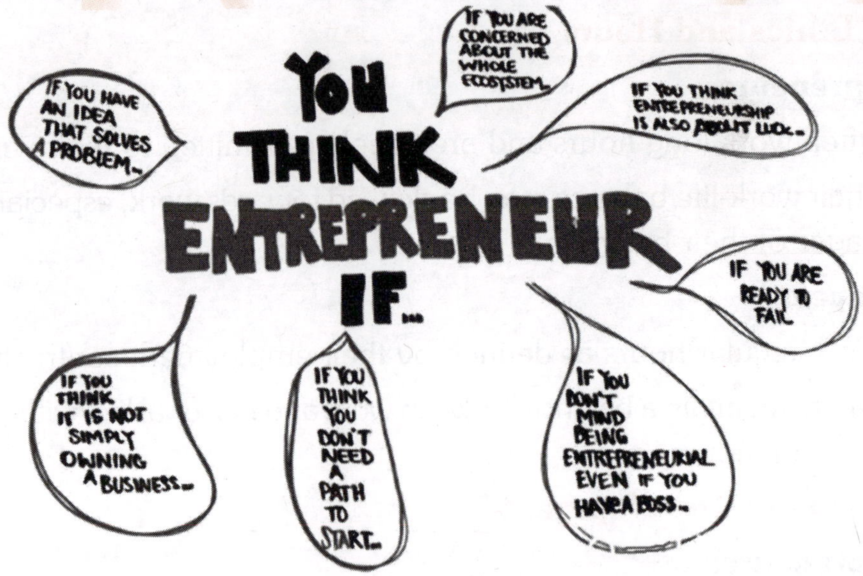

Fig. 4.1 Thinking like an entrepreneur

4.2. Problems Faced by Entrepreneurs

Entrepreneurs face numerous challenges, including:

1. **Problem-Solving:** Entrepreneurs often need to solve specific problems to improve their businesses. This process starts with identifying the problems and finding solutions. They might ask themselves questions such as:
    - Which idea should I start with? How do I know it will work?
    - How much money is needed? How can I arrange funds if I need more?
    - Where do I get raw materials, and at what cost?
    - How do I manufacture the product? How do I start the manufacturing process?
    - What should be the selling price to make a profit? How do I know what price customers are willing to pay?
    - How do I advertise my product?
    - How will customers buy from me?
    - How do I keep track of expenses and profits?
    - How can I offer a better product than what's available?
    - How can I grow my business and improve?

4.3. Story of Dr. Arokiaswamy Velumani: Founder of Thyrocare

Dr. Velumani, born to a poor farmer in Tamil Nadu, sought government aid for his education. Despite starting with a humble job, he founded Thyrocare, the world's largest thyroid testing company, with 1,122 outlets across India, Bangladesh, Nepal, and the Middle East.

After working at BARC (Bhabha Atomic Research Centre) for 14 years, he used his savings to start a thyroid testing lab. Today, Thyrocare is worth over ₹3,377 crore. Dr. Velumani's success is due to his problem-solving skills and innovative approach to thyroid testing.

4.4. Thinking Like an Entrepreneur

Entrepreneurs use various strategies to solve problems, such as:

1. **Creativity:** Coming up with new ideas. For instance, Dr. Velumani's idea of affordable thyroid testing.
2. **Innovation:** Implementing new ideas in real life. Dr. Velumani turned his idea into a successful business.
3. **Critical Thinking:** Understanding problems by asking questions and researching. Dr. Velumani identified a gap in thyroid testing and addressed it effectively.

Practical Activities

1. How did Dr. Velumani come up with the idea of a thyroid testing company?
2. Why is critical thinking important for entrepreneurs? Provide an example.

SESSION 5: COMING UP WITH A BUSINESS IDEA

5.1. Coming up with a Business Idea

Coming up with a business idea is the first step toward becoming an entrepreneur. This session will guide you through the process of brainstorming, evaluating, and refining your business ideas.

To see **Coming up with a Business Idea** in Action

Scan QR Code

5.2. Importance of a Good Business Idea

A good business idea is the foundation of a successful business. It should:

(i) **Solve a Problem:** Identify and address a need or problem that people face.

(ii) **Be Feasible:** Ensure that the idea is practical and can be implemented with available resources.

(iii) **Have Market Potential:** Make sure there is a demand for the product or service.

5.3. Steps to Generate a Business Idea

1. **Brainstorming:**
   - Think about problems you or others face daily.
   - Consider your interests, hobbies, and skills.
   - Look for gaps in the market or ways to improve existing products/services.
2. **Research and Analysis:**
   - Conduct market research to understand the needs and preferences of potential customers.
   - Analyse current trends to identify opportunities.
3. **Evaluate Ideas:**
   - Assess the feasibility of each idea considering resources, time, and skills required.
   - Consider the potential market size and competition.
   - Choose the most promising idea that aligns with your interests and skills.
4. **Refine the Idea:**
   - Develop a clear and concise description of your business idea.
   - Identify the unique selling proposition (USP) that differentiates your idea from others.
   - Seek feedback from potential customers, mentors, or peers and refine the idea based on their input.

PRACTICAL ACTIVITIES: DEVELOPING YOUR BUSINESS IDEA

STEP 1: BRAINSTORMING SESSION

1. **Individual Brainstorming:** Take 10 minutes to write down as many business ideas as you can think of. Focus on:
   - Problems you face in your daily life.
   - Things you are passionate about.
   - Improvements you wish existed in products/services you use.
2. **Group Discussion:** Form groups of 4-5 students. Share your ideas with your group and discuss:
   - Which ideas seem most feasible?
   - Which ideas address significant problems?
   - Which ideas have the most market potential?

STEP 2: MARKET RESEARCH

1. **Identify Your Target Market:**
   - Who are your potential customers?
   - What are their needs and preferences?
2. **Conduct a Survey:**
   - Create a short survey with questions related to your business idea.
   - Distribute the survey to classmates, friends, and family.
   - Collect and analyse the responses to understand the demand and preferences.

STEP 3: IDEA EVALUATION

1. **Feasibility Assessment:**
   - List the resources, time, and skills needed to implement each idea.
   - Evaluate whether you have or can acquire these resources and skills.
2. **Market Potential:**
   - Estimate the size of your target market.
   - Identify existing competitors and analyze their strengths and weaknesses.
3. **Select the Best Idea:**
   - Choose the idea that is most feasible and has the highest market potential.

STEP 4: IDEA REFINEMENT

1. **Define Your Idea:**
   - Write a clear and concise description of your business idea.
   - Highlight the unique selling proposition (USP).
2. **Seek Feedback:**
   - Present your refined idea to classmates, teachers, or mentors.
   - Incorporate their feedback to improve your idea.

STEP 5: PRESENTATION

1. **Prepare a Presentation:**
   - Create a short presentation about your business idea.
   - Include the problem it solves, the target market, the unique selling proposition, and the market potential.
2. **Present to the Class:**
   - Present your idea to the class.
   - Be prepared to answer questions and receive feedback.

5.4. Example Business Idea Development

Fig. 5.1 Business idea Tips

Idea: Eco-Friendly School Supplies

STEP 1: BRAINSTORMING:

- Problem: Traditional school supplies contribute to environmental pollution.
- Idea: Create a line of eco-friendly school supplies made from recycled and sustainable materials.

STEP 2: MARKET RESEARCH:

- Target Market: Students, parents, and environmentally-conscious consumers.
- Survey Results: 70% of respondents are willing to pay more for eco-friendly products.

STEP 3: IDEA EVALUATION:

- Feasibility: Materials like recycled paper and biodegradable plastics are available. The initial investment required is moderate.
- Market Potential: The growing trend towards sustainability; few competitors in the local market.

STEP 4: IDEA REFINEMENT:

- Clear Description: Eco-friendly school supplies including notebooks, pens, and backpacks made from recycled materials.
- USP: Combines high quality with environmental responsibility.

STEP 5: PRESENTATION:

- Prepare slides detailing the problem, solution, target market, USP, and market potential.
- Present to the class and gather feedback for further improvement.

5.5. Story of Munaf Kapadia: Founder of The Bohri Kitchen

Munaf Kapadia, a business management graduate, wanted to share his mother's culinary skills. He started The Bohri Kitchen, a home-dining concept, and later expanded to multiple outlets. Despite initial challenges, he persisted and his business now generates significant revenue.

WHAT IS A BUSINESS IDEA?

A business idea is a solution that an entrepreneur provides creatively to meet customer needs. It can be product-based, service-based, or a hybrid model.

5.6. Principles of Idea Creation

Entrepreneurs can create ideas based on:

1. **Customer Need:** Identifying and meeting existing demands in the market.
2. **Entrepreneur's Interest or Talent:** Turning personal interests or talents into a business.
3. **Innovation:** Using new methods or original ideas to start a business.

5.7. Ways to Come Up with Business Ideas

1. **Location-Based Ideas:** Serving specific needs at a particular location.
2. **Seasonal Ideas:** Offering products or services based on seasonal demand.
3. **Event-Based Ideas:** Catering to specific events or festivals.
4. **Interest-Driven Ideas:** Starting a business based on personal interests.
5. **Vocation-Driven Ideas:** Using professional skills or family business knowledge to start a new venture.

Case Studies

Shabana, the Fashion Designer: Shabana started making and selling fashionable hijabs due to her personal interest and market need. Now, she has a successful boutique and online store.

Ramesh, the Special Auto-Wala: Ramesh turned his auto-rickshaw into a unique experience with snacks, music, and Wi-Fi. His innovative service became popular, and he now manages a team of auto-walas.

SHORT ANSWER QUESTIONS

1. What principles did the entrepreneurs follow to get their ideas?
2. How did Shabana and Ramesh come up with their business ideas?
3. If you could start a business, what would your idea be?
4. Why did Munaf start his restaurant?

By the end of this session, students should have a clear understanding of how to generate, evaluate, and refine business ideas, along with practical experience in developing their own business concepts.

❑❑❑

UNIT 5 GREEN SKILLS—III

UNIT OUTLINE

- **Session 1:** The Concept of Green Economy
- **Session 2:** Sectors of Green Economy
- **Session 3:** Policies for Green Economy
- **Session 4:** Stakeholders of Green Economy

SESSION 1: THE CONCEPT OF GREEN ECONOMY

1.1. The Concept of Green Economy

Fig. 1.1 Green Economy: Powering Progress, Preserving the Planet

1.2. Understanding the Environment

The term 'environment' refers to nature. It encompasses the natural landscape along with all its non-human features, characteristics, and processes. Essentially, the environment is everything that surrounds a living organism, including natural forces and other living things, which provide conditions for growth, development, and potential harm. The environment consists of both living and non-living things-, and includes physical, chemical, and other natural forces. Living organisms interact with their environment and adapt to its conditions. This interaction includes relationships between animals, plants, soil, water, and other living and non-living elements.

1.3. Economic Development and Environmental Pollution

With societal economic development, environmental pollution has increased. The expansion of society has led to the adoption of various new agricultural methods, which often involve the use of fertilizers and pesticides to boost agricultural output. This practice has resulted in soil pollution and environmental degradation, posing a significant threat to the environment. In response, there is a shift towards eco-friendly agricultural methods, such as using solar panels, organic fertilizers, and innovative, sustainable farming techniques.

1.4. Green Growth

The Green Growth Strategy is a framework that guides countries in achieving economic growth and development while addressing climate change and preventing costly environmental degradation and inefficient resource use. This strategy offers a new perspective for re-examining the current economic growth model and provides an actionable policy framework for policymakers in advanced, emerging, and developing economies.

The Ministry of Environment, Forest and Climate Change, Government of India, views green growth as a tool to eradicate poverty. The effectiveness of a green economy depends on its ability to reduce the quantity of resources required over time to support economic growth. This, in turn, enhances social equity and job creation. Implementing green growth strategies varies by country, influenced by policy and institutional settings, development levels, resource endowments, and specific environmental challenges.

1.5. What is a Green Economy?

The term "green economy" was first introduced in a 1989 report titled "Blueprint for a Green Economy" by a group of leading environmental economists for the Government of the United Kingdom. A green economy improves human well-being and social equity while significantly reducing environmental risks and ecological scarcities. It is characterised by being low in carbon, resource-efficient, and socially inclusive. This concept acknowledges the interconnectedness of ecosystems, the economy, and human well-being.

To see **What is a Green Economy?** in Action

Scan QR Code

The Green Skills Agreement defines skills for sustainability as the technical skills, knowledge, values, and attitudes needed in the workforce to support sustainable social, economic, and environmental outcomes in business, industry, and the community. According to the United Nations Environment Program (UNEP), a green economy is low in carbon, resource-efficient, and socially inclusive.

1.6. Components of a Green Economy

1. **Renewable Energy:** Renewable energy is produced from inexhaustible sources like solar, hydropower, wind, and tidal energy. These sources reduce the environmental impact and support economic growth by providing sustainable power.
2. **Green Buildings:** Green buildings are designed, constructed, and operated to reduce or eliminate negative impacts on the environment, creating positive effects on our climate and natural environment. They help preserve natural resources and improve quality of life.
3. **Green Transport:** Sustainable transportation relies on renewable energy sources and produces minimal or no greenhouse gas emissions. Technologies like electric vehicles and public transport powered by electricity play a significant role in reducing pollution and supporting economic growth.

To see **Components of a Green Economy** in Action

Scan QR Code

4. **Water Management:** Effective water management includes reducing water waste and replenishing groundwater through systems like rainwater harvesting. This ensures sustainable water resources for future generations.

5. **Waste Management:** Proper waste management involves practices like refusing, reducing, reusing, recycling, and upcycling. Segregating waste at the source and following the 4 R's (Refuse, Reduce, Reuse, Recycle) and 1 U (Upcycle) helps manage waste sustainably and minimise environmental degradation.

1.7. Goals and Principles of a Green Economy

The main goals of a green economy include:

- Preserving, sustaining, and restoring the natural environment.
- Protecting and nurturing public health.
- Increasing social justice through green economics.
- Strengthening local independent businesses and institutions.
- Reducing poverty by creating green-collar jobs.

The common principles of a green economy are:

1. Achieving sustainable development.
2. Creating decent work and green jobs.
3. Being resource- and energy-efficient.
4. Respecting ecological limits.
5. Using integrated decision-making.
6. Measuring progress beyond GDP using appropriate indicators.
7. Ensuring equity, fairness, and justice within and between countries and generations.
8. Protecting biodiversity and ecosystems.
9. Delivering poverty reduction, well-being, livelihoods, social protection, and access to essential services.
10. Improving governance and the rule of law through inclusiveness, democracy, participation, accountability, transparency, and stability.

1.8. Green Consumers

Green consumers are individuals who prefer eco-friendly products. They choose products that have a minimal environmental impact, such as hybrid vehicles, products made from recycled materials, and those with little or no packaging. Green Consumer Day, held annually on September 28, promotes the idea of choosing environmentally friendly products.

1.9. Skill Development for a Green Economy

The demand for green skills arises from public policies and targets aimed at sustainability. It is driven by three main trends:

1. Greening requires upgrading skills and adjusting qualifications in all job types.
2. New economic activities create new occupations, requiring new skills and training frameworks.
3. Structural changes will realign sectors, necessitating workforce adaptation.

A successful transition to a low-carbon economy relies on ensuring that workers can adapt and shift to industries with increasing employment opportunities.

1.10. Green Jobs

Green jobs are positions in businesses that produce goods or services benefiting the environment or conserving natural resources. These jobs span various sectors, including agriculture, industry, services, and administration, and contribute to preserving or restoring environmental quality.

1.10.1 Green Projects

Various individuals and organisations are implementing green projects to save the environment. Examples include:

Fig. 1.2 Building a Safer Environment, One Project at a Time

- **SwacH Cooperative:** Waste mana-gement cooperative in Pune.
- **Digital Green:** Multimedia solutions for rural education in agriculture, health, and nutrition.
- **Waste Ventures India:** Environmentally and financially sustainable waste management.
- **Encashea:** Collecting waste in exchange for cash.
- **Fourth Partner Energy:** Financing and building rooftop solar projects.
- **Banyan Nation:** Recycling plastic waste.
- **SayTrees:** Organising tree plantation drives.
- **Priti International:** E-commerce for products made from waste materials.

ACTIVITIES

1. **Class Discussion:** Explain the importance of green skills and a green economy.
2. **Poster Making:** Create a poster on the importance of a green economy using magazine and newspaper cuttings.
3. **Quiz:** Identify which options correctly describe a green economy:
   - Uses fewer resources
   - Uses more resources
   - Wastes fewer items
   - Wastes more items
4. **Presentation:** Prepare a presentation on important initiatives taken in India to promote a green economy, highlighting their impact on environmental protection and suggesting changes for improvement.

SESSION 2: SECTORS OF GREEN ECONOMY

2.1. Sectors of Green Economy

Introduction to the Green Economy

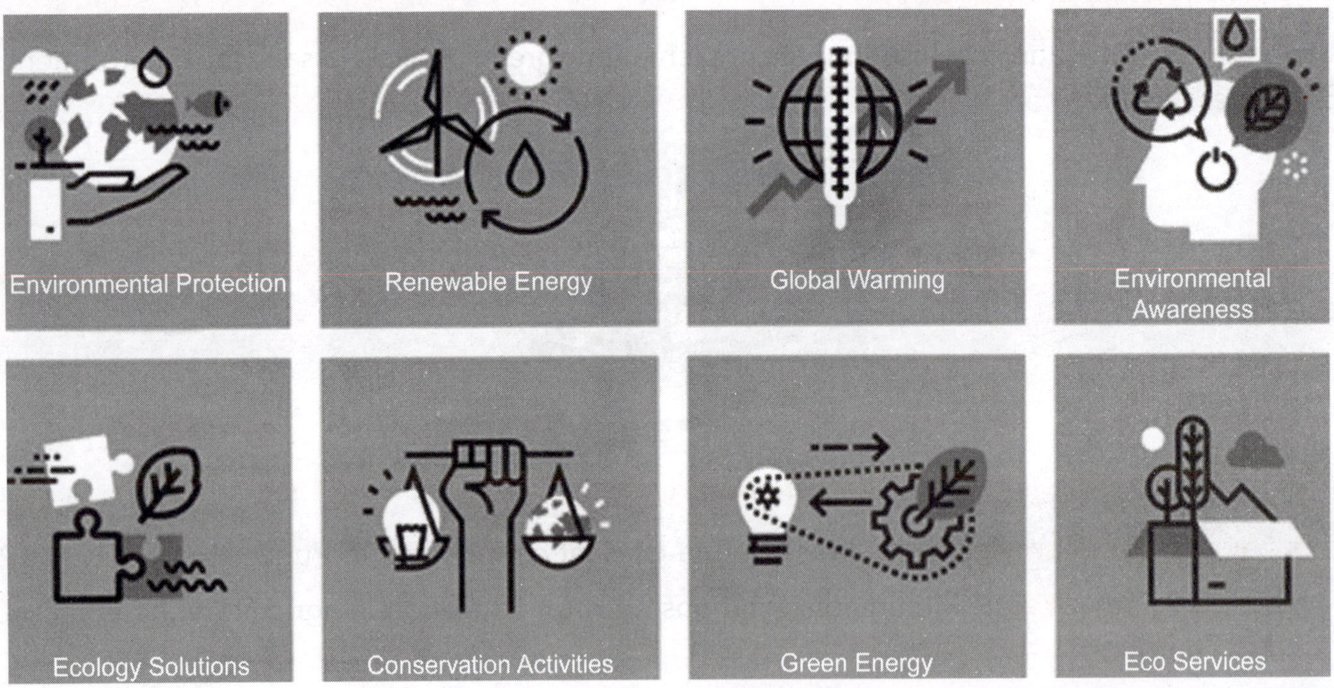

Fig. 2.1 From Energy to Innovation – Sectors Powering a Greener Tomorrow

A green economy aims for economic growth that protects the environment. This term was first introduced in 1989 in a UK government report called "Blueprint for a Green Economy." Different parts of the economy, like agriculture, transportation, and healthcare, make up what we call sectors. Some of these sectors are closely linked to the environment and can have significant impacts on it.

2.2. How Different Sectors Can Go Green

2.2.1 Agriculture Sector

To see
How Different Sectors Can Go Green
in Action

Scan QR Code

Agriculture is crucial as it provides us with food, but it can also harm the environment by overusing land, cutting down trees, and polluting with chemicals.

WHAT CAN WE DO?

- Support local, organic, and natural farming that avoids harmful chemicals.
- Grow your vegetables in a kitchen garden.
- Choose seasonal and locally produced food.

ENERGY RESOURCES

We rely on energy for almost everything, but traditional sources like oil, coal, and gas are harmful and running out.

WHAT CAN WE DO?

- Promote clean and renewable energy like solar and wind.
- Save electricity and avoid wasting it.
- Use bikes or public transport that runs on cleaner fuels instead of petrol and diesel.

FISHERIES

Overfishing depletes fish populations and threatens species, which can disrupt ecosystems and affect fishermen's livelihoods.

WHAT CAN WE DO?

- Promote sustainable fishing practices that allow fish populations to recover.
- Support fish farming.
- Buy fish that are farmed sustainably and in season.

FORESTRY

Forests are vital for rainfall, soil protection, and wildlife. Deforestation causes climate change, soil erosion, and loss of biodiversity.

WHAT CAN WE DO?

- Reduce, reuse, and recycle paper to save trees.
- Avoid buying products made from endangered species.
- Support products that are harvested sustainably, like honey collected without harming beehives.

2.3. Construction Sector

Construction can lead to deforestation, pollution, and inefficient buildings that waste energy and water.

WHAT CAN WE DO?

- Use local materials for construction.
- Report large construction projects that cause pollution.
- Design and support green buildings that are energy-efficient and use renewable energy.

2.4. Tourism Sector

Tourism boosts local economies but can also harm the environment if not managed responsibly.

WHAT CAN WE DO?

- Promote eco-tourism that protects natural environments.
- Travel in groups, conserve water and energy-, and avoid waste.

2.5. Transport Sector

Transportation consumes a lot of petrol and diesel, contributing to pollution.

WHAT CAN WE DO?

- Use public transport like buses or trains.
- Walk or cycle when possible.
- Opt for electric vehicles if available.

2.6. Water Management

Fig. 2.2 Managing Water, Sustaining Life

Water is essential, but many people lack access to clean drinking water and sanitation.

WHAT CAN WE DO?

- Use water efficiently and fix leaks immediately.
- Turn off taps when not in use.
- Ensure polluted water is treated before being released back into the environment.

2.7. Waste Management

Throwing away items can waste resources and pollute the environment.

WHAT CAN WE DO?

- Reduce, reuse, and recycle items before discarding them.
- Separate waste for recycling and composting.

2.7.1 Manufacturing Industry

Industries create jobs and drive economic growth but can also harm the environment.

WHAT CAN WE DO?

- Support industries that use clean energy and minimise pollution.
- Buy environmentally friendly products to encourage sustainable manufacturing.

KEY QUESTIONS FOR PRACTICES

1. What is the role of agriculture in protecting our environment?
2. How is tourism responsible for preserving the environment?
3. What is the importance of energy resources in a green economy?

By understanding these sectors and making small changes, we can all contribute to a greener, more sustainable economy.

SESSION 3: POLICIES FOR GREEN ECONOMY

3.1. Policies for Green Economy

POLICIES FOR A GREEN ECONOMY

A policy is a guideline or set of rules set up by the controlling agency that must be followed by all government and private organisations. A policy tells us what is to be done, who has to do it, how it is to be done, and for whom it is to be done. For example, the National Policy on Skill Development and Entrepreneurship 2015 is a policy of the Indian Government that aims to provide skill knowledge to people quickly and with high quality. Different stakeholders, or those involved in this process, have various responsibilities to ensure the success of this policy. The government has adopted many policies for sustainable development, ensuring economic growth without harming the environment.

3.2. Policies for Green Economy in India

India has adopted 'Sustainable Development' as a policy, aiming to reduce poverty, inequalities, and provide food, education, employment, energy resources, and sanitation while caring for natural resources. Special policies address problems like air and water pollution, waste disposal, and conserving biodiversity. Important steps taken by the Government under the green economy policy include the National Action Plan on Climate Change, the Green India Mission, the Mahua Economy, and the National Solar Mission.

3.3. National Action Plan on Climate Change (NAPCC)

The NAPCC is an action plan that includes various missions aimed at sustainable development. A policy with a fixed action date and the budget becomes a 'mission'. NAPCC includes eight important missions covering different environmental aspects.

To see
National Action Plan on Climate Change (NAPCC)
in Action

Scan QR Code

3.4. Green India Mission (GIM)

The Green India Mission is one of the eight missions under the NAPCC, aimed at protecting, restoring, and increasing India's forest cover. It includes plans for ecosystems, biodiversity, water, biomass, and preserving mangroves, wetlands, and critical habitats, along with services like fuel, fodder, timber, and non-wood forest products.

To see
Green India Mission (GIM)
in Action

Scan QR Code

3.5. The Mahua Economy

Fig. 3.1 Mahua Flowers

Mahua flowers form a sweet-smelling yellow carpet in forest areas of Madhya Pradesh, Jharkhand, Chhattisgarh, Odisha, Maharashtra, and Bihar. Forest sellers, like the Gond and Baiga tribes, collect Mahua flowers, fruits, seeds, and leaves from February to April and sell them to forest departments. Mahua fruits are used to extract oil, a biofuel with medicinal properties. Mahua leaves are used to make eco-friendly plates, cones, and bowls. Mahua flowers are also used to make sweets like laddoo, halwa, and kheer. Mahua oil cakes are used as eco-friendly manure. Recognising its cultural and economic importance, state forest departments promote products made from Mahua flowers, supporting economic development without damaging forests.

3.6. Jawaharlal Nehru National Solar Mission

Launched on June 30, 2008, this mission promotes ecologically sustainable growth while addressing India's energy security challenge. It aims to make India a global leader in solar energy, a renewable source, and supports local production and distribution of energy.

To see **Jawaharlal Nehru National Solar Mission** in Action

Scan QR Code

3.7. Swachh Bharat Abhiyan (Clean India Mission)

This mission aims to clean up Indian cities, towns, and villages and achieve an open-decation-free India by constructing toilets across the country. It became a campaign with nationwide participation, resulting in around ten crore toilets being built.

To see **Swachh Bharat Abhiyan (Clean India Mission)** in Action

Scan QR Code

3.8. National Green Tribunal (NGT)

The NGT acts like a court for environmental protection cases, the conservation of forests, and other natural resources. It handles disputes related to environmental issues,

imposes heavy fines on violators, and takes actions to stop and correct environmental damage, even sending violators to jail.

3.9. Policy Initiatives for Green Economy in India

Various measures have been taken by the Government of India to promote sustainable development through different policies.

(*i*) **Environment Protection Act, 1986:** This Act was enacted after the Bhopal Tragedy to implement the decisions of the United Nations Conference on the Human Environment.

(*ii*) **National Forest Policy, 1988:** This policy aims to ensure environmental stability and maintain ecological balance for sustaining all life forms.

(*iii*) **National Environment Tribunal Act, 1995:** Established to provide for strict liability for damage from handling hazardous substances.

To see **Policy Initiatives for Green Economy in India** in Action

Scan QR Code

(*iv*) **National Green Tribunal Act, 2010:** The NGT was established for effective and quick disposal of cases related to environmental protection, conservation of forests, and other natural resources.

(*v*) **Biological Diversity Act, 2002:** This Act aims at the conservation of biological diversity, sustainable use of its components, and fair sharing of benefits from the use of genetic resources.

(*vi*) **National Water Policy:** Formulated by the Ministry of Water Resources, this policy governs the planning and development of water resources. It was first adopted in 1987 and updated in 2002 and 2012.

(*vii*) **National Project on Organic Farming:** Implemented in October 2004, this project focuses on capacity building, technology development, awareness creation, and quality control for organic farming.

(*viii*) **Wildlife Protection Act, 1972:** This Act protects plant and animal species, establishing schedules of protected species and regulating hunting or harvesting.

(*ix*) **Water Prevention and Control of Pollution Act, 1974:** This legislation regulates agencies responsible for checking water pollution and covers pollution control boards at both central and state levels.

(*x*) **Central Pollution Control Board (CPCB):** Established in 1974, the CPCB provides technical services and guidance under the Environment Protection Act, of 1986, and resolves disputes among state pollution control boards.

(*xi*) **Territorial Waters, Continental Shelf, Exclusive Economic Zones, and Other Maritime Zones Act, 1976:** Regulates fishing by foreign vessels in India's maritime zones.

(*xii*) **Forest Conservation Act, 1980:** This Act aims to conserve forests and related matters, in effect since October 25, 1980.

Note: The details of the policies have been taken from https://www.mondaq.com/india/waste-management/624836/environment-laws-in-india. My sincere thanks to the online resource.

PRACTICAL ACTIVITIES

1. Make a list of various Acts made to protect our environment.
2. Write a brief note on how the Mahua plant controls the economy of that area.
3. Which projects have been made to promote solar energy?

SESSION 4: STAKEHOLDERS OF GREEN ECONOMY

4.1. Stakeholders of Green Economy

A stakeholder is anyone who has an interest in the decisions or activities of an organisation, whether it be a business, policy, or activity. The green economy affects everyone and requires support from various people, making us all stakeholders. Sustainable development requires the active participation of all sectors of society and all types of people. Stakeholders in a green economy can be grouped into the following major categories:

(i) **Government:** Governments and local authorities create and implement sustainable development laws, policies, strategies, standards, programs, and agreements with other countries. The government plays a crucial role in the green economy by planning, budgeting, and implementing policies to protect the environment. Key government branches involved include the Ministry of Environment, Forest, HRD Ministry, Education Ministry, Ministry of Tourism, Ministry of Transport, Ministry of Health and Wellness, Ministry of Petroleum, and Ministry of Finance.

Roles of the Government:

- Formulating policies and providing funds for implementation.
- Enacting legislation like 'The Environment (Protection) Act, 1986' to protect the environment.
- Establishing missions such as the Green India Mission and National Solar Mission.
- Collaborating with scientists to educate the public on environmentally safe practices.

(ii) **Non-Governmental Organisations (NGOs):** NGOs and individual social workers support the government and society in promoting the green economy. They engage in activities such as waste management, promoting organic farming, and creating employment opportunities in waste management.

Roles of NGOs:

- Supporting government initiatives.
- Educating the public on green practices.
- Reporting violations of environmental laws.

(iii) **Business, Industry, and Private Agencies:** The success of the green economy depends on the active participation of both public and private sectors. Companies need to follow responsible business practices to protect the environment. Private agencies play a significant role in executing policies and ensuring their success.

Roles of Private Agencies:

- Complying with government laws and policies.
- Participating in government missions.
- Reporting violations and educating the public.
- Providing information to the government and helping implement green policies.

(iv) **Farmers:** Farmers produce food and agricultural products, maintaining a balance between nature and people. They play a significant role in the success of a green economy by adopting sustainable farming practices.

(v) **Women:** Women, making up half the population, have a crucial role in households, society, and the economy. Their participation is vital for sustainable development.

(vi) **Workers and Trade Unions:** Workers are essential to the economy. Green policies aim to provide them with a healthy working environment, proper drinking water, and sanitation. Workers also support skills training and interact with nature through their industries.

(vii) **Native Tribes:** Indigenous people, who depend on forests for their survival, play a key role in conserving the environment. The green economy can benefit many such tribes.

(viii) **Scientific and Technological Community:** Science and technology are vital for sustainable development. Scientists can provide sustainable solutions, educate the public, and advise policymakers on the benefits and limitations of technology.

(ix) **Children and Youth:** Youth are the present and future of our economy. Their active participation is crucial for the success of green policies and the promotion of economic and social development.

4.2. Examples of Green Projects

1. **Deep Modern Chulha:** Developed a biomass-based stove that reduces wood consumption by 50% and smoke by 80%, improving environmental and health outcomes.
2. **Enbiolet Green Solution Foundation (GSF):** Created bio-toilets for hygienic sanitation in villages and city slums, providing training and employment opportunities.
3. **Liter of Light:** A global movement using recycled plastic bottles to make solar lamps, providing lighting to areas with limited electricity access.

4.3. Success Stories from Developing Countries

- Renewable Energy in China
- Organic Agriculture in Uganda

- Rural Ecological Infrastructure in India
- Sustainable Urban Planning in Brazil
- Solar Energy in Tunisia

PRACTICAL ACTIVITIES QUESTIONS

1. Prepare a poster on the Green Economy related to cities, buildings, tourism, industry, transport, renewable energy, waste management, agriculture, water, forests, and fisheries.
2. Make a chart showing some of the latest Green Economy projects in India.
3. Highlight the impact of government and tourism in promoting the Green Economy.

❑❑❑

PART B

SUBJECT SPECIFIC SKILLS

UNIT 1 Role of Physical Education in the Development of a Child

1.1 Introduction

In today's fast-paced, technology-driven world, the role of physical education (PE) has become increasingly vital. Modern children and adolescents face unique challenges, making regular physical activity more important than ever. From countering sedentary lifestyles to supporting mental well-being, PE has become an essential part of a holistic and balanced education."

Fig. 1.1: Physical Activities

Physical activity is essential not only for maintaining a healthy body but also for the brain's development and function. For children and adolescents, regular physical activity is particularly important as it can positively influence their cognitive development, learning capabilities, and emotional well-being.

1.2 Physical and Emotional Needs of Children

Children's physical and emotional needs are fundamental to their overall development and well-being. Meeting these needs supports their growth into healthy, confident, and resilient individuals.

1.2.1 Physical Needs of Children

1. **Nutrition:** A balanced diet rich in essential nutrients is vital for a child's growth, brain development, and immune system.

2. **Sleep:** Adequate sleep is crucial for physical health, cognitive function, and emotional regulation.
3. **Physical Activity:** Regular exercise promotes muscle and bone strength, cardiovascular health, and helps maintain a healthy weight.
4. **Healthcare:** Routine medical and dental check-ups ensure early detection and prevention of health issues.
5. **Safe Environment:** A secure and clean living space protects children from harm and supports their physical well-being.
6. **Hygiene:** Teaching and maintaining personal hygiene practices prevent illnesses and promote self-care habits.
7. **Clothing and Shelter:** Appropriate clothing for weather conditions and stable housing provide comfort and protection.
8. **Affection and Touch:** Physical affection, such as hugs, supports emotional bonding and can positively impact physical health.

1.2.2 Emotional Needs of Children

1. **Love and Affection:** Consistent expressions of love help children feel valued and secure.
2. **Safety and Security:** A stable environment where children feel protected fosters trust and emotional stability.
3. **Acceptance and Belonging:** Feeling accepted by family and peers contributes to a positive self-image and social development.
4. **Recognition and Encouragement:** Acknowledging achievements and efforts boosts self-esteem and motivation.

Fig. 1.2: Modern Exercise

5. **Listening and Understanding:** Being heard and understood validates children's feelings and encourages open communication.
6. **Guidance and Boundaries:** Clear expectations and consistent discipline help children understand acceptable behaviours and develop self-control.
7. **Opportunities for Play:** Engaging in play supports emotional expression, creativity, and stress relief.

1.3 Health Triangle

1.3.1 Physical Development

Physical health encompasses the condition of the body and its ability to perform daily activities.

Nutrition: Consuming a balanced diet rich in essential nutrients.

- **Exercise:** Engaging in regular physical activity to maintain fitness and prevent chronic diseases.
- **Sleep:** Ensuring adequate rest for recovery and overall health.
- **Preventive Care:** Regular medical check-ups and vaccinations.

Maintaining physical health not only enhances bodily functions but also positively influences mental clarity and social interactions.

1.3.2 Mental Development

Mental health involves emotional, psychological, and cognitive well-being.

- **Emotional Regulation:** Managing emotions effectively.
- **Stress Management:** Utilizing techniques like mindfulness and relaxation to cope with stress.
- **Cognitive Function:** Engaging in activities that stimulate thinking and learning.

A sound mental state enhances decision-making, relationships, and resilience against life's challenges.

1.3.3 Social Development

Social health pertains to the ability to form satisfying interpersonal relationships and adapt to social situations.

- **Communication Skills:** Expressing oneself clearly and listening actively.
- **Relationship Building:** Establishing and maintaining healthy connections with others.
- **Community Engagement:** Participating in social activities and contributing to society.

Strong social ties provide support, increase feelings of belonging, and can improve both mental and physical health

Fig. 1.3: Road to Fitness

Fig. 1.4: Physical Development

Fig. 1.5: Social Development

Fig. 1.6: Mental Development

Fig. 1.7: Social Development

Fig. 1.8: Free Bee

Fig. 1.9: Icons of Action

Fig. 1.10: Bodyweight Blast

1.4 Health Development

Early childhood development encompasses several critical domains that lay the foundation for a child's future growth and success. These domains include physical, cognitive, social, emotional, and language development. Each domain interrelates with the others, contributing to a child's overall well-being and readiness for lifelong learning.

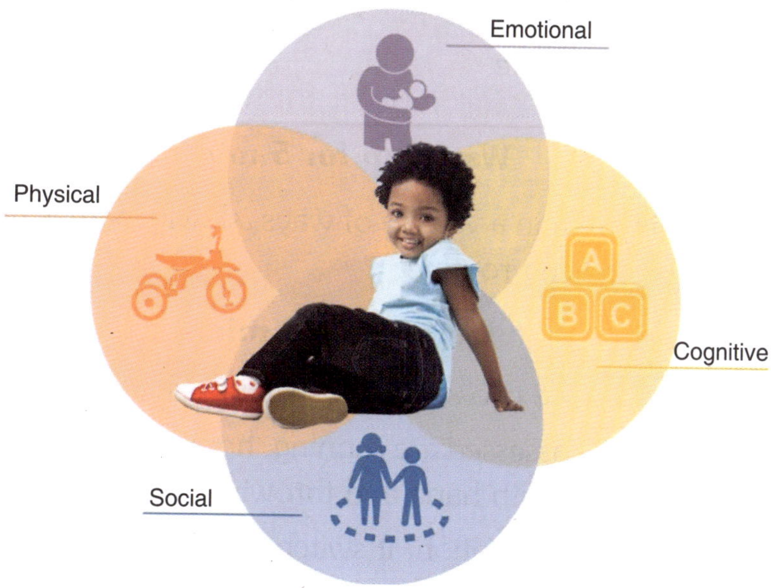

Fig. 1.11: Health Triangle

To see
Cognitive Activity
in Action

Scan QR Code

1. **Physical Development:** Physical development in early childhood involves the growth and strengthening of the body, including the development of gross and fine motor skills.
2. **Mental Development:** Mental advancement alludes to youngsters' thought process, being investigative, and ability to sort things out. It is the growth of knowledge,

ability to solve problems, and comprehension of the world around them.. Children learn by exploring their environment, asking questions, and trying out new things. Cognitive tasks such as puzzles, games, and building shapes help to develop problem-solving abilities. Children begin to understand concepts such as numbers, shapes, and colours, and how things relate to one another.

3. **Social Development:** Social development involves learning to interact with others, developing relationships, and understanding social norms and behaviours.

   Learning to play and communicate with other children helps to develop social skills. Children learn about sharing, taking turns, and following rules through social interactions. Developing bonds with family, friends, and caregivers is crucial for social growth.

4. **Emotional Development:** Emotional development focuses on understanding and managing emotions, developing self-regulation, and building self-esteem and empathy. Children learn to identify their own emotions and express them appropriately developing the ability to control impulses, manage stress, and handle frustration. Understanding and responding to the feelings of others is a key aspect of emotional growth.

ACTIVITY

Prepare a chart on health triangle

Warm-up for 5 min

Move around the activity area in a variety of ways, slowly increasing their speed. Lead, or have a student lead, a stretching routine.

Duration: 25 min

- Make two groups and make two stations as circuits shown in figure 1 and 2.
- The skills which would be assessed are running, hopping, dribbling with feet, twisting/turning, striking, dribbling with hand and throwing.
- Once a group completes the station, it switches over to the other station.
- You need to go through the circuit using the above skills and your trainer should watch how you perform.
- If you are not able to perform a particular skill well, you should practise more to improve.

Cool Down for 5 min

Multiple Choice Questions with Answers

1. **Which of the following is NOT considered a component of physical fitness?**
   (a) Cardiovascular endurance (b) Muscular strength
   (c) Flexibility (d) Cognitive ability
2. **Which component of physical fitness refers to the ability of a muscle or group of muscles to perform continuously without fatigue?**
   (a) Muscular endurance (b) Flexibility
   (c) Body composition (d) Balance
3. **Which component of physical fitness measures the ratio of lean mass to fat mass in the body?**
   (a) Muscular strength (b) Cardiovascular endurance
   (c) Body composition (d) Flexibility
4. **What is the primary benefit of cardiovascular endurance?**
   (a) Improved muscle tone (b) Increased flexibility
   (c) Enhanced heart-and-lung function (d) Better balance and coordination
5. **Flexibility is the ability to:**
   (a) Lift heavy weights repeatedly
   (b) Maintain stability while stationary or moving
   (c) Move joints through their full range of motions
   (d) Sustain prolonged physical activity
6. **Which stage of child development is characterised by rapid physical growth and the development of fine and gross motor skills?**
   (a) Infancy (b) Early Childhood
   (c) Adolescence (d) Adulthood
7. **What is the primary focus of physical education in early childhood?**
   (a) Competitive sports (b) Motor skill development
   (c) Academic achievement (d) Weight training
8. **Which motor skill is typically developed first in young children?**
   (a) Skipping (b) Throwing
   (c) Walking (d) Catching
9. **Which of the following is NOT a benefit of physical activity in children?**
   (a) Improved cardiovascular health

(b) Enhanced social skills

(c) Increased risk of chronic diseases

(d) Better academic performance

10. At what age do children generally start to develop the ability to understand and follow game rules?

(a) 2-3 years (b) 4-5 years

(c) 6-7 years (d) 8-9 years

11. Why is it important to include activities that promote balance and coordination in a child's physical education program?

(a) To prepare them for professional sports

(b) To reduce the risk of injury

(c) To improve their artistic skills

(d) To increase their muscle mass

12. Which type of play is crucial for developing social skills and teamwork in children?

(a) Solitary play (b) Parallel play

(c) Associative play (d) Cooperative play

13. What is the recommended amount of daily physical activity for children aged 6-17 according to the World Health Organization (WHO)?

(a) 30 minutes (b) 45 minutes

(c) 60 minutes (d) 90 minutes

14. Which factor is most likely to positively influence a child's physical activity levels?

(a) Parental involvement (b) Watching television

(c) Lack of access to play areas (d) Excessive academic pressure

15. What is the term for the period of significant physical and emotional development that occurs during adolescence?

(a) Puberty (b) Infancy

(c) Senescence (d) Menopause

ANSWERS

1. (d)	2. (a)	3. (c)	4. (c)	5. (c)	6. (b)	7. (b)
8. (c)	9. (c)	10. (b)	11. (b)	12. (d)	13. (c)	14. (a)
15. (a)						

Subjective Questions

1. What you mean by physical education in modern era ?
2. What do you mean by motor fitness skill ?
3. How does physical fitness affect our mental and physiological state?
4. Explain fine and gross motor skills with examples.

1.5 Factor Affecting Physical Fitness

Actual work is impacted by a perplexing interchange of different variables. Individual, social, environmental, and policy-related influences are all examples of these. For effective interventions and policies to promote physical activity among various populations, it is essential to understand these factors.

1.5.1 Individual Factors

(a) Biological and Physical Factors

- **Age:** Physical activity levels tend to decrease with age due to factors like declining health, reduced energy, and/or increased responsibilities.
- **Gender:** Males and females often have different activity patterns and preferences influenced by social norms and biological differences.
- **Genetics:** Genetic makeup can affect physical abilities and predisposition to certain health conditions, influencing one's ability to engage in physical activity.
- **Health Status:** Chronic illnesses, injuries, or disabilities can limit the ability to participate in physical activities.

Fig. 1.12: Biological Factor

(b) Psychological Factors

- **Motivation and Attitude:** Personal interest, enjoyment, and attitudes towards physical activity strongly impact participation.
- **Self-Efficacy:** Confidence in one's ability to perform physical activities can drive engagement and persistence.
- **Mental Health:** Mental health conditions, such as depression or anxiety can either act as barriers or motivators for engaging in physical activity.

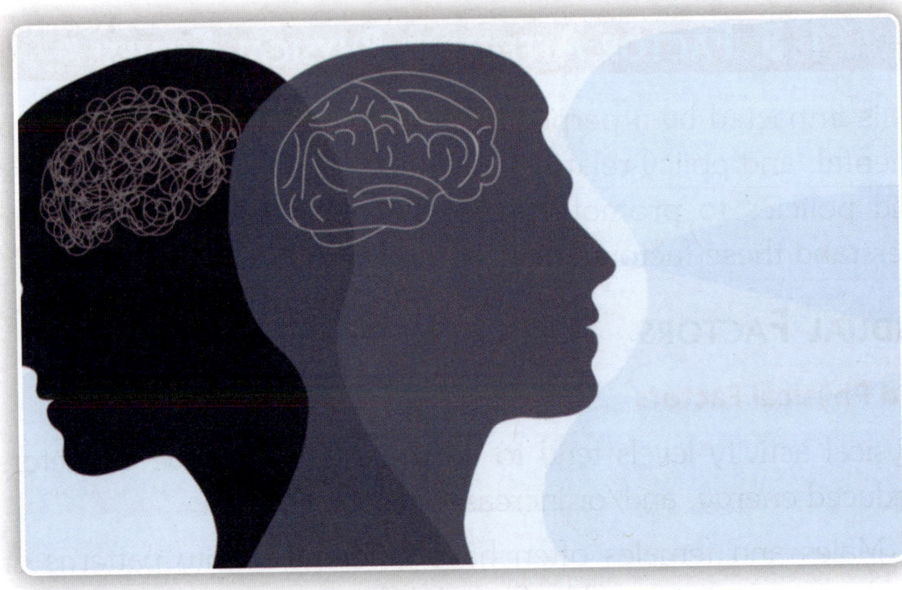

Fig. 1.13: Psychological Factor

(c) Knowledge and Skills

- **Awareness:** Knowledge of the benefits of physical activity can encourage participation.
- **Skills:** Having the necessary skills and experience for specific activities can boost confidence and involvement.

1.5.2 Social Factors

(a) Family and Peer Influence

- **Support:** Encouragement and participation from family and friends can foster regular physical activity.
- **Role Models:** Observing active individuals can inspire similar behaviours.

(b) Cultural Influences

- **Norms and Values:** Cultural expectations and norms regarding physical activity can promote or hinder engagement.
- **Community Engagement:** Active participation in community events or sports can increase physical activity levels.

Fig. 1.14: Social Factor

1.5.3 Environmental Factors

(a) Built Environment

To see **Environmental Factors** in Action

Scan QR Code

- **Accessibility:** Proximity to parks, gyms, and recreational facilities makes it easier to engage in physical activities.
- **Safety:** Safe neighbourhoods, well-lit streets, and low crime rates encourage outdoor activities.
- **Infrastructure:** Availability of sidewalks, bike paths, and pedestrian zones supports physical activity.

(b) Natural Environment

- **Climate and Weather:** Extreme weather conditions can limit outdoor physical activity opportunities.
- **Geography:** The type of terrain and extent of natural spaces influence the types of activities people can engage in.

Fig. 1.15: Natural Factor

1.6 Sports in Well-being

- **Teamwork and Cooperation:** Participating in team sports fosters collaboration, communication, and understanding among individuals.
- **Building Relationships:** Sports provide opportunities to meet new people, strengthening social networks and reducing feelings of isolation.
- **Community Engagement:** Local sports events and teams can enhance community spirit and provide a sense of belonging.
- **Development of Leadership Skills:** Taking on roles such as team captain or coach can cultivate leadership and organizational abilities.

1.6.1 Holistic Well-being

The integration of physical, mental, and social benefits from sports leads to a holistic improvement in quality of life. Whether it's the joy of playing, the thrill of competition, or the camaraderie among teammates, sports offer a multifaceted approach to enhancing well-being.

1.7 Influence of Society on Sports

1.7.1 Environmental Influence

Fig. 1.16: Environmental Influence

Environmental conditions and concerns significantly impact sports:

- **Climate Change:** Rising temperatures and extreme weather events disrupt training schedules and competitions. For instance, heatwaves can pose health risks to athletes and spectators alike.
- **Venue Location and Community Impact:** The placement of sports facilities can lead to environmental justice concerns.

1.7.2 Economic Influence

Sports have a profound economic impact on societies:

- **Job Creation and Revenue Generation:** Major sporting events and local clubs generate employment opportunities and stimulate local economies.
- **Infrastructure Development:** Hosting large-scale events often leads to infrastructure improvements, such as transportation and hospitality services, benefiting the broader community.
- **Economic Disparities:** While sports can boost economies, they can also exacerbate inequalities.

1.7.3 Technological Influence

Fig. 1.17: Technological Influence

Technology is revolutionizing sports in various ways:

- **Performance Enhancement:** Wearable devices and data analytics help athletes monitor and improve their performance
- **Fan Engagement:** Innovations like AI-powered apps enhance the spectator experience by providing personalized content and interactive features.
- **Training and Safety:** Virtual reality and simulation technologies offer immersive training environments, allowing athletes to practice safely and efficiently.

1.7.4 Political Influence

Fig. 1.18: Political Influence

- **Regulation and Governance:** Governments establish regulatory bodies to oversee sports organizations, ensuring fair play and financial integrity.
- **Diplomacy and National Identity:** Sports often serve as a platform for political expression and diplomacy. Historical examples include the U.S. boycott of the 1980 Moscow Olympics in protest of the Soviet invasion of Afghanistan.
- **Social Movements:** Athletes have used their platforms to advocate for social justice, bringing attention to issues like injustice and other policies.

1.8 Influence of Sports on Well-being

Sports have always been an integral part of human society, offering not just entertainment but also a means to enhance individual and collective well-being.

1. **Physical Well-being** Sports are synonymous with physical activity, which is a cornerstone of good health. Regular participation in sports improves cardiovascular fitness, strengthens muscles, enhances flexibility, and promotes overall body coordination.
2. **Mental Well-being** Sports have a profound impact on mental health. Physical activity triggers the release of endorphins, commonly known as "feel-good" hormones, which help combat stress, anxiety, and depression.
3. **Emotional Well-being** Sports play a significant role in shaping emotional health. Athletes experience various emotions, from the thrill of victory to the lessons of defeat.
4. **Social Well-being** Sports are inherently social activities that bring people together. Team sports such as football, basketball, and volleyball promote cooperation, communication, and leadership.
5. **Character Development** Sports instill valuable life skills such as discipline, perseverance, and time management. Athletes learn to balance practice, competition, and personal life, fostering a sense of responsibility. They also experience the importance of hard work, dedication, and continuous improvement.
6. **Promotion of Healthy Lifestyle** Regular participation in sports encourages individuals to adopt a healthy lifestyle. Athletes tend to maintain a balanced diet, stay hydrated, and avoid harmful substances like tobacco and excessive alcohol. The positive influence of sports extends beyond the field, promoting lifelong habits that contribute to overall well-being.

ACTIVITY

1. Group activity on demonstration of factors influencing physical activities

Multiple Choice Questions with Answers

1. Which of the following factors has the most direct impact on an individual's cardiovascular fitness?

(a) Diet (b) Sleep
(c) Genetics (d) Aerobic exercise

2. How does age affect physical fitness?

(a) Fitness levels remain the same regardless of age.
(b) Fitness levels generally decrease with age due to changes in muscle mass and metabolism.
(c) Fitness levels increase with age as people gain more experience.
(d) Age has no effect on fitness as long as one maintains a regular exercise routine.

3. Which of the following is a psychological factor that can influence fitness levels?

(a) Exercise frequency (b) Motivation
(c) Diet (d) Hydration

4. How does proper nutrition affect physical fitness?

(a) It only impacts muscle growth.
(b) It has no significant impact on fitness.
(c) It provides the necessary energy and nutrients for overall health and performance.
(d) It is less important than exercise.

5. Which environmental factor can negatively affect outdoor physical activities?

(a) Availability of sports facilities
(b) Weather conditions
(c) Access to fitness information
(d) Support from family and friends

ANSWERS

1. (d) 2. (b) 3. (b) 4. (c) 5. (b)

Subjective Questions

1. What is body type?
2. What are the factors that affect physical fitness?
3. Define physical and mental fitness traits.
4. List out six factors affecting our physical fitness.
5. What do you mean by cardiovascular fitness?
6. What are the three body types according to somatotype?

1.9 Plan Physical Activities

Thinking in advance about "what is to be done, when it is to be done, how it is to be done, and by whom it should be done," is one definition of planning. We could put it this way: planning helps us to take us from where we are now to where we want to be. Planning entails establishing goals and determining the best way to achieve those goals in advance. We can likewise characterise arranging as setting up of goals and targets and figuring out an activity to accomplish them. Macro planning is the term for this because it provides an overview of the entire year.

There are mostly two types of plans:

1. Long-term plan – Macro plan
2. Short-term plan – Micro plan

1.9.1 Importance of Planning

1. Goal Setting

- **Clarity:** Clear goals help athletes focus their efforts and understand what they are working towards.
- **Motivation:** Specific, measurable goals provide motivation and a sense of direction.
- **Benchmarking:** Goals allow for tracking progress and making necessary adjustments.

2. Performance Optimisation

- **Training Efficiency:** Well-structured plans ensure that training sessions are effective and efficient.
- **Periodisation:** Planning allows for periodisation, which cycles different types of training (e.g., endurance, strength, speed) to peak at the right time.
- **Skill Development:** Focused practice on specific skills or techniques leads to improvement and mastery.

3. Performance Optimisation

- **Balanced Workload:** Proper planning prevents overtraining and ensures adequate rest and recovery.
- **Individualisation:** Plans can be tailored to an athlete's specific needs, taking into account their strengths, weaknesses, and history of injury.
- **Safety Measures:** Incorporating proper warm-ups, cool-downs, and flexibility exercises reduces the risk of injuries.

Fig. 1.16

4. Progression and Adaptation

- **Progressive Overload:** Gradually increasing the intensity, volume, and complexity of training helps in continuous improvement.
- **Adaptation:** Planned variations in training (e.g., different drills, activities) help athletes adapt and avoid plateaus.
- **Feedback Loop:** Regular assessment and adjustments based on performance data keep the training relevant and effective.

5. Time Management

- **Efficiency:** A well thought-out plan helps athletes to make the most of their available time.
- **Prioritisation:** Identifying key areas that need improvement ensures that critical aspects of training are not overlooked.
- **Balance:** Allows athletes to balance training with other commitments (e.g., school, work, family).

Fig. 1.17: The Power of Every Minute

6. Mental Preparation

- **Confidence:** Knowing that there is a plan in place can boost an athlete's confidence.
- **Stress Reduction:** Reduces uncertainty and anxiety by providing a clear roadmap.
- **Focus:** Keeps athletes concentrated on their long-term objectives rather than getting distracted by short-term setbacks.

Fig. 1.18: Bright Ideas and Bold Expressions

To see **Teamwork and Cooperation** in Action

Scan QR Code

7. Team Coordination

- **Alignment:** Ensures that all team members are working towards the same goals.
- **Cohesion:** Facilitates coordination among coaches, trainers, and athletes.
- **Role Clarity:** Defines roles and responsibilities within the team, leading to better teamwork.

8. Resource Management

- **Effective Use of Facilities:** Ensures that training facilities and equipment are used optimally.
- **Financial Planning:** Helps in budgeting for travel, competitions, and equipment.
- **Human Resources:** Maximise the effective use of coaches, medical staff, and support personnel.

1. Aims/ Goals/ Objectives of the School for Physical Education and Sports
2. Management and Communication Structure.
3. Infrastructure and Resources.
4. Scheduling
5. Intermediate Milestones /Dependencies

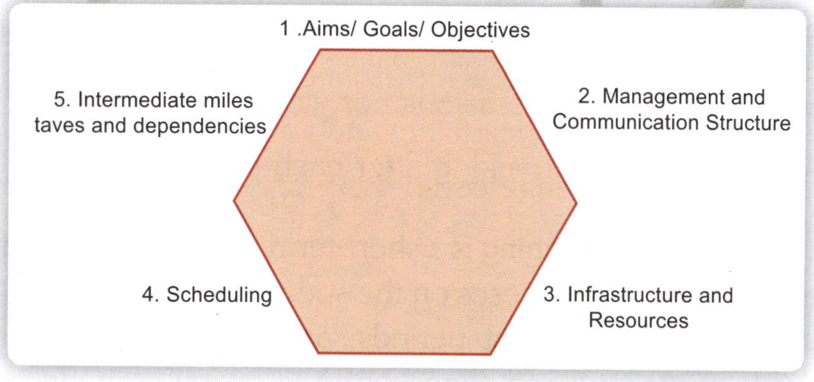

Fig. 1.19

1.10 Structuring Physical Activity Sessions

Effective physical activity sessions require careful planning to ensure safety, progress, and desired outcomes. This document outlines the structured approach to planning physical activity sessions using four key levels: Macro-planning, Meso-planning, Micro-planning, and Weekly Planning.

1. Macro-planning

Particular	Details
Duration	6 months to 1 year
Goal	Overall objectives (e.g., improving fitness, training for an event)
Phases	Divided into distinct phases (e.g., endurance, strength, flexibility)
Participant Profile	Age, fitness level, health status, and specific goals
Evaluation	Periodic assessments to track progress

2. **Meso-planning** Meso-planning is a medium-term approach to physical activity planning, typically covering several weeks to a few months. It divides the macro-plan into smaller, manageable phases, each focused on specific objectives. This approach allows for systematic progress and prevents plateaus by varying training intensity, duration, and type.

Particular	Details
Duration	Several weeks to a few months
Phases	Divided into smaller cycles (e.g., strength, hypertrophy, endurance)
Objectives	Specific goals for each phase (e.g., muscle growth, fat loss)
Activities	Types of exercises (e.g., cardio, strength training)

Intensity	Adjusted according to phase (e.g., high intensity, moderate)
Frequency	Number of sessions per week
Evaluation	Progress tracking after each phase

Micro-planning: Micro-planning is a short-term, highly detailed approach to planning physical activity sessions. It focuses on the specific structure of each session, including exercises, sets, repetitions, rest periods, and techniques. This approach ensures each session is purposeful and aligns with the overall training objectives.

Aspect	Details
Duration	One week to a few sessions
Focus	Specific exercises, techniques, and skill development
Components	Warm-up, main activity, cool-down
Intensity	Adjusted based on the session's goal (e.g., light, moderate, high)
Sets/ Repetitions	Clearly defined for each exercise
Rest Periods	Specific rest duration between exercises
Evaluation	Immediate feedback and adjustments

Weekly Planning Weekly planning is a short-term approach that outlines daily activities for a specific week. It provides a clear schedule for different types of physical activities, ensuring variety, balance, and proper recovery. This method helps participants stay consistent, organized, and aware of their progress.

Aspect	Details
Duration	One week
Structure	Day-wise plan (e.g., Monday - Cardio, Tuesday - Strength)
Activity Types	Balanced mix (e.g., cardio, strength, flexibility)
Rest Days	Pre-planned for optimal recovery
Intensity	Adjusted for each session type (e.g., moderate, high)
Flexibility	Allows adjustments based on performance and fatigue
Evaluation	Quick review at the end of the week

1.11 Yoga and Their Benefits

Asana	Description	Benefit
Mountain Pose (Tadasana)	Standing straight with arms by the side.	Improves posture, enhances balance, strengthens legs.
Tree Pose (Vrikshasana)	Standing on one leg with the other foot placed on the thigh.	Enhances balance, strengthens legs, improves focus.
Butterfly Pose (Baddha Konasana)	Sitting with soles of feet touching, knees bent.	Improves hip flexibility, aids digestion, relieves stress.
Child's Pose (Balasana)	Kneeling, leaning forward with arms extended.	Provides relaxation, relieves back pain, calms the mind.
Cobra Pose (Bhujangasana)	Lying on stomach, lifting chest with hands on the ground.	Strengthens back, improves spine flexibility, relieves stress.
Cat-Cow Pose (Marjaryasana-Bitilasana)	Alternating arching and dipping of the back.	Enhances spine flexibility, improves digestion, relieves back pain.
Downward-Facing Dog (Adho Mukha Svanasana)	An inverted V-shape with hands and feet on the ground.	Stretches spine, strengthens arms and legs, improves blood circulation.
Bridge Pose (Setu Bandhasana)	Lying on back, lifting hips with feet on the ground.	Strengthens back, stretches chest, reduces anxiety.
Warrior Pose (Virabhadrasana)	Standing with one leg bent, arms extended overhead.	

1.12 Lesson Plan for Physical Activities

A lesson plan for physical activities involves setting clear objectives, organising activities, and ensuring that the session is engaging and informative.

A physical education class lesson plan should contain the following:

Grade Level

Duration

Objectives

Materials Needed

Lesson Outline

1. Introduction
2. Warmup
3. Main Activity
4. Cool Down
5. Conclusion and reflection

Grade Level:	Unit:	Lesson Focus:
2nd Grade	Ball Skills	Dribbling With Hand

Essential Question:	
What are the key elements to dribbing a ball?	
1.	Finger pads
2.	Head looking up
3.	Dribble ball waist level
4.	Push ball towards the floor (not slap)

Intended Student Performance of Objectives:	
Paychomotor:	The student will be able to ...dribble in their own space with good form
Cognitive:	The student will be able to...tell the teacher what part of the hand you dribble a ball with
Affective:	The student will be able to...cooperate with others to 'peel' student's bananas to get them free in the Banana Bunch game

Intended Student Performance of Objectives:	
Paychomotor:	The student will be able to ...dribble in their own space with good form
Cognitive:	The student will be able to...tell the teacher what part of the hand you dribble a ball with
Affective:	The student will be able to...cooperate with others to 'peel' student's bananas to get them free in the Banana Bunch game

Intended Teacher Performance Objectives:	
Buring The Lesseon The teacher will...	...attempt to use each student's name at least once. ...attempt to give each student specific feedback pertaining to skill development and improvement. ...move around the gym so that all students can be observed.

Equipment Needs:	Quantity Needed:	Equipment Needs:	Quantity Needed:
Bear bags	1 for every 2 students	Foam bananas	2 or 3
Playground balls	1 for every student	Cones	4
Pinnies	2 or 3		

Reference:
Instantly Active poster of "Banana Bunch" game.
P.E. Central. "Red Light, Green Light, 3-2-1" game.

Warmup/Instant Activity		
Time needed:	**Description of activity:**	**Diagram of activity:**
	Banana Bunch Game:	
10 minutes	1. Tow student are selected as taggers (The Monkeys)	
	2. If you get tagged, put both arms up and pose your body in the shape of a banana.	
	3. To get free, two students must "peel" you (one on each arm)	
	4. All students must use a locomotor skill to move other than running.	

Movement Awareness/Fitness Activity

Time needed:	Description of activity:	Diagram of activity:
	High Five Bean Bag Grab:	
5 minutes	1. All students have a partner	
	2. Place the bear bag in between partners and get into a push-up position while the song is being played	
	3. When the song goes off, try to grab the bear bag first	

Skill Development/Lead up Game:

Time needed:	Description of activity:	Diagram of activity:
	"Dribbling practise"	
10 minutes	1. Students get a ball and practise dribbling for a few minutes moving in and out of each other.	
	2. Students should dribble with: • Finger pads • Head looking up • Dribble ball waist level • Push ball towards the floor (not slap)	
15 minutes	1. RED LIGHT, GREEN LIGHT, 3-2-1. Students try to dribble the ball from one side of the gym to the other. Each time they cross the gym they get 1 point.	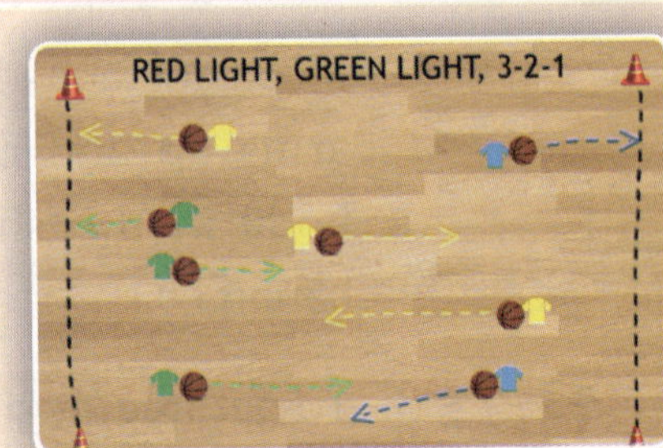
	2. Students can dribble when they hear "Green Light" but must stop when they hear "Red Light".	
	3. It the student is not holding the ball against their belly by the count of 3-2-1, then they lose 1 point.	

Close of Class/Cool Down		
Time needed:	Description of activity:	Essential question:
5 minutes	Students are seated in their coloured lines	What are the key elements of dribbling a ball? 1. Finger pads 2. Head looking up 3. Dribble ball waist level 4. Push ball towards the floor (not slap)

To see **Skill Development** in Action

Scan QR Code

ACTIVITY

Materials Required: None

1. Prepare a lesson plan for 4-6-year old children (for a session of 35 min). Mention the duration for each element of your lesson plan. Add extra sheets if required.

Activity	
Aim:	
Props & Equipment Required:	

Warm-up

Activity -1

2. Prepare flow chart on planning cycle.
3. Preparation of lesson plans for various physical activities

Subjective Questions

1. What is the importance of planning?
2. What are the elements of a lesson plan?
3. How should we prepare a lesson plan?

Unit 2

Props and Equipment

2.1 Selection of Prop and Equipment

A sports facility, also known as a sports venue, encompasses buildings, structures, or spaces designed for sports training or competitions. When planning the design and funding for a sports facility, it is essential to have a clear understanding of its intended purpose, which may range from serving as a community recreation center to a venue for competitive events. The popularity and success of a sports facility hinge on its utilisation, requiring proper equipment, maintenance, and a well-equipped environment. The crucial components of a sports facility are the props and equipment used, which are essential for optimising the user experience. Before delving further, let's differentiate between props and equipment.

2.2 Equipment

Definition: Equipment refers to the essential items and gear that athletes use to participate in their sport. This includes protective gear, uniforms, and any items necessary for playing the game.

Examples:

- **Baseball:** Bat, glove, helmet, cleats.
- **Football:** Pads, helmet, cleats, football.
- **Soccer:** Shin guards, cleats, soccer ball, goalposts.
- **Tennis:** Racquet, tennis balls, tennis shoes.

2.3 Props

Definition: Props in sports are items used to enhance the presentation, entertainment, or ceremonial aspects of a sport. They are not essential for playing the game itself but are often used in activities surrounding the sport, such as fan engagement, team celebrations, or media events.

Examples:

- **Cheerleading:** Pom-poms, megaphones, banners.

- **Sports events:** Mascot costumes, team flags, confetti cannons.
- **Ceremonies:** Trophy presentations, victory podiums, ceremonial first pitch items.

2.3.1 Key Differences

- **Purpose:** Equipment is necessary for the actual playing of the sport, while props are used for enhancing spectator experience or for ceremonial purposes.
- **Usage:** Equipment is used by players during the game, while props are used by cheerleaders, fans, event organisers, or during special ceremonies.
- **Regulations:** Equipment is typically regulated by sports governing bodies to ensure safety and fairness, whereas props do not usually have strict regulations.

2.4 Purpose and Importance of Props and Equipment

Props and equipment in sports must be age-appropriate for several important reasons related to safety, skill development, engagement, and overall experience.

To see **Fitness with Props** in Action

Scan QR Code

2.4.1 Safety

- **Proper Fit and Protection:** Age-appropriate equipment ensures that protective gear fits properly, providing necessary protection and reducing the risk of injuries. For example, helmets, pads, and guards that are too large for children or small for adults may not offer adequate protection to either.
- **Material and Design:** Equipment designed for children often uses lighter and softer materials to minimise injury risks. For instance, youth footballs are smaller and lighter, making them easier and safer for children to handle.

2.4.2 Skill Development

To see **Skill Development** in Action

Scan QR Code

- **Appropriate Size and Weight:** Using equipment suited to an age group aids in proper development of skills. For example, smaller basketballs for younger players help them to learn shooting and dribbling techniques more effectively. Similarly, shorter cricket balls and bats are easier for young children to swing.
- **Progressive Learning:** Age-appropriate equipment allows for a gradual increase in complexity and difficulty, of building they young athletes skills step by step. As they grow and improve, they can move on to more advanced equipment.

2.4.3 Engagement and Enjoyment

- **Encouraging Participation:** When equipment is appropriate for an athlete's age and size, it makes the sport more enjoyable and less frustrating. Children are more likely to stay engaged and develop a love for the sport if they can handle the equipment comfortably.

- **Confidence Building:** Using the right equipment helps young athletes achieve success in their sports activities, boosting their confidence and motivation. This positive reinforcement is crucial for their continued interest and development.

2.4.4 Performance

- **Optimal Performance:** Age-appropriate equipment enhances performance by ensuring that young athletes can use it effectively. For instance, a soccer ball that is too large or heavy for a child can hinder their ability to kick and control the ball properly.
- **Preventing Overuse Injuries:** Properly sized equipment reduces the risk of overuse injuries by ensuring that young athletes use their bodies correctly. For example, using and adult size racquet size in tennis can inflict strain on a child's wrist and arm.

2.4.5 Developmental Appropriateness

- **Cognitive and Physical Development:** Children's cognitive and physical abilities vary greatly with age. Age-appropriate props and equipment cater to these developmental stages, ensuring that activities are challenging yet achievable. For example, simple and brightly coloured props are more suitable for younger children who are still developing their coordination and focus skills.
- **Social and Emotional Development:** Appropriate equipment and props also support social interactions and emotional growth. Team sports equipment that fosters cooperative play is vital for developing social skills among younger children.

2.4.6 Regulatory Compliance

- **Adhering to Standards:** Many sports organisations and educational institutions have guidelines and standards for age-appropriate equipment to ensure safety and proper development. Compliance with these standards is essential to meet legal and institutional requirements.

List of Some commonly used props and equipment

Prop / Equipment	Prop/Equipment name	Description
	Pom-Poms	Fluffy, colourful hand-held items used by cheerleaders to encourage the crowd
	Mascot Costumes	Costumes worn by individuals representing the team mascot, used to entertain the crowd.
	Banners and Flags	Large, colourful pieces of fabric with team logos or slogans, waved by fans or displayed in stadia.
	Foam Fingers	Large foam hands with a pointing finger, used by fans to show support for their team.

	Confetti Cannons	Devices that shoot confetti into the air, used during celebrations and ceremonies.
	Medals	Small, often round metal discs given to athletes as awards for their achievements.
	Trophy	A decorative cup or statuette awarded to winners of a sporting event.
	Whistles	Small devices blown by referees and coaches to signal plays or fouls.
	Team Flags	Flags representing team colours and logos, waved by fans to show support.
	Cheerleader Megaphones	Cone-shaped devices used by cheerleaders to amplify their voices.
	Football Helmet	A protective helmet with a faceguard used in American football to prevent head injuries.
	Tennis Racquet	A racquet used in tennis, with a handle and a large oval frame strung with tightly pulled cords.
	Baseball Glove	A large leather glove worn by baseball players to catch the ball.
	Soccer Ball	A spherical ball used in soccer, typically black and white, made of leather or other synthetic materials.
	Basketball Shoes	Specially designed shoes with ankle support and non-slip soles for playing basketball.
	Hockey Stick	A long stick with a curved end used in ice hockey to hit the puck.
	Golf Clubs	Clubs of various types (driver, iron, putter) used to hit the golf ball.
	Cricket Bat	A flat-faced bat made of wood used to hit the cricket ball.
	Volleyball Net	A net placed vertically in the centre of the court, used in volleyball to separate the two teams.
	Boxing Gloves	Padded gloves worn by boxers to protect their hands and reduce the impact of punches.
	Swim Goggles	Protective eyewear used by swimmers to see clearly under water
	Badminton Shuttlecock	A feathered projectile used in badminton, hit back and forth over a net.
	Table Tennis Paddle	A small, handheld paddle used to hit the ball in table tennis.
	Ski Poles	Poles are used by skiers to aid in balancing and propulsion.
	Lacrosse Stick	A long stick with a net at one end used to catch, carry, and throw the ball in lacrosse.

	Field Hockey Ball	A small, hard ball used in field hockey.
	Equestrian Helmet	A protective helmet worn by horse riders to prevent head injuries.
	Archery Bow	A curved piece of equipment used to shoot arrows in archery.
	Ice Skates	Boots with blades attached to the bottom, used for skating on ice.
	Wrestling Mat	A padded mat used in wrestling to provide a safe surface for the athletes.

2.5 Factors Affecting Selection of Equipment

To see **Selection of Equipment** in Action

Scan QR Code

1. **Sport-Specific Requirements:** Every sport has its unique equipment needs tailored to the nature of the game. For example, American football requires helmets, shoulder pads, and cleats, while tennis racquets rackets and specific types of shoes. The equipment must align with the rules and gameplay mechanics of the sport.
2. **Safety:** Safety is paramount in sports, and the equipment is often selected based on its ability to protect athletes from injuries. For instance, helmets in American football and hockey, mouthguards in boxing and martial arts, and shin guards in soccer are critical for players' safety. The material and design of such equipment are scrutinised to provide maximum protection.
3. **Quality and Durability:** High-quality and durable equipment can withstand the rigours of sports activities. For example, a durable tennis racquet will maintain its integrity longer under heavy use, and high-quality soccer balls will perform consistently over time. Athletes and teams often invest in equipment that offers the best performance over its lifespan.
4. **Regulations and Standards:** Sports governing bodies set strict standards for equipment to ensure fairness and safety. For example, the International Tennis Federation (ITF) regulates the size, weight, and bounce of tennis balls, while FIFA has standards for soccer ball size and weight. Compliance with these standards is crucial for official competitions.
5. **Performance:** Equipment that enhances performance is highly valued. Lightweight materials, ergonomic designs, and advanced technologies improve players' perform anal. For instance, aerodynamic cycling helmets reduce drag, and high-grip basketball shoes improve traction on the court.
6. **Comfort and Fit:** Properly fitting equipment enhances comfort and can improve performance. Ill-fitting gear can lead to discomfort and even injuries. Custom-fitted mouthguards, adjustable helmets, and size-specific shoes are examples of equipment designed for comfort and fit.

7. **Cost:** Budget constraints can however, influence equipment selection. While professional teams and athletes may afford high-end gear, amateur players and small schools might opt for less costly options. For the latter, balancing cost and quality is a key consideration for many.

8. **Brand and Sponsorship:** Brand reputation and sponsorship deals often influence equipment choices. Sponsored athletes may use and endorse specific brands, and teams might have contracts with equipment manufacturers. Brand loyalty and perceived quality also play roles in selection.

2.6 Factors Affecting Selection of Props

1. **Event Purpose and Theme:** The purpose and theme of the event greatly influence the choice of props. For example, props used in a national championship might include patriotic elements, while a club-level event might use props reflecting team colours and mascots. The theme of the event guides the visual and emotional tone of the props.

2. **Audience Engagement:** Props are selected to enhance audience engagement and enjoyment. Cheerleaders use pom-poms and megaphones to energise the crowd, while interactive props like foam fingers and noise-makers involve fans in the action. Engaging props contribute to the overall atmosphere and excitement of the event.

3. **Aesthetics:** Visual appeal is crucial for props used in ceremonies and presentations. The design, colour, and overall look of the props must align with the event's branding and aesthetic goals. Attractive and well-designed props enhance the visual experience for both live and broadcast audiences.

4. **Safety:** Safety considerations are important, especially for the props used in large crowds or by performers. Props should be made from non-toxic, flame-retardant materials and should not pose any hazards. For example, confetti cannons should be safe for indoor use, and large props should be stable to prevent accidents.

5. **Ease of Use and Transport:** Props should be easy to set up, use, and transport. For touring events or those held in large stadia, props that are lightweight, collapsible, and easy to pack and assemble are preferred. This logistical consideration ensures smooth operations and reduces the risk of delays or complications.

6. **Cost:** Budget constraints also play a role in prop selection. Event organisers often seek cost-effective props that still deliver the desired visual and emotional impact. Renting props or opting for reusable ones can be cost-effective solutions for managing expenses.

7. **Durability:** Durable props that can be reused for multiple events offer better value. Props made from sturdy materials are more likely to withstand wear and damage from repeated use, reducing the need for frequent replacements. This is particularly important for props used in recurring events or by touring teams.

8. **Regulations:** Specific regulations may govern the types of props allowed, especially in professional sports arenas. For example, pyrotechnics might be restricted, and certain types of signage or displays might need approval. Compliance with these regulations is essential to avoid fines or penalties.

9. **Innovation and Creativity:** Unique and creative props can make an event engaging and memorable for the audience. Innovative props that surprise and delight spectators can enhance the overall experience. For instance, creative halftime show props or unique award presentation setups can leave a lasting impression.

ACTIVITIES

1. List down factors affecting selection of props and equipment.
2. Preparation of poster of props and equipment.
3. Preparation of list of equipment for conducting physical and sports activities.

Differentiate Between

After completing this session, you should be able to:

1. Identify age-appropriate props and equipment to conduct sports activities
2. Select props and equipment as per specific requirement
3. Determine props correctly for age-appropriate lessons and skills
4. Minimise the risk associated with using of non-age-specific props and equipment

Subjective Questions

1. List the factors affecting the selection of props and equipment.
2. Why props and equipment should be age-appropriate?
3. What are the negative effects of selecting non-age-appropriate props and equipment during play activities?

Multiple Choice Questions with Answers

1. **What is the primary purpose of using props and equipment in physical education classes?**

   (a) To make classes more competitive (b) To enhance motor skill development
   (c) To reduce the duration of classes (d) To increase academic learning

2. **Which piece of equipment is commonly used for balance and coordination exercises?**
   (a) Basketball (b) Balance beam
   (c) Soccer ball (d) Tennis racket
3. **What type of ball is typically used in primary school physical education for developing throwing and catching skills?**
   (a) Medicine ball (b) Soccer ball
   (c) Foam ball (d) Bowling ball
4. **Which of the following is NOT considered a prop in physical education?**
   (a) Hula hoop (b) Jump rope
   (c) Resistance band (d) Textbook
5. **For which activity would you most likely use a parachute as a piece of equipment?**
   (a) Weight training (b) Aerobics
   (c) Group games and activities (d) Gymnastics
6. **Which piece of equipment is essential for teaching and practicing gymnastics?**
   (a) Football (b) Gymnastics mat
   (c) Baseball glove (d) Cricket bat
7. **Which equipment would be best suited for improving cardiovascular endurance in children?**
   (a) Dumbbells (b) Jump ropes
   (c) Yoga mats (d) Balance balls
8. **Which type of equipment is often used to develop upper body strength in young children?**
   (a) Resistance bands (b) Pool noodles
   (c) Cones (d) Bean bags
9. **What is the primary benefit of using cones in physical education classes?**
   (a) To mark boundaries and create obstacle courses
   (b) To provide hydration stations
   (c) To use as weights for strength training
   (d) To measure students' height
10. **Which piece of equipment is commonly used to improve flexibility in physical education?**
   (a) Medicine ball (b) Balance board
   (c) Yoga mat (d) Soccer ball

ANSWERS

1. (b) 2. (b) 3. (c) 4. (d) 5. (c) 6. (b) 7. (b)
8. (a) 9. (a) 10. (c)

2.7 Inspection of Playfields

2.7.1 Low-Frequency Inspections

(a) Long-Term Condition Assessment:

- Evaluate the overall health and condition of the turf, soil, and drainage systems.
- Identify the areas prone to wear, compaction, or drainage issues that may not be apparent during regular use.

(b) Safety and Compliance:

- Ensure that the field meets safety standards and regulatory requirements set by sports governing bodies and local authorities.
- Identify potential hazards or structural issues that could pose risk to players or spectators.

(c) Planning for Major Maintenance:

- Plan and schedule major maintenance activities such as renovation, overseeding, or soil amendments based on inspection findings.
- Assess the effectiveness of previous maintenance practices and adjust strategies as needed.

2.7.2 Components of Low-Frequency Inspections:

(i) Field Surface Evaluation:

- Assess the overall turf quality, including colour, density, and uniformity.
- Look for signs of stress, disease, or invasive species that may require specialised treatment.

(ii) Soil Analysis:

- Conduct soil tests to evaluate nutrient levels, pH balance, and compaction.
- Determine the need for fertilisation, aeration, or other soil amendments to promote healthy turf growth.

(iii) Drainage and Irrigation Assessment:

- Inspect drainage systems, including pipes, channels, and surface drains, for blockages or damage.
- Evaluate the effectiveness of irrigation systems in delivering adequate water distribution across the field.

(iv) Inspection of Infrastructure and Equipment:

- Check structural components such as goalposts, nets, fencing, and seating for stability and safety.

- Evaluate the condition of equipment such as field lighting, scoreboards, and sound systems.

(v) Documentation and Reporting:

- Maintain detailed records of inspection findings, including photographs and measurements.
- List out recommendations for corrective actions, maintenance priorities, and budget considerations.

2.7.3 High Frequency Inspections

(a) Checking of Surface and Equipment:

- Inspect the field surface for evenness, divots, and signs of wear after each use.
- Check equipment such as goalposts, nets, and safety barriers for stability and functionality.

(b) Line Markings and Visibility:

- Ensure that all field markings, including boundary lines, goal lines, and centre circles, are clear and correctly positioned.
- Verify the visibility of markings under different lighting conditions to meet the requirements of the game.

(c) Player and Spectator Safety:

- Evaluate spectator areas, seating, fencing, and walkways for hazards or obstructions.
- Monitor player benches, medical equipment, and emergency exits for accessibility and readiness.

(d) Drainage and Irrigation Monitoring:

- Assess the effectiveness of drainage systems in managing water runoff and preventing waterlogging.
- Check irrigation systems for proper function, ensuring uniform distribution of water across the field.

(e) Immediate Action and Reporting:

- Address any identified issues promptly, such as repairing divots, clearing debris, or adjusting field equipment.
- Report inspection findings, actions taken, and recommendations for further maintenance or repairs.

Use the following checklist for the inspection of play area.

Particular	Question	Corrective Action	Person Responsible	Completion Date
Surface Condition	Ensure that the surface is free from hazards such as cracks, holes, or unevenness. Verify that the adequate cushioning material (e.g., rubber, mulch) is intact and evenly distributed.			
Equipment Safety	Inspect all play structures (e.g., swings, slides) for stability and signs of wear. Check for any sharp edges, protrusions, or pinch points. Ensure that the equipment meets safety standards (e.g., ASTM, CPSC).			
Fall Zones	Assess fall zones around the equipment to ensure that they are clear and covered with impact-absorbing material. Measure the depth of surfacing material (e.g., minimum 6 inches of loose fill or 12 inches of engineered wood fibre			
Accessibility	Verify accessibility features (e.g., ramps, transfer systems) comply with ADA guidelines. Ensure pathways to play equipment are accessible for all users.			
Signage and Instructions	Check for safety signs, age-appropriate use instructions, and emergency contact information. Ensure that signage is clear, visible, and in good condition.			
Maintenance	Inspect for cleanliness and general maintenance (e.g., litter, graffiti). Check for loose bolts, missing hardware, or damaged components. Review maintenance logs for completeness			
Environmental Factors	Assess surroundings for potential hazards (e.g., proximity to roads, and bodies of water). Consider the availability of shade and exposure to the sun. Check for insect nests or animal activity			
Sanitation	Ensure that adequate trash receptacles are available and are emptied regularly. Check the cleanliness of seating areas and restroom facilities (if applicable).			

To keep the quality of sports surfaces, it is necessary to do regular maintenance, like:

- Ensure that the pitch is free from any leaves, stones, pebbles, flints, or sharp objects.
- Clean the floor daily, especially if it is made of cement.
- Only use recommended footwear on the court.
- Keep the pitch and its surroundings clean.
- Maintain the quality and cleanliness of all equipment and props.
- Regularly inspect the maintenance of goal posts, volleyball poles, basketball posts, etc.
- Ensure that enough dustbins are available.

2.8 Maintenance of Sport Facilities

2.8.1 Regular Inspection:

- **Purpose:** Regularly inspect props and equipment before and after each use.
- **Focus:** Check for signs of wear, damage, or malfunction that could compromise safety.
- **Action:** Promptly repair or replace any damaged equipment to prevent injuries during use.

2.8.2 Cleaning and Sanitisation:

- **Routine:** Establish a routine schedule for cleaning and sanitising the equipment.
- **Methods:** Use appropriate cleaning agents and techniques recommended by manufacturers.
- **Attention:** Pay special attention to high-touch areas and surfaces to prevent the spread of infections.

2.8.3 Storage and Organisation:

- **Proper Storage:** Store equipment in a clean, dry, and well-ventilated area.
- **Organization:** Arrange the equipment to prevent overcrowding and ensure easy access for inspection and use.
- **Separation:** Store different types of equipment separately to prevent damage and maintain organisation.

2.8.4 Training and Proper Use:

- **Education:** Train personnel on proper handling, use, and maintenance procedures for each type of equipment.
- **Guidelines:** Follow manufacturer guidelines and safety protocols for setting up and using equipment.

- **Supervision:** Ensure that the equipment is used only by trained individuals who understand its proper operation.

2.8.5 Replacement and Upgrades:

- **Lifecycle:** Monitor the lifecycle of equipment and props to schedule their timely replacements.
- **Safety Standards:** Ensure that replacements meet current safety standards and regulations.
- **Technology:** Consider upgrades or improvements to the equipment to enhance safety and performance.

2.8.6 Emergency Preparedness:

- **Protocols:** Establish and communicate emergency protocols for handling equipment-related accidents or malfunctions.
- **First Aid:** Ensure the availability of first aid supplies and personnel trained in emergency response.

2.8.7 Weather and Environmental Conditions:

- **Protection:** Protect the equipment from extreme weather conditions, such as rain, heat, or cold.
- **Covering:** Use covers or shelters when the equipment is not in use, to prolong its lifespan and maintain functionality.

2.8.8 Documentation and Record-Keeping:

- **Maintenance Logs:** Maintain detailed records of equipment inspections, cleaning schedules, repairs, and replacements.
- **History:** Use historical data to track equipment performance, identify trends, and plan future maintenance or upgrades.

After completing this session, you should be able to:

- Identify the reasons affecting the playground and equipment condition
- Plan for playground and equipment inspection
- Create a checklist for inspection
- Inflate balls with correct air pressure
- Demonstrate how to maintain sports facilities

ACTIVITY

1. Prepare a timetable for the inspection of playfield area
2. List down the safety measure to be kept in mind while doing playfield inspection

Differentiate Between

1. Low frequency and high frequency inspections
2. The amount of pressure for basketball, volleyball and football
3. Maintenance procedure for balls before and after use

Subjective Questions

1. Explain the factors affecting the condition of the play area and equipment
2. Describe low frequency and high frequency inspections
3. How should props and equipment be maintained?
4. How should balls, props and equipment be stored be stored?
5. What is the correct pressure to inflate football, basketball and volleyball?

Unit 3 Hygiene and Safety

3.1 Introduction

Hygiene is the practice of keeping yourself and your surroundings clean, especially in order to prevent the spread of disease. Having good personal hygiene practices means taking care of yourself and leading a healthy life. Good personal hygiene is the first step to good health. It not only protects you from poor health, but also shields those around you from illness that arises from poor personal habits. Habits such as washing your hands, bathing, brushing, may all look monotonous and boring, but they all come under the am bit of important personal hygiene. They make you feel good about yourself and keep you free from bacteria, viruses, and illnesses. To protect your health, you must clean your body, hair, mouth and teeth regularly. You must also wear clean clothes.

To see **Cleaning and Sanitisation** in Action

Scan QR Code

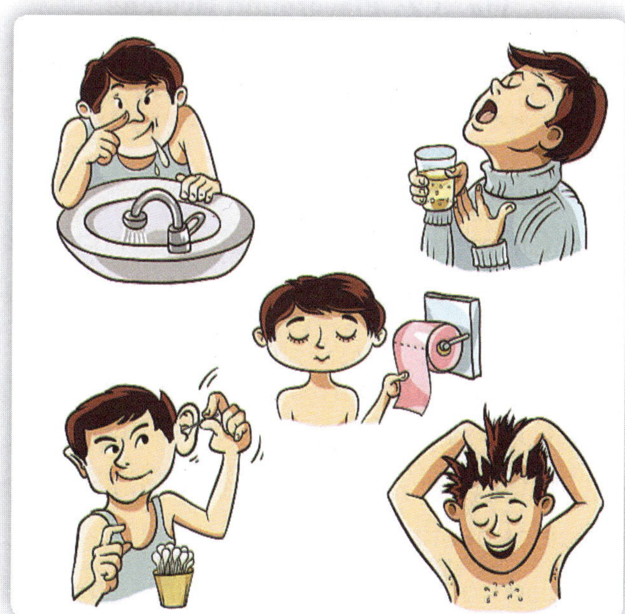

Fig. 3.1: Healthy Habits

3.1.1 Some General Hygiene and Sanitation Rules

- **Regular Handwashing:** Wash hands thoroughly with soap and water for at least 20 seconds, especially after using the restroom, before eating, and after coughing or sneezing.

- **Bathing:** Take regular showers or baths to keep the body clean and prevent the buildup of sweat and bacteria.
- **Oral Hygiene:** Brush teeth at least twice a day and floss daily to prevent dental issues.
- **Nail Care:** Keep nails trimmed and clean to avoid the buildup of dirt and bacteria.
- **Hair Care:** Wash hair regularly and maintain a clean scalp.
- **Clothing:** Wear clean clothes and wash them regularly to avoid odour and skin infections.

Below, you will learn essential rules of hygiene and sanitation. By adopting these healthy practices, you can enjoy a longer, healthier life and increase your productivity and efficiency.

Fig. 3.2: Playground Hygiene

3.2 Maintenance of Hygiene in Play Area

3.2.1 Playground Hygiene Guidelines

To see **Some General Hygiene and Sanitation Rules 1** in Action

Scan QR Code

- **Regular Cleaning:** Clean the playground equipment regularly using appropriate disinfectants, especially high-touch surfaces like swings, slides, and monkey bars.
- **Trash Disposal:** Provide adequate trash bins and ensure that they are emptied regularly to prevent littering.
- **Sand and Mulch:** Rake and replace sand or mulch periodically to ensure that it remains clean and free of debris.
- **Water Areas:** If the playground has water features, ensure that the water is clean and changed regularly to prevent the growth of bacteria and algae in it.
- **Handwashing Stations:** Install handwashing stations or hand sanitiser dispensers at the entrance and exit of the playground.
- **Hand Hygiene:** Encourage children and caregivers to wash their hands before and after using playground equipment.

To see **Some General Hygiene and Sanitation Rules** in Action

Scan QR Code

- **Clean Clothing:** Ensure that children wear clean clothes and encourage them to change out of dirty clothes after playing.
- **Supervision:** Ensure adult supervision to monitor and guide children in safe and hygienic play practices.
- **Footwear:** Encourage children to wear appropriate footwear to protect their feet from injuries and infections.
- **Food and Drinks:** Discourage eating and drinking on playground equipment to prevent spills and contamination.
- **Sick Children:** Advise parents to keep sick children at home to prevent spreading illnesses.
- **First Aid:** Have a first aid kit readily available and ensure that the staff is trained to handle minor injuries.
- **Hygiene Education:** Educate children and caregivers about the importance of hygiene and proper handwashing techniques.
- **Routine Checks:** Conduct routine inspections of playground equipment to ensure it is in good condition and free from hazards.
- **Repair and Replace:** Promptly repair or replace damaged equipment to maintain safety.
- **Pest Control:** Implement pest control measures to prevent the presence of insects and rodents.
- **Shade and Sun Protection:** Provide shaded areas to protect children from excessive exposure to the sun and ensure that surfaces are not too hot to touch.

Fig. 3.3: Hygienic Play Zones

Survey your school playground and fill the questionnaire given below:
Date of Survey:
Name of Supervisor:
Location of Playground:

S.No	Measures	Particulars	Options
	General Cleanliness	Are there visible trash or litter on the playground?	Yes/No
		Are trash bins available and regularly emptied?	Yes/No
		Is the ground free of chewing gum, food, and other debris?	Yes/No
	Condition of the Equipment	Is the playground equipment clean?	Yes /No
		Are there any broken or damaged pieces of equipment?	Yes/No
		Is the equipment well-maintained and free of rust?	Yes/No
	Cleanliness of all Surface	Is the ground surface (sand, mulch, rubber mats) clean and free of hazardous materials?	Yes/No
		Is the sand or mulch regularly raked and replaced?	Yes/No
		Is the rubber matting intact and not worn out?	Yes/No
	Hygiene Facilities	Are handwashing stations or hand sanitiser dispensers available?	Yes/No
		Are restrooms nearby and in clean condition?	Yes/No
		Are soap and paper towels or hand dryers available in restrooms?	Yes/No
	Safety Measures	Are there any sharp objects, broken glass, or other hazardous materials present?	Yes/No
		Is there adequate shading to protect children from excessive sun exposure?	Yes/No
		Is there soft surfacing under playground equipment to cushion falls?	Yes/No

Survey your school's common areas and fill out the questionnaire

S.No	Area	Particulars	Options
	General Cleanliness	Are there visible trash or litter in common areas?	Yes/No
		Are trash bins available and regularly emptied?	Yes/No
		Are floors and surfaces clean and free of spills and stains?	Yes/No
	Restroom Condition	Are restrooms clean and well-maintained?	Yes/No
		Are toilets and sinks in good working condition?	Yes/No
		Are toilets and sinks in good working condition?	Yes/No
		Is there sufficient soap and toilet paper?	Yes/No
		Are handwashing facilities clean and stocked?	Yes/No

	Cafeteria and Eating Areas	Are eating areas clean and free of food debris?	Yes/No
		Are tables and chairs in good condition and regularly cleaned?	Yes/No
		Are food preparation and serving areas clean and hygienic?	Yes/No
	Hallways and Corridors	Are hallways and corridors clean and free of obstacles?	Yes/No
		Are walls and floors in good condition?	Yes/No
		Are there any safety hazards present (e.g., wet floors, exposed wires)?	Yes/No
	Classrooms	Are classrooms clean and well-organized?	Yes/No
		Are desks and chairs in good condition and regularly cleaned?	Yes/No
		Is there adequate ventilation and lighting?	Yes/No

3.3 Maintenance of Safest Conditions Around Swimming Area

Maintaining safety around swimming areas is essential to prevent accidents, ensure hygiene, and promote a secure recreational environment.

1. **Proper Supervision**
   - Lifeguards should be present and alert at all times.
   - Clear safety rules must be displayed and enforced.
2. **Cleanliness and Hygiene**
   - Regular cleaning of pool water using filtration systems and chlorine.
   - Showers and footbaths should be functional and used before entering the pool.
3. **Safety Equipment**
   - Life jackets, rescue tubes, first-aid kits, and reaching poles should be available and accessible.
   - Emergency contact information should be posted.
4. **Slip-Resistant Surfaces**
   - Pool decks and walking areas should be made of non-slip materials to avoid falls.
5. **Water Quality Checks**
   - Regular testing of pH, chlorine levels, and temperature.
   - Immediate action if contamination is detected.
6. **Restricted Access**
   - Children should only enter under adult supervision.
   - Fencing or barriers should prevent unsupervised entry.

7. **Lighting and Visibility**
    - Adequate lighting during evening hours to ensure visibility.
    - Underwater lights should be functional.

8. **Signage and Markings**
    - Depth markers, "No Diving" signs, and emergency exits should be clearly visible.

9. **Emergency Protocols**
    - Staff should be trained in CPR and first aid.
    - Regular drills and preparedness checks are important.

10. **Regular Maintenance**
    - Inspection of pool tiles, ladders, railings, and drainage systems.
    - Fix cracks, leaks, or damage immediately.

3.4 Safety in Swimming Pool

Always supervise children and inexperienced swimmers. An adult should always be present to monitor activities in and around the pool.

Encourage swimmers to always swim with a buddy, even if they are experienced swimmers.

Enroll children and inexperienced swimmers in swimming lessons to teach them how to swim and handle themselves in the water.

To see **Maintenance of Safest Conditions Around Swimming Area** in Action

Scan QR Code

Trained lifeguards on duty.

Fig. 3.4: Swimming Pool

Install a fence around the pool area with a self-latching gate to prevent unsupervised access, especially by young children.

Consider installing pool alarms that alert you if someone enters the pool area.

Use non-slip materials around the pool to prevent slips and falls.

Keep the area around the pool free of toys, furniture, and other items that could be tripped over.

Clearly mark the depth of the pool at various levels so swimmers are aware of where it is safe to dive or jump.

Prohibit diving in shallow areas to prevent head injuries.

Use buoys and floats to designate swimming zones and to keep swimmers within safe areas.

Rescue equipment such as life rings, reaching poles, and a first aid kit near the pool.

Encourage swimmers to take shower before entering the pool to reduce the introduction of contaminants.

Discourage swimming if someone has diarrhoea or some other illnesses that can contaminate the water.

Keep a list of emergency contact numbers readily available in the pool area.

Use a pool cover when the pool is not in use to prevent accidental tripping.

After completing this session, you should be able to:

- Identify the steps to maintain playground hygiene
- Identify the steps to maintain environmental hygiene

ACTIVITY

1. Conduct hygiene survey in your school playground using a checklist.

Differentiate Between

1. Playground and common area hygiene
2. Municipal waste and medical waste
3. Hazardous waste and non-hazardous waste

Subjective Questions

1. Explain the factors affecting the condition of the play area and equipment.
2. List the steps to maintain hygiene at playground.
3. Why is it important to keep oneself and one's environment clean?

3.5 First Aid

3.5.1 Concept of First Aid

First aid is the immediate care provided to a person who has been injured or taken ill suddenly, before professional medical assistance is available. The primary goal of first aid is to preserve life, prevent the condition from worsening, and promote recovery.

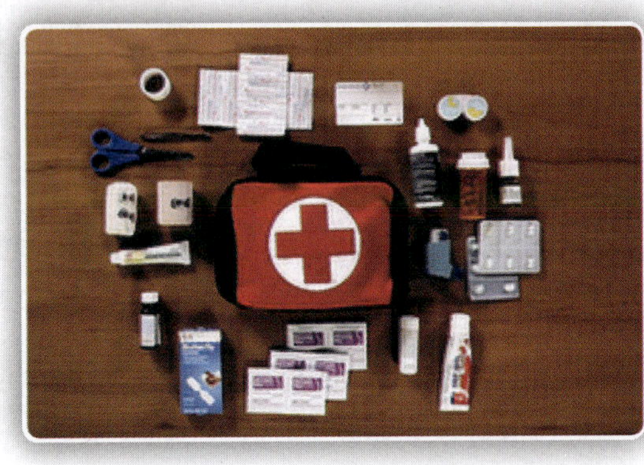

Fig. 3.5: Aid Kit Contents

3.5.2 Purpose and Basic Principles of First Aid

To see **Purpose and Basic Principles of First Aid** in Action

Scan QR Code

Purpose of First Aid

- **Preserve Life:** The primary objective is to save lives by providing immediate care in life-threatening situations.
- **Prevent Further Harm:** First aid aims to stabilise the patient's condition, preventing the situation from worsening. This includes actions that stop bleeding, immobilise fractures, and protect the injured from further injury.
- **Promote Recovery:** Early intervention can facilitate faster recovery. First aid can reduce pain, minimise the risk of complications, and provide psychological reassurance to the patient.

3.5.3 Principles of First Aid

1. Assess the Situation:

- Ensure your own safety first. Check for any dangers or hazards before approaching the injured person. Quickly evaluate the nature of the injury or illness to determine the appropriate course of action.

2. Call for Help:

- In severe cases, contact emergency services immediately. Provide clear and concise information about the location, nature of the emergency, and the condition of the injured person.

3. Perform a Primary Survey (DRABC):

- **Danger:** Ensure that the area is safe for both you and the injured person.
- **Response:** Check if the injured person is responsive by gently shaking them and asking if they are okay.
- **Airway:** Ensure that the airway is open and clear. If necessary, perform the head-tilt, chin-lift manoeuvre.
- **Breathing:** Check for normal breathing. Look, listen, and feel for breaths.
- **Circulation:** Check for signs of circulation, such as movement, coughing, or normal breathing. If absent, begin CPR.

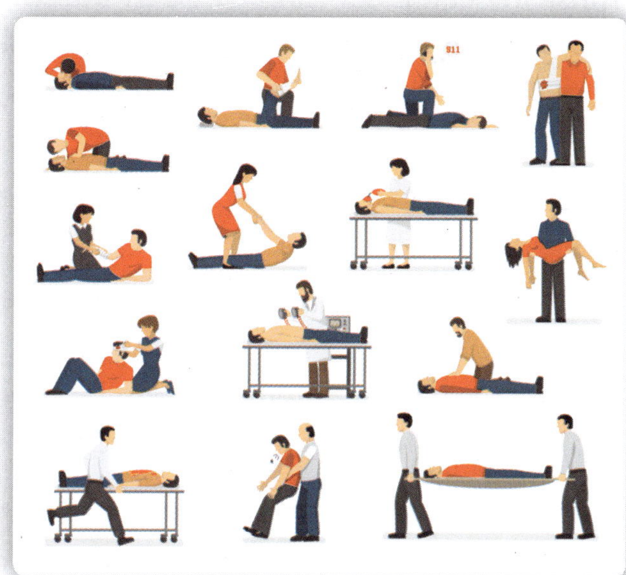

Fig. 3.6: DRABC

4. Perform a Secondary Survey:

- Once that immediate life-threatening conditions are addressed, conduct a more thorough checks for other injuries or medical issues. Check that vital signs, look for bleeding, fractures, burns, or other injuries, and gather information about the person's medical history, if possible.

3.5.4 Conditions Requiring Immediate Attention

1. Cuts and bruises; 2. Heat exhaustion; 3. Breathing difficulties; 4. Basic sports injury.

1. Cuts and Bruises

Cuts and bruises are part of growing up. Do not become paranoid about the children's safety and stop them from exploring. At the same time know what to do when they injure themselves. If cuts are deep and do not stop bleeding, seek medical help.

Types of Cuts:

- **Minor Cuts:** Shallow cuts that do not involve severe bleeding.
- **Major Cuts:** Deeper cuts that may involve profuse bleeding, large areas of skin, or deep tissues.

First Aid for Minor Cuts:

1. **Wash Your Hands:** Clean your hands thoroughly with soap and water to prevent infection.
2. **Stop the Bleeding:** Apply gentle pressure to the cut with a clean cloth or bandage until the bleeding stops.
3. **Clean the Cut:** Rinse the cut under running water to remove dirt and debris. Then use mild soap if necessary, but avoid getting soap inside the cut.
4. **Apply an Antiseptic:** Use an antiseptic wipe or ointment to reduce the risk of infection.
5. **Cover the Cut:** Apply a sterile bandage or adhesive bandage to keep the cut clean and protected.
6. **Change the Bandage:** Replace the bandage daily or whenever it becomes wet or dirty.
7. **Watch for Signs of Infection:** Look out for redness, swelling, increased pain, or pus. Seek medical attention if these symptoms occur.

Bruises

- A bruise, also known as a contusion, occurs when small blood vessels under the skin break, causing blood to leak into the surrounding tissues. This results in discolouration, swelling, and pain.

First Aid for Bruises:

Use the concept of RICE, i.e., rest, ice, compression and elevation.

1. **Rest:** Minimise movement of the bruised area to prevent further injury and to promote healing.
2. **Ice:** Apply an ice pack or a cold compress to the bruised area for 15-20 minutes every hour for the first 24-48 hours.

   Use a cloth to wrap the ice pack to protect the skin.
3. **Compression:** Apply a compression bandage to the area if it is swollen, but ensure that it is not too tight as to restrict blood flow within the body.
4. **Elevation:** Raise the bruised area above the level of the heart, if possible, to reduce swelling.

5. **Pain Relief:** Over-the-counter pain relievers, such as acetaminophen or ibuprofen, can help to manage pain and reduce inflammation. Follow the dosage instructions on the packaging.

Fig. 3.7: R I C E

3.5.5 Heat Exhaustion

If is a heat-related illness that can occur after being exposed to high temperatures, often combined with high humidity and strenuous physical activity. It is important to recognise the signs and symptoms of heat exhaustion to prevent it from progressing to heat stroke, which is a more severe and life-threatening condition.

Signs and Symptoms of Heat Exhaustion

1. **Heavy Sweating:** Excessive sweating, often accompanied by moist, cool skin.
2. **Weakness or Fatigue:** Feeling weak, tired, or fatigued, often with a sense of being overwhelmed.
3. **Dizziness or Fainting:** Light-headedness, dizziness, or even fainting spells.
4. **Nausea or Vomiting:** Feeling of nausea or vomiting.
5. **Muscle Cramps:** Painful muscle cramps, especially in the legs, arms, or abdomen.
6. **Headache:** Throbbing headache.
7. **Rapid Heartbeat:** Fast but weak pulse.

Prevention of Heat Exhaustion

1. **Stay Hydrated:** Drink plenty of fluids, especially water, before, during, and after outdoor activities. Avoid alcohol, caffeine, and sugary drinks, which can contribute to dehydration.

2. **Wear Appropriate Clothing:** Wear lightweight, loose-fitting, light-coloured clothes to help your body stay cool. A wide-brimmed hat and sunglasses can provide additional protection.
3. **Take Breaks:** Take frequent breaks in a cool or shaded area if you are working or exercising outdoors. Take rest often and avoid over-exertion.
4. **Avoid Peak Sun Hours:** Limit your outdoor activities to the cooler parts of the day, such as early morning or late evening. Avoid strenuous activities during the hottest part of the day, typically between 10 a.m. and 4 p.m.

Fig. 3.8: Heat Exhaustion

3.5.6 Breathing Difficulties

Breathing difficulties can range from mild shortness of breath to severe respiratory distress. They can be caused by various factors, including medical conditions, environmental factors, and physical exertion. Recognising the signs and symptoms and knowing how to provide first aid can be critical.

(A) Causes of Breathing Difficulties

(i) **Asthma:** Chronic condition where airways become inflamed and narrow.

(ii) **Chronic Obstructive Pulmonary Disease (COPD):** Includes chronic bronchitis and emphysema, which obstruct airflow.

(iii) **Allergic Reactions:** Can cause swelling of the airways.

(iv) **Infections:** Such as pneumonia or bronchitis.

(v) **Heart Conditions:** Including heart failure or heart attack.

(vi) **Anxiety or Panic Attacks:** Can lead to hyperventilation.

(vii) **Obstructions:** Choking on food or foreign objects.

(viii) **Environmental Factors:** Exposure to smoke, pollutants, or allergens.

(B) Signs and Symptoms of Breathing Difficulties

(i) **Shortness of Breath:** Feeling like you can't get enough air.

(ii) **Rapid Breathing:** Breathing faster than usual.

(iii) **Laboured Breathing:** Using extra muscles to breathe, indicated by the chest or abdomen moving more than usual.

(iv) **Wheezing:** A high-pitched sound during breathing.

(v) **Coughing:** Persistent or severe coughing.

(vi) **Chest Tightness:** A feeling of constriction in the chest.

(vii) **Cyanosis:** Bluish tint to lips, face, or fingernails due to lack of oxygen.

(viii) **Fatigue:** Feeling unusually tired.

(ix) **Confusion:** Difficulty thinking clearly due to lack of oxygen.

(x) **Anxiety:** Feeling panicked or anxious about not being able to breathe.

(C) First Aid for Breathing Difficulties

(a) **Assess the Situation:**

- Determine the cause of the breathing difficulty, if possible.
- Check for any obvious signs of airway obstruction, allergic reactions, or injury.

(b) **Help the Person to a Comfortable Position:**

- Often, sitting upright or leaning slightly forward can improve breathing.
- Avoid lying the person flat on their back.

(c) **Loosen Tight Clothing:** Loosen any tight clothing around the neck and chest to help with breathing.

(d) **Encourage Slow, Deep Breaths:** If the person is hyperventilating, encourage them to breathe slowly and deeply. Using a paper bag to breathe into can help if they are hyperventilating due to anxiety.

(e) **Use Medications if Available:** If the person has a prescribed inhaler or medication for a known condition (like asthma), assist them in using it.

(f) **Monitor and Reassure:** Stay with the person and keep them calm. Anxiety can worsen breathing difficulties.

(g) **Perform CPR if Necessary:** If the person stops breathing, be prepared to perform CPR. Ensure the airway is open and begin chest compressions and rescue breaths as needed.

(D) Preventive Measures

(a) **Avoid Triggers:** Identify and avoid known triggers for conditions like asthma or allergies.

(b) **Use Medications as Prescribed:** Take medications regularly and as prescribed for chronic conditions.

(c) **Stay Hydrated:** Drink plenty of fluids to keep mucus thin and easier to clear from the airways.

(d) **Maintain a Healthy Lifestyle:** Exercise regularly to strengthen the respiratory system and maintain a healthy weight.

(e) **Avoid Smoking and Pollutants:** Avoid smoking and exposure to second-hand smoke and other pollutants.

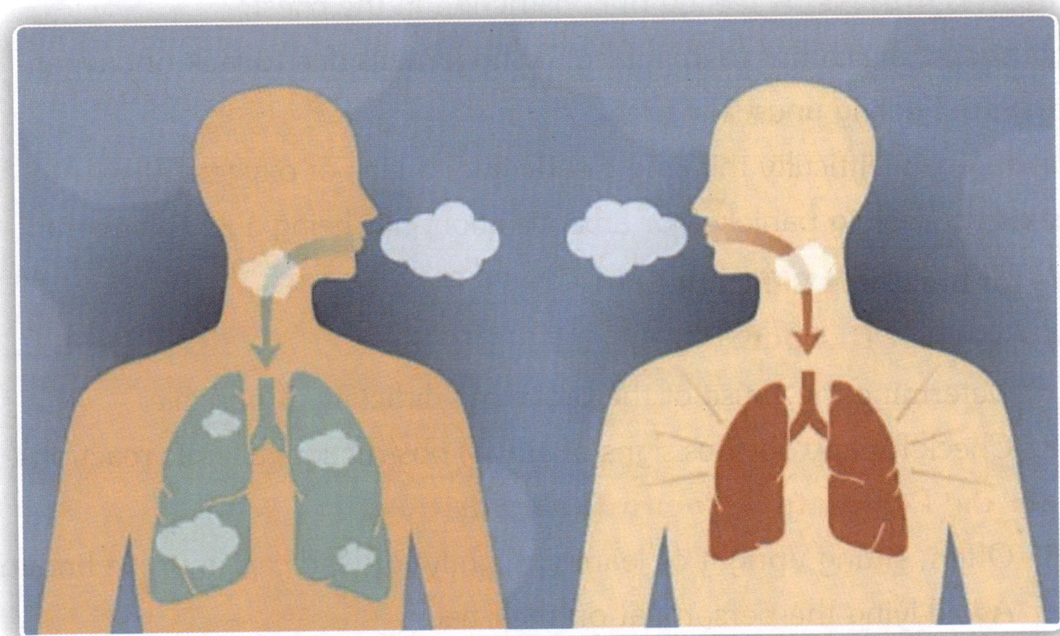

Fig. 3.9: Breathing

3.5.7 Basic Sports Injury

(i) Sprains

- **Description:** Stretching or tearing of ligaments (the tissue connecting bones to each other).
- **Common Areas:** Ankles, knees, wrists.
- **Symptoms:** Pain, swelling, bruising, and limited ability to move the affected joint.

(ii) Strains

- **Description:** Stretching or tearing of muscles or tendons (the tissue connecting muscles to bones).
- **Common Areas:** Hamstrings, back, shoulders.
- **Symptoms:** Pain, muscle spasms, swelling, and limited muscle movement

(iii) Fractures

- **Description:** Breaks in the bone.

- **Common Areas:** Arms, legs, feet, hands.
- **Symptoms:** Severe pain, swelling, bruising, and inability to move the affected area.

(iv) Dislocations

- **Description:** Bones forced out of their normal position in the joint.
- **Common Areas:** Shoulders, fingers, knees.
- **Symptoms:** Visible deformity, intense pain, swelling, and immobility of the joint

(v) Concussions

- **Description:** Traumatic brain injuries caused by a blow to the head or body, shaking of brain inside the skull.
- **Symptoms:** Headache, confusion, dizziness, nausea, and sometimes loss of consciousness.

(vi) Tendinitis

- **Description:** Inflammation of a tendon.
- **Common Areas:** Elbows (tennis elbow), shoulders, knees (patellar tendinitis).
- **Symptoms:** Pain and tenderness along a tendon, especially near joints.

(vii) Bursitis

- **Description:** Inflammation of the bursae (small sacs of fluid that cushion the bones, tendons, and muscles near joints).
- **Common Areas:** Shoulders, elbows, hips, knees.
- **Symptoms:** Pain, swelling, and reduced range of motion in the affected joint.

(viii) Shin Splints

- **Description:** Pain along the shin bone (tibia), often due to overuse.
- **Symptoms:** Tenderness, soreness, or pain along the inner side of the shin bone and mild swelling in the lower leg.

(ix) Achilles Tendon Injuries

- **Description:** Injuries to the tendon connecting the calf muscles to the heel bone, including tendinitis and ruptures.
- **Symptoms:** Pain and stiffness along the Achilles tendon, especially in the morning, and swelling or thickening of the tendon.

(x) Runner's Knee (Patellofemoral Pain Syndrome)

- **Description:** Pain around the kneecap often due to overuse, misalignment, or damage to the cartilage.
- **Symptoms:** Pain around or behind the knee cap, especially when bending the knee, walking downstairs, or sitting cross-legged on floor for long periods.

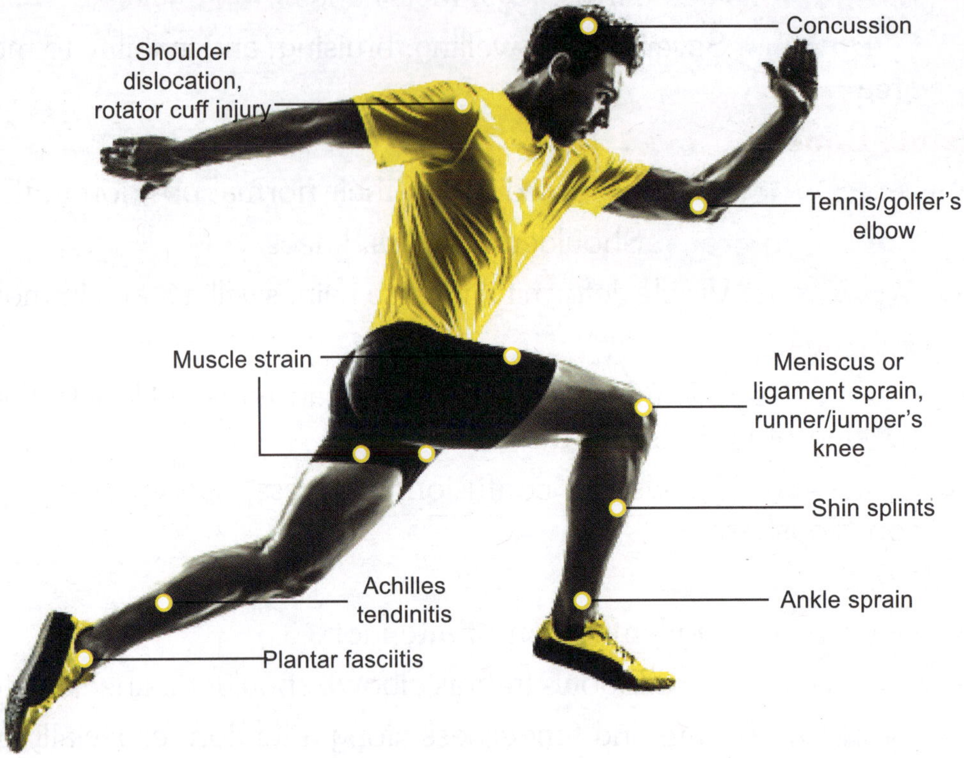

Fig. 3.10: Basic Injuries

3.5.8 First Aid for Sprains

First aid for sprains is essential to reduce pain, swelling, and prevent further injury. The RICE method is commonly recommended

Rest

- **Action:** Avoid putting weight on the injured area.
- **Reason:** Resting prevents further injury and allows the healing process to begin.

Ice

- **Action:** Apply ice to the injured area for 15-20 minutes every 2-3 hours during the first 48 hours.
- **Reason:** Ice reduces swelling and numbs the pain. Do not apply ice directly to the skin; use a cloth or towel as a barrier.

Compression

- **Action:** Use an elastic bandage to wrap the injured area.
- **Reason:** Compression helps to reduce swelling and provides support. Ensure that the bandage is snug but not so tight that it restricts normal blood flow.

Elevation

- **Action:** Elevate the injured limb above heart level, if possible.

- **Reason:** Elevation helps to reduce swelling by allowing fluids to drain away from the injured area.

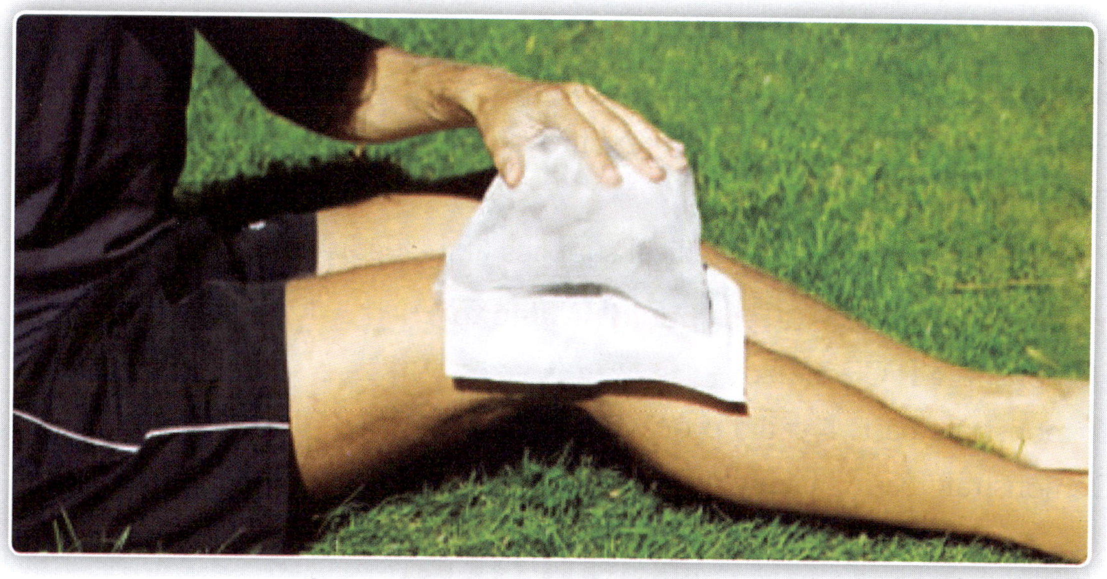

Fig. 3.11: First AID

3.6 Concept of First Aid Kit

A first aid kit is a collection of essential supplies and equipment used to provide initial medical treatment for injuries or illnesses. It is important to have a well-stocked first aid kit at home, in your car, and when participating in outdoor activities or sports. Here are the key concepts and components of a basic first aid kit.

Components of a Basic First Aid Kit:

- Adhesive bandages (various sizes)
- Sterile gauze pads
- Rolled bandages (e.g., conforming gauze)
- Triangular bandage (for slings or wraps)
- Antiseptic wipes or solution (e.g., alcohol pads, iodine solution)
- Antibiotic ointment (e.g., Neosporin)
- Sterile gloves
- Scissors
- Tweezers (remove to splinter)
- Thermometer
- CPR face shield or mask
- Splint (e.g., SAM splint for stabilising fractures)
- Pain relievers (e.g., acetaminophen, ibuprofen)

- Antihistamine (for allergic reactions)
- Aspirin (if recommended by a healthcare provider for heart conditions)
- Adhesive tape
- Safety pins
- Emergency contact information and first aid manual
- Flashlight with extra batteries
- Personal medications and medical supplies (if needed)

After completing this session, you should be able to

- Demonstrate RICE method
- Demonstrate basic first aid procedure for sprains
- Demonstrate basic first aid procedure for bleeding and cuts

ACTIVITY

Materials Required:

Chart-paper, First aid kit

1. Write the basic principles of first aid on a chart paper and display it in yoursports and physical education lab.
2. Conduct on-ground demonstration of first aid. Remember the actionmeasures of first aid while demonstrating.

Differentiate Between

1. Heat exhaustion and heat stroke.
2. A first aid box and a medical kit.

Subjective Questions

1. What is RICE?
2. What are the basic sports injuries?
   (a) What are the basic principles of first aid?
   (b) What is the basic first aid for sprain and strain?
   (c) What are the signs and symptoms of heat exhaustion and heat stroke?
   (d) What are the six principles of first aid?

3.7 Types of Sports Injurie

Sports injuries are commonly caused by overuse, direct impact, or an impact that is greater than a body part can withstand. There are two kinds of sports injuries: acute and chronic. An injury that occurs suddenly, such as a sprained ankle caused by an awkward landing, is known as an acute injury. Chronic injuries are caused by repeated overuse of muscle groups or joints. Poor technique and structural abnormalities can also contribute to the development of chronic injuries. Medical attention to any sports injury is important, because you may be hurt more severely than you think.

Some common types of injury are discussed below.

3.7.1 Musculoskeletal Injuries:

- **Sprains:** Stretching or tearing of ligaments.
- **Strains:** Stretching or tearing of muscles or tendons.
- **Fractures:** Breaks in bones.
- **Dislocations:** Joint injuries where bones are forced out of normal alignment.
- **Tendinitis:** Inflammation of tendons.
- **Bursitis:** Inflammation of bursae (small fluid-filled sacs that provide cushion to joints).
- **Shin Splints:** Pain along the shin bone.
- **Achilles Tendon Injuries:** Injuries to the tendon connecting the calf muscles to the heel bone.

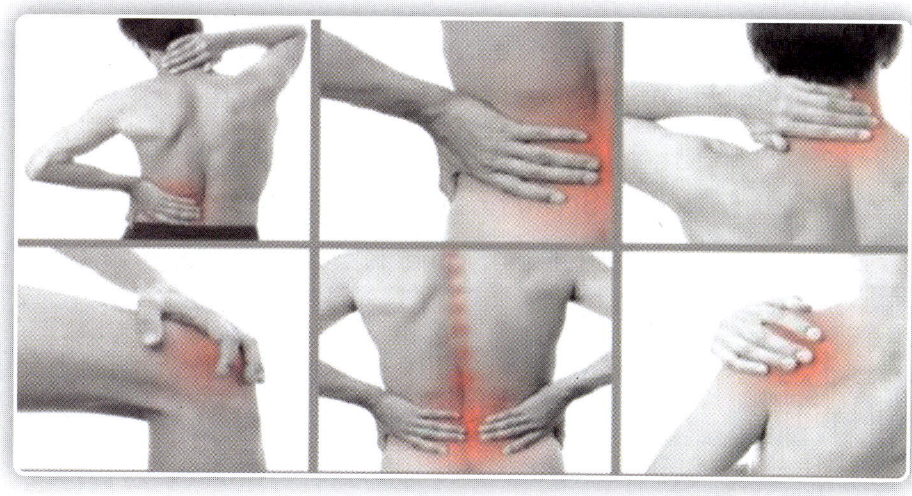

Fig. 3.12: Musculoskeletal Injuries

2. **Soft Tissue Injuries:**
   - **Contusions:** Bruises caused by impact or trauma to the soft tissue.
   - **Lacerations:** Cuts or tears in the skin or soft tissue.
   - **Abrasions:** Scrapes or grazes on the skin's surface.

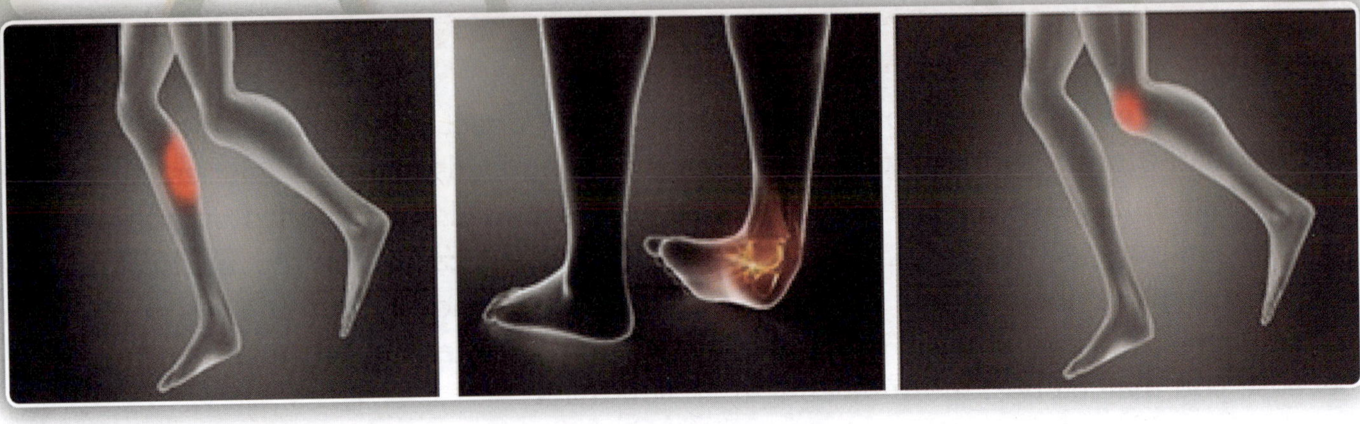

Fig. 3.13: Soft Tissue Injuries

3. **Head and Neck Injuries:**
   - **Concussions:** Traumatic brain injuries often caused by a blow to the head.
   - **Whiplash:** Neck injury due to a sudden backward and forward movement of the head, often in car accidents.
4. **Overuse Injuries:**
   - **Tennis Elbow:** Pain on the outside of the elbow due to repetitive motion.
   - **Runner's Knee:** Pain around the knee cap due to overuse.
5. **Burns:**
   - **First-degree Burns:** Minor burns affecting only the outer layer of the skin.
   - **Second-degree Burns:** Burns that damage both the outer layer and underlying layer of the skin.
   - **Third-degree Burns:** Severe burns that penetrate all layers of the skin, potentially affecting muscles and bones.
6. **Eye Injuries:**
   - **Corneal Abrasions:** Scratches on the surface of the eye.
   - **Foreign Objects:** Particles or objects that enter and irritate the eye.
7. **Environmental Injuries:**
   - **Heat Exhaustion:** Heat-related illness with symptoms like heavy sweating and rapid pulse.
   - **Heat Stroke:** Severe heat-related illness with symptoms such as confusion, seizures, and loss of consciousness.
   - **Hypothermia:** Abnormally low body temperature due to exposure to cold weather or water.

Fig. 3.14: Prevent Sports Injuries

1. **Warm-Up and Cool Down:**

   Warm-Up: Engage in dynamic stretching and light aerobic activity to increase blood flow to muscles and prepare them for exercise.

   Cool Down: Gradually decrease the intensity of exercise and include static stretching to help muscles to relax and improve flexibility.

2. **Proper Technique and Form:** Learn and use correct techniques for your sport or exercise to minimise the risk of overuse injuries and strain on muscles and joints.
3. **Gradual Progression:** Gradually increase the intensity, duration, and frequency of your workouts to allow your body time to adapt and strengthen.
4. **Appropriate Equipment:** Wear proper footwear and any necessary protective gear (e.g., helmets, pads) that fit well and are suitable for your sport or activity.
5. **Stay Hydrated:** Drink plenty of fluids before, during, and after exercise to maintain hydration and prevent heat-related illnesses.
6. **Cross-Train:** Incorporate a variety of exercises and activities into your routine to reduce the risk of overuse injuries and promote overall fitness.
7. **Listen to Your Body:** Pay attention to pain, discomfort, or signs of fatigue. Rest when needed and avoid pushing through serious pain.
8. **Conditioning and Strength Training:** Build strength, endurance, and flexibility through regular conditioning exercises and strength training tailored to your sport or activity.
9. **Balance and Stability Exercises:** Improve balance and stability with exercises that strengthen core muscles and help to prevent falls and joint injuries.

10. **Seek Professional Guidance:** Consult with coaches, trainers, or healthcare professionals to ensure that you are using proper techniques, conditioning effectively, and addressing any specific concerns related to your sport or activity.

11. **Warm Environment:** Ensure that exercise areas are appropriately heated in cold weather to prevent muscle stiffness and potential injury.

12. **Rest and Recovery:** Allow adequate time for rest and recovery between workouts or competitions to prevent overtraining and fatigue-related injuries.

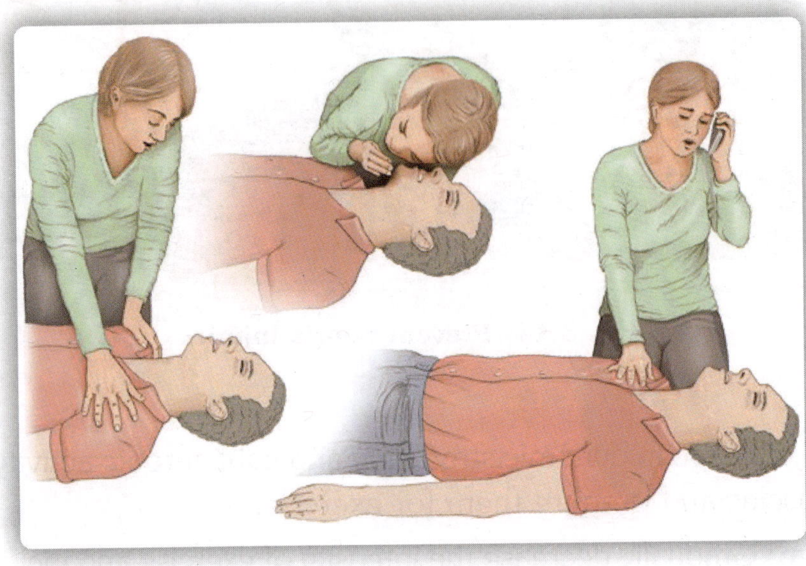

Fig. 3.15: Breathing Check

3.8 Cardiopulmonary Resuscitation (CPR)

CPR, or cardiopulmonary resuscitation, is a lifesaving technique used in emergencies to manually keep blood circulation and oxygenation going when a person's heart and breathing have stopped.

Steps for Performing CPR

1. **Check the Scene Safety:** Ensure that the area is safe for both you and the person needing help.

2. **Check Responsiveness:** Tap the person's shoulder and shout, "Are you okay?" Look for signs of responsiveness, such as movement or verbal response.

3. **Check for Breathing:** Tilt the person's head back slightly and look, listen, and feel for signs of breathing for up to 10 seconds. If they are not breathing normally, proceed with CPR.

4. **Perform Chest Compressions:**
    - Place the heel of one hand on the centre of the person's chest (between the nipples).
    - Place your other hand on top and interlock your fingers.

- Position yourself vertically above the person's chest and perform chest compressions:
    - Push down firmly and quickly, compressing the chest about 2 inches (5 centimetres) deep.
    - Perform compressions at a rate of about 100-120 compressions per minute. Let the chest rise completely between compressions.

5. **Rescue Breaths (if trained and willing):**
    - After 30 compressions, give 2 rescue breaths. Ensure that the airway is open (head tilted back, chin lifted).
    - Pinch the person's nose closed, place your mouth over theirs, and give 2 full breaths, each lasting about 1 second and causing the chest to rise.
    - Continue cycles of 30 compressions and 2 breaths until help arrives or the person starts breathing on their own.

6. **Continue CPR:** Continue performing cycles of chest compressions and rescue breaths until:
    - Emergency help arrives and takes over.
    - The person shows signs of life, such as breathing normally.
    - You are too exhausted to continue (if possible, have someone else take over).

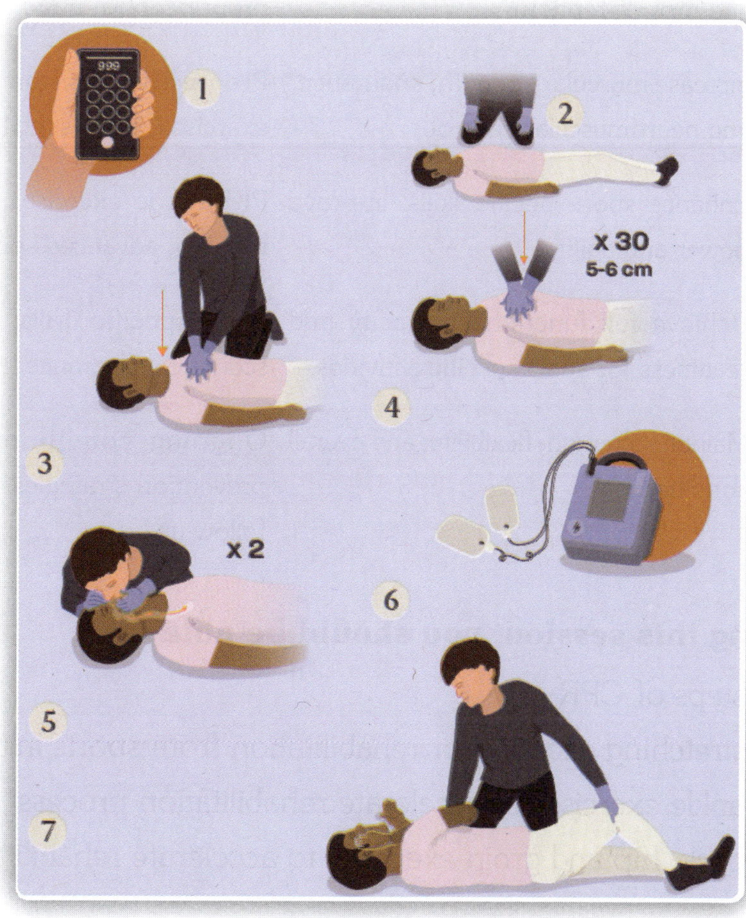

Fig. 3.16: CPR

3.8.1 Rehabilitation of Sports Injuries

Rehabilitation of sports injuries is a structured process aimed at restoring function, reducing pain, and preventing recurrence of further injury. The specific approach to rehabilitation depends on the type and severity of the injury,Each stage of rehabilitation builds upon the previous one, focusing on progressively challenging activities to facilitate recovery and prepare the athlete for a safe return to sports or physical activities. It is crucial to tailor the rehabilitation plan to the specific injury and individual needs, under the guidance of healthcare professionals such as physical therapists or sports medicine specialists.

3.8.2 Exercise for Rehabilitation

Stage	Objective	Activities
1. Acute Stage	Control pain and inflammation, protect injured tissue.	Rest, ice therapy, gentle range-of-motion exercises, compression, elevation.
2. Sub-acute Stage	Restore range of motion and flexibility.	Passive and active stretching, gentle joint mobilisation, manual therapy.
3. Early Rehabilitative Stage	Regain strength, improve muscle control and proprioception.	Low-resistance exercises, isometric exercises, proprioceptive training, balance exercises.
4. Intermediate Stage	Increase muscular strength, endurance, and neuromuscular control.	Progressive resistance training, functional exercises, sport-specific drills.
5. Advanced Strengthening	Enhance sport-specific skills, improve power and agility.	Plyometric exercises, high-intensity interval training, advanced sport-specific drills.
6. Return to Sport Phase	Achieve full functional capacity and readiness for sport-specific activities.	Sport-specific drills, simulated competition scenarios, clearance from healthcare provider.
7. Maintenance Phase	Maintain strength, flexibility, and overall conditioning.	Ongoing conditioning exercises, injury prevention strategies, regular monitoring and follow-up.

After completing this session, you should be able to:

- Demonstrate steps of CPR
- Demonstrate stretching exercise for rehabilitation from sports injuries
- Demonstrate ankle exercises to accelerate rehabilitation process
- Demonstrate back, hip and groin exercises to accelerate rehabilitation process

ACTIVITIES

1. Preparation of flowchart on the sequential steps of CPR
2. Perform rehabilitation for common sports injuries

Differentiate Between

1. Functional activities and sport specific activities at an injured ankle
2. Different stages of rehabilitation
3. Different steps of CPR

Subjective Questions

1. What are the five stages of rehabilitation during the treatment of sports injuries?
2. What are the steps to preform CPR?
3. What are common points one should keep in mind to prevent the occurrence of sports injuries?
4. What are the common symptoms of ankle sprain?

Multiple Choice Questions with Answers

1. What is the most common type of sports injury?

(a) Fractures
(b) Sprains and strains
(c) Dislocations
(d) Concussions

2. Which of the following is a common symptom of a concussion?

(a) Joint swelling
(b) Nausea and confusion
(c) Muscle cramps
(d) Increased appetite

3. What does the "R" in the R.I.C.E. method for treating sports injuries stand for?

(a) Rest
(b) Rotate
(c) Recover
(d) Rehabilitate

4. Which of the following injuries is characterised by a stretch or tear of a ligament?

(a) Strain
(b) Sprain
(c) Fracture
(d) Contusion

5. **What type of injury is commonly referred to as "tennis elbow"?**

(a) Lateral epicondylitis
(b) Medial epicondylitis
(c) Carpal tunnel syndrome
(d) Rotator cuff tear

6. **Which of the following is a chronic injury often caused by overuse?**

(a) Acute fracture
(b) Stress fracture
(c) Dislocation
(d) Concussion

7. **Which type of injury involves the inflammation of a tendon?**

(a) Bursitis
(b) Tendinitis
(c) Arthritis
(d) Myositis

8. **What is the recommended initial treatment for a suspected muscle strain?**

(a) Heat application
(b) Rest, ice, compression, and elevation (R.I.C.E.)
(c) Massage
(d) Stretching exercises

9. **Which of the following injuries is typically caused by a direct blow or impact?**

(a) Concussion
(b) Shin splints
(c) Tendinitis
(d) Stress fracture

10. **What is the primary purpose of using a compression bandage on a sports injury?**

(a) To improve flexibility
(b) To reduce swelling
(c) To increase blood flow
(d) To promote muscle growth

ANSWERS

1. (b) 2. (b) 3. (a) 4. (b) 5. (a) 6. (b) 7. (b)
8. (b) 9. (a) 10. (b)

UNIT 4

SPORTS AND FITNESS

4.1 HEALTH AND PHYSICAL FITNESS

Sports and fitness encompass a wide range of activities designed to improve physical health, mental well-being, and overall quality of life. These activities can be competitive sports or recreational exercises.

Physical fitness is akin to fine-tuning an engine for the human body, enabling us to maximize our capabilities. It encompasses the ability to perform daily tasks with vigour, while still having energy for leisure activities and meeting unforeseen demands. Enduring stress, persevering in challenging circumstances, and contributing to good health and overall well-being are all integral parts of physical fitness.

4.2 TYPES OF SPORTS

4.2.1 INDIVIDUAL SPORTS

- **Examples:** Running, swimming, cycling, gymnastics, martial arts.
- **Benefits:** Focus on personal goals and performance, flexibility in training schedules.

Fig. 4.1: Individual Sports

To see **Individual Sports** in Action

Scan QR Code

4.2.2 TEAM SPORTS

- **Examples:** Soccer, basketball, volleyball, rugby, cricket.
- **Benefits:** Promotes teamwork, communication, and strategic thinking.

To see **Team Sports** in Action

Scan QR Code

Fig. 4.2: Team Sports

4.2.3 Recreational Activities:

- **Examples:** Hiking, dancing, rock climbing, skiing, kayaking.
- **Benefits:** Enjoyment, stress relief, and a sense of adventure.

Fig. 4.3: Recreational Activity

4.2.4 Competitive Sports:

- **Examples:** Track and field, competitive swimming, triathlons, tennis, golf.
- **Benefits:** Provides a structured environment for skill development and competition.

Fig. 4.4: Competitive Activity

4.3 Benefits of Physical Fitness

4.3.1 Regular Aerobic Exercise:

Activities: Running, brisk walking, swimming, cycling, aerobic classes.

Benefits:

- Improves cardiovascular health by strengthening the heart and lungs.
- Increases endurance and energy levels.
- Helps with weight management by burning calories.
- Reduces the risk of chronic diseases such as heart disease, stroke, and diabetes.

4.3.2 Strength Training:

Activities: Weightlifting, resistance band exercises, bodyweight exercises (push-ups, squats, lunges).

Benefits:

- Builds and maintains muscle mass and strength.
- Enhances bone density, reducing the risk of osteoporosis.
- Boosts metabolism, aiding in weight control.
- Improves functional performance and daily activities.

4.3.3 Flexibility and Stretching:

Activities: Yoga, pilates, static and dynamic stretching routines.

Benefits:

- Increase range of motion and flexibility.
- Reduce muscle tension and stiffness.
- Prevent injuries by preparing muscles and joints for activity.
- Enhance overall physical performance.

4.3.4 Balancing and Coordination Exercises:

Activities: Balancing exercises, tai chi, certain yoga poses.

Benefits:

- Improve stability and reduces the risk of falls, especially in older adults.
- Enhance overall coordination and body control.
- Support efficient and safe movement patterns.

4.3.5 High-Intensity Interval Training (HIIT):

Activities: Short bursts of intense exercise followed by rest or low-intensity exercise (e.g., sprinting, high-intensity cycling, circuit training).

Benefits:

- Improves cardiovascular fitness and burns calories efficiently.
- Increases metabolism for hours after the workout.
- Enhances both aerobic and anaerobic fitness.

4.3.6 Mind-Body Exercises:

Activities: Yoga, tai chi, meditation.

Benefits:

- Reduce stress and promote mental well-being.
- Improve focus, concentration, and mindfulness.
- Enhance relaxation and sleep quality.

4.3.7 Recreational Activities and Sports:

Activities: Hiking, dancing, playing team sports (soccer, basketball), individual sports (tennis, golf).

Benefits:

- Provide enjoyment and social interaction.

To see **Recreational Activities** in Action

Scan QR Code

- Encourage consistent physical activity through fun and engaging activities.
- Improve overall fitness and skill levels.

4.3.8 Proper Nutrition:

Focus: Balanced diet with adequate macronutrients (proteins, fats, carbohydrates) and micronutrients (vitamins, minerals).

Benefits:

- Fuels physical activity and supports muscle recovery.
- Enhances overall health and immune function.
- Promotes healthy weight management and body composition.

4.3.9 Adequate Hydration:

Importance: Staying well-hydrated before, during, and after exercise.

Benefits:

- Maintains optimal physical performance.
- Prevents dehydration-related issues such as muscle cramps and fatigue.
- Supports overall bodily functions and recovery.

4.3.10 Rest for Recovery:

Strategies: Regular sleep, rest days, and active recovery (light activities such as walking or stretching).

Benefits:

- Allows muscles to repair and grow stronger.
- Prevents overtraining and reduces the risk of injury.
- Enhances mental and physical readiness for subsequent workouts.

Fig. 4.5: Rest and Recovery

4.3.11 Mental Health Focus:

Activities: Incorporate stress-reducing activities and maintain a positive mindset.

Benefits:

- Reduces anxiety and depression symptoms.
- Improves mood and overall mental well-being.
- Enhances concentration and motivation for physical activities.

To see **Fitness Activities** in Action

Scan QR Code

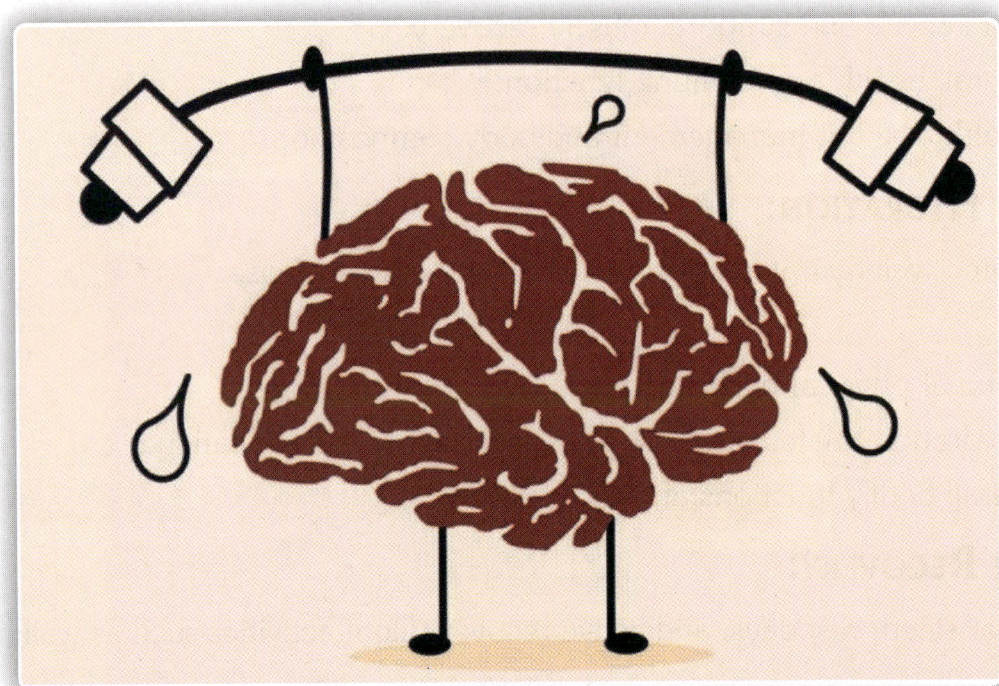

Fig. 4.6: Mental Health

4.4 Stages of Team Selection

The school's yearly sports activities are planned at the beginning of each academic year and are directly aligned with the school's vision, mission, and goals, with the consent of the school management. Various factors like the available infrastructure, employed PE teachers/ coaches and their expertize, the school's history in sports, type of school, students' skill levels in different sports, and sports popularity in the region are considered in determining the sports activities for the school.

Once the objectives are established, it is the responsibility of the PE and sports department to assemble teams for different sports and categories. In a school environment, it is crucial to consider that the selection for various sports and categories can only take place once the students have received training in the specific sport to a certain extent. Therefore, the team selection process requires careful planning and execution. The commonly adopted process for team selection in a school setting typically involves three stages. Given below is the three-stage talent identification process:

1. **Talent Detection:** Students are exposed to a variety of sports and then grouped based on their interest levels and the skill sets required for their chosen sport.
2. **Talent Identification:** This stage involves recognising current participants who have the potential to excel in their chosen sport. It involves predicting performance over various periods by measuring physical, physiological, psychological, and sociological attributes.
3. **Talent Development:** Students are provided with a suitable learning environment so that their sporting talent can be realised.

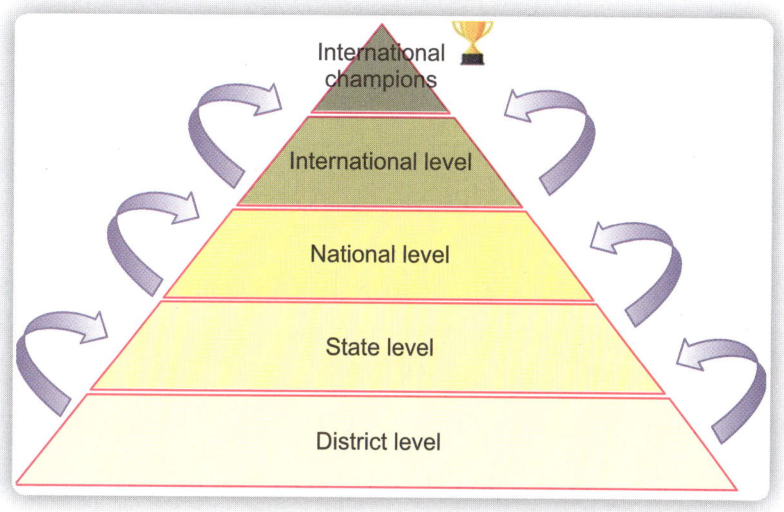

Fig. 4.7: Talent Identification

4.4.1 Process of Talent Detection, Identification and Development

Fig. 4.8: Talent Development Process

Stage	Activities
Grassroots Engagement	Community outreach, local competitions, open trials.
Initial Assessment	Physical assessments, technical skills evaluation, tactical understanding.
Academy Recruitment	Intensive trials, age-appropriate development phases (U8-U22, U13-U16, U17-U21).
Development Programmes	Individual training plans, educational support, life skills workshops.
Continuous Monitoring	Regular evaluations, individual development plans, holistic support (nutrition, psychology, mentorship).
Advanced Scouting	Match observation, video analysis, performance metrics.
Elite Development	National/regional development centres, professional integration, contracts, and scholarships.

An indicative weekly training plan for after-school coaching sessions.

Day	Focus	Key activities
Monday	Technical skills development	Dribbling, passing, ball control drills, small-sided games
Tuesday	Tactical awareness and small-sided games	Positional drills, tactical play, small-sided games
Wednesday	Physical conditioning and speed/agility	Speed drills, agility exercises, endurance training
Thursday	Technical skills and shooting practice	Shooting drills, combination play, small-sided shooting games
Friday	Game simulation and review	Full/half-pitch game simulation, team discussion, and review
Saturday	Optional extra training or recovery	Optional skills practice or recovery session
Sunday	Rest and recovery	Rest, light activities, hydration, and nutrition

Age-Wise Skill Development Structure for Football Players

Age group	Focus	Key activities	Goals
5–7	Basic motor skills, fun, fundamentals	Basic coordination, ball familiariation, fun games	Develop basic motor skills and coordination, introduce football
8–10	Fundamental skills, tactical awareness	Dribbling, passing, shooting, small-sided games	Improve technical skills, understand basic game concepts

11–13	Skill refinement, tactical introduction	Advanced dribbling, passing, shooting, tactical drills, physical conditioning	Enhance proficiency, develop team tactics, build fitness
14–16	Advanced skills, game intelligence	Technical mastery, advanced tactical training, game intelligence, physical conditioning, mental training	Achieve high skill level, develop advanced tactics, build strength
17–19	Elite performance, competitive readiness	Technical precision, tactical sophistication, match simulations, advanced conditioning, psychological prep	Technical precision, tactical sophistication, match simulations, advanced conditioning, psychological prep

Basketball

Process of Talent Detection, Identification and Development

Stage	Activities
Grassroots Engagement	Community outreach, local competitions, open trials.
Initial Assessment	Physical assessments, technical skills evaluation, tactical understanding.
Academy Recruitment	Intensive trials, age-appropriate development phases (U8-U12, U13-U16, U17-U21).
Development Programmes	Individual training plans, educational support, life skills workshops.

An indicative weekly training plan for after-school coaching sessions.

Day	Focus	Key activities
Monday	Technical skills development	Dribbling, passing, ball control drills, small-sided games
Tuesday	Tactical awareness and small-sided games	Positional drills, tactical play, small-sided games
Wednesday	Physical conditioning and speed/ agility	Speed drills, agility exercises, endurance training
Thursday	Technical skills and shooting practice	Shooting drills, combination play, small-sided shooting games
Friday	Game simulation and review	Full/half-pitch game simulation, team discussion, and review
Saturday	Optional extra training or recovery	Optional skills practice or recovery session
Sunday	Rest and recovery	Rest, light activities, hydration, and nutrition

Fig. 4.9: Basketball

Age-Wise Skill Development Structure for Basketball Players

Age group	Focus	Key activities	Goals
5-7	Basic motor skills, fun, fundamentals	Basic coordination, ball familiarisation, fun games	Develop basic motor skills and coordination, introduce volleyball
8-10	Fundamental skills, tactical awareness	Passing, setting, serving, ball control, small-sided games	Improve technical skills, understand basic game concepts
11-13	Skill refinement, tactical introduction	Advanced passing, setting, serving, hitting, blocking, tactical drills, physical conditioning	Enhance proficiency, develop team tactics, build fitness
14-16	Advanced skills, game intelligence	Technical mastery, advanced tactical training, game intelligence, physical conditioning, mental training	Achieve high skill level, develop advanced tactics, build strength
17-19	Elite performance, competitive readiness	Technical precision, tactical sophistication, match simulations, advanced conditioning, psychological prep	Prepare for professional competition, perfect skills, optimise readiness

Process of Talent Detection, Identification and Development Volleyball

Age group	Focus	Key activities	Goals
5-7	Basic motor skills, fun, fundamentals	Basic coordination, ball familiariation, fun games	Develop basic motor skills and coordination, introduce volleyball
8-10	Fundamental skills, tactical awareness	Passing, setting, serving, ball control, small-sided games	Improve technical skills, understand basic game concepts
11-13	Skill refinement, tactical introduction	Advanced passing, setting, serving, hitting, blocking, tactical drills, physical conditioning	Enhance proficiency, develop team tactics, build fitness

14-16	Advanced skills, game intelligence	Technical mastery, advanced tactical training, game intelligence, physical conditioning, mental training	Achieve high skill level, develop advanced tactics, build strength
17-19	Elite performance, competitive readiness	Technical precision, tactical sophistication, match simulations, advanced conditioning, psychological prep	Prepare for professional competition, perfect skills, optimie readiness

Process of Talent Detection, Identification and Development

Stage	Activities
Grassroots engagement	Community outreach, local competitions, open trials.
Initial assessment	Physical assessments, technical skills evaluation, tactical understanding.
Academy recruitment	Intensive trials, age-appropriate development phases (U8-U12, U13-U16, U17-U21).
Development programmes	Individual training plans, educational support, life skills workshops.

Fig. 4.10: Grassroot Engagement

Age-Wise Skill Development Structure for Volleyball Players

Age group	Focus	Key activities	Goals
5-7	Basic motor skills, fun, fundamentals	Basic coordination, ball familiarisation, fun games	Develop basic motor skills and coordination, introduce volleyball
8-10	Fundamental skills, tactical awareness	Service, passing, shooting, small-sided games	Improve technical skills, understand basic game concepts
11-13	Skill refinement, tactical introduction	Advanced passing, tactical drills, physical conditioning	Enhance proficiency, develop team tactics, build fitness
14-16	Advanced skills, game intelligence	Technical mastery, advanced tactical training, game intelligence, physical conditioning, mental training	Achieve high skill level, develop advanced tactics, build strength
17-19	Elite performance, competitive readiness	Technical precision, tactical sophistication, match simulations, advanced conditioning, psychological prep	Prepare for professional competition, perfect skills, optimise readiness

Fig. 4.11: Skill Development

What have you learn?

After completing this session, you should be able to:

- Conduct warm up exercises, aerobic exercises and cool down exercises to detect the physical strength, endurance and flexibility of an individual.
- Demonstrate the competency of teaching various skills related to ball control, use of hand, sense of direction, stance, passing, and shooting.
- Fill in the checklist after assessing the ability of the students regarding space awareness, ball control, use of hand, sense of direction, stance, passing, and shooting.

ACTIVITIES

1. Identify talented players from 6-8 standard school students and create teams and make them participate in local tournaments. Map their skill and fitness progress a on regular basis.
2. Make a coaching session plan in any sport of your choice.
3. Explain the process of school team selection on the basis of Talent Detection, Talent Identification and Talent Development. You may take any sport of your choice. (Do it on a separate sheet of paper).

Differentiate Between

1. Talent Detection, Talent Identification and Talent Development

Subjective Questions

1. What is talent detection?
2. What is talent identification?
3. What is talent development?
4. In addition to the skill part during talent detection what are the other attributes that you can detect with regard to a team sport?

4.5 Organise Sports Activities (Events)

In this section, we will explore the detailed strategies for organising a variety of sports events within a school setting. Below is a comprehensive list of events suitable for any month at a school. We will also delve into the specific planning processes and execution tools required for each of these events during the month of execution.

List of important events in a year

- Sports Day
- Intramural Tournaments
- Extramural Tournaments
- Father's Day/ Mother's Day/ Grandparent's Day/ Children's Day
- Summer/Winter Cam

Preparation	Sports Day	Post Sports Day
Form an Organising Committee Choose a Date and Venue: Budgeting: Activity Planning: Equipment and Supplies: Volunteers	• Ceremonies • Speeches • Script • Activities- Finals • Prize distribution • Vote of thanks	• Winding up • Feedback and Learnings • Payments • Settling of accounts

4.5.1 Sports Day Planning

1. Initial Planning (6-8 Weeks Before the Event)

Form an Organising Committee:

- **Assign roles:**
- **Event Coordinator:** Oversees overall planning and execution.
- **Equipment Manager:** Handles logistics for sports equipment and supplies.
- **Volunteer Coordinator:** Recruits and manages volunteers.
- **Safety Officer:** Ensures that all safety measures are in place.
- **Communications Manager:** Manages promotions and communications.

Choose a Date and the Venue:

- Select a date considering school/holiday calendars and potential weather conditions.
- Secure a venue that has the necessary facilities (restrooms, water stations, shaded areas).

Budgeting:

- Draft a budget covering all potential expenses (equipment, refreshments, awards, first aid supplies).
- Seek sponsorships or donations to cover costs.

2. Detailed Planning (4-6 Weeks Before the Event)

Activity and Event Planning:

- Decide on the sports and activities to be included (e.g., running races, relay races, sack races, obstacle courses, team games).
- Categorise events by age group for fair competition.
- Plan a mix of competitive and fun activities to cater to different interests and abilities.

Equipment and Supplies:

- List all required equipment and supplies (cones, markers, bean bags, whistles, first aid kits).

- Arrange for rental or purchase of these items.

Volunteer Recruitment:

- Recruit volunteers (teachers, parents, older students) and assign specific roles.

Safety and Emergency Planning:

- Develop a safety plan, including first aid stations and emergency procedures.
- Ensure the presence of medical staff or trained first aiders on-site.

3. Communication and Promotion (3-4 Weeks Before the Event)

Inform Participants:

- Send permission slips and information packets to parents detailing the event schedule, what to bring, and any special instructions.

Promotion:

- Create promotional materials (flyers, posters, social media posts) to generate excitement.
- Use school newsletters, websites, and community boards for wider reach.

Registration:

- Set up a registration system (online or in-person) to track participants and their event preferences.

4. Final Preparations (1-2 Weeks Before the Event)

Schedule Creation:

- Create a detailed event schedule, including start and end times for each activity.
- Share the schedule with participants, parents, and volunteers.

Confirm Arrangements:

- Confirm venue booking and equipment delivery.
- Double-check all logistics and ensure that everything is in place.
- Brief volunteers on their roles and responsibilities.

Logistics Planning:

- Plan the layout of the event area, including event stations, registration desks, and first aid points.
- Arrange transportation of equipment to the venue.

Weather Contingency Plan:

- Develop a backup plan for bad weather (indoor location or reschedule date).

5. Final Checks (1-2 Days Before the Event)

Equipment Check:

- Verify that all equipment and supplies are ready and in good condition.
- Pack a kit with extra items like markers, water bottles, sunscreen, and first aid supplies.

Volunteer Briefing:

- Conduct a final briefing with all volunteers to review the schedule, roles, and emergency procedures.

Venue Setup:

- If possible, set up the event area a day before (marking tracks, setting up stations, etc.).

Participant Reminder:

- Send a reminder to participants and parents, including final details and any last-minute instructions.

Example of a Detailed Schedule for Pre-Sports Day Preparation

Time frame	Task	Details
6-8 weeks before	Objective Setting	Define goals, form the organising committee, choose the date and venue.
6-8 weeks before	Budgeting	Draft budget, seek sponsorships/donations.
4-6 weeks before	Activity Planning	Decide on activities, categorise by age group, plan mix of competitive/fun activities.
4-6 weeks before	Equipment and Supplies	List out required items, arrange rental/purchase.
4-6 weeks before	Volunteer Recruitment	Recruit and assign roles to volunteers.
4-6 weeks before	Safety and Emergency Planning	Develop safety plan, ensure that medical staff/first aiders are available.
3-4 weeks before	Inform Participants	Send permission slips and information packets to parents.
3-4 weeks before	Promotion	Create and distribute promotional materials.
3-4 weeks before	Registration	Set up the registration system.
1-2 weeks before	Schedule Creation	Create and share detailed event schedule.
1-2 weeks before	Confirm Arrangements	Confirm bookings, double-check logistics, brief volunteers.
1-2 weeks before	Logistics Planning	Plan layout, arrange transportation of equipment.
1-2 weeks before	Weather Contingency Plan	Develop backup plan for bad weather.

Time frame	Task	Details
1-2 days before	Equipment Check	Verify all equipment and supplies, pack extra items.
1-2 days before	Volunteer Briefing	Conduct final briefing with volunteers.
1-2 days before	Venue Setup	Set up event area (if possible).
1-2 days before	Participant Reminder	Send final details and instructions to participants and parents.

On the Sports Day

Time	Activity	Details
8:00 - 9:00 am	Setting up	Volunteers set up registration, equipment, and event areas.
9:00 - 9:30 am	Registration and Check-In	Participants check in, receive schedules and numbers.
9:30 - 10:00 am	Opening Ceremony	Welcome speech, introductions, overview of the day.
10:00 - 10:30 am	Running Races	Age-group specific races (50m, 100m dashes).
10:30 - 11:00 am	Team Games	Tug-of-war, relay races.
11:00 - 11:30 am	Obstacle Course	Fun obstacle courses for different age groups.
11:30 - 12:00 pm	Jumping Events	Long jump, high jump.
12:00 - 1:00 pm	Lunch Break	Lunch break with access to water and shade.
1:00 - 1:30 pm	Fun Activities	Sack race, three-legged race, bean bag toss.
1:30 - 2:00 pm	Ball Games	Soccer drills, basketball free throws.
2:00 - 2:30 pm	Relay Races	Various relay races (baton relay, shuttle run).
2:30 - 3:00 pm	Yoga and Stretching	Fun and relaxing yoga session.
3:00 - 3:30 pm	Cool Down and Relaxation	Gentle stretching, hydration, and relaxation.
3:30 - 4:00 pm	Awards Ceremony	Announcement of winners, distribution of medals and certificates.
4:00 - 5:00 pm	Cleanup	Volunteers clean up the event area and pack away the equipment.

Post Sports Day Activities

Timeframe	Activity	Details
Immediately After	Cleanup and Equipment Return	Volunteers clean the area, dispose of the waste, return and store the equipment.

Timeframe	Activity	Details
1-2 days after	Volunteer and Staff Debrief	Hold briefing meeting, discuss feedback, and recognise volunteers.
1 week after	Participant Feedback	Distribute and review feedback surveys.
1-2 weeks after	Financial Reconciliation	Track expenses, and prepare financial reports.
2 weeks after	Documentation and Reporting	Create event reports, compile photos/videos, and share highlights.
Ongoing	Planning for Future Events	Document the lessons learned, and plan for continuous improvement.

Avitvit 1	What do you like about your existing sports day

Avitvit 2	What would you like to add in the existing Sports Day

PART A

Subjective Questions

1. Write four elements of a good mass display.

   (a) ....

   (b) ....

   (c) ....

   (d) ....

2. What are the three typical items on a Sports Day agenda?

   (a) ....

   (b) ....

   (c) ....

PART B

Subjective Questions

1. Demonstrate six different types of free hand exercises that can be done during a mass drill.
2. Practise march past in your physical education period – every student should get the opportunity to command.
3. Prepare a model agenda for a Sports Day

Multiple Choice Questions with Answers

1. **What is the primary purpose of organising a Sports Day in schools?**

   (a) To complete academic lessons (b) To promote physical activity and teamwork

   (c) To watch professional sports (d) To have a day off from school

2. **Which event is commonly included in a Sports Day for young children?**

(a) Marathon (b) Sack race

(c) Weightlifting (d) High jump

3. **What is a typical role of a teacher or coach during Sports Day?**

(a) Participate in all events (b) Ensure safety and fair play

(c) Grade academic papers (d) Organise classroom activities

4. **Which of the following is a benefit of participating in Sports Day?**

(a) Increased screen time (b) Improved social skills

(c) Decreased physical fitness (d) Isolation from peers

5. **What type of activity is a relay race considered to be?**

(a) Individual sport (b) Team sport

(c) Solo performance (d) Spectator sport

6. **Which of the following is NOT typically an event during a Sports Day?**

(a) 100-meter dash (b) Long jump

(c) Math competition (d) Tug of war

7. **How can schools ensure inclusivity during Sports Day?**

(a) Only allow the best athletes to participate

(b) Organise a variety of activities catering to different abilities

(c) Focus solely on competitive events

(d) Limit participation to specific age groups

8. **Which piece of equipment is essential for measuring time in track events during Sports Day?**

(a) Stopwatch (b) Measuring tape

(c) Whistle (d) First aid kit

9. **Why is a warm-up session important before starting Sports Day activities?**

(a) To tire out the participants (b) To reduce the risk of injuries

(c) To delay the start of events (d) To teach academic lessons

10. **What is a common way to conclude a Sports Day event?**

(a) Academic awards ceremony (b) Sports awards ceremony

(c) Classroom lecture (d) Silent reading time

ANSWERS

1. (b) **2.** (b) **3.** (b) **4.** (b) **5.** (b) **6.** (c) **7.** (b)

8. (a) **9.** (b) **10.** (b)

4.5.2 Organising Tournaments and Events

Tournaments

Organising sports tournaments, such as those for football, basketball, and cricket, bears resemblance to orchestrating a sports day. Effective pre-event planning stands as the paramount factor influencing the event's success. The checklist utilised for the sports day can be suitably adapted and applied to tournament organisation.

Fig. 4.12: Tournament

Committee Structure for a Tournament

Position	Responsibilities
Tournament Director	Oversee overall planning and execution, coordinate with all committee members.
Logistics Coordinator	Arrange venue, equipment setup, and logistics for the event day.
Registration Manager	Handle participant registrations, payments, and paperwork.
Marketing Manager	Promote the tournament through various channels, manage social media and advertising.
Volunteer Coordinator	Recruit, train, and manage volunteers for event roles.
Finance Manager	Manage budgeting, sponsorships, expenses, and financial reporting.
Safety and First Aid Coordinator	Ensure safety protocols, coordinate first aid services.

Surface Preparation

- **Grass Fields:**
  - ★ **Mowing:** Ensure that the grass is mowed to the proper height for the sport being played.
  - ★ **Levelling:** Address any uneven areas or divots that could affect gameplay.
  - ★ **Fertilisation and Irrigation:** Ensure that the grass is healthy and adequately watered before the tournament.
- **Artificial Turf:**
  - ★ **Cleaning:** Remove debris, dirt, and contaminants from the turf surface.
  - ★ **Brushing:** Brush the turf fibres to maintain uniformity and prevent compaction.
  - ★ **Infill Inspection:** Check the infill levels and add more if necessary to ensure consistent playing conditions.

- **Court Surfaces (e.g., Tennis, Basketball):**
  - ★ **Cleaning:** Sweep or vacuum the court surface to remove dust, dirt, and debris.
  - ★ **Line Markings:** Ensure that lines are freshly painted or re-taped to clearly define the court boundaries and markings.

4.5.3 Referees / Umpires / Officials

Role: Officiate matches, enforce rules, and make decisions on fouls, penalties, and game infractions.

Qualifications: Usually certified or licensed by a governing body or association specific to the sport.

Responsibilities:

- Ensure fair play and sportsmanship.
- Control the pace and flow of the game.
- Resolve disputes between players and teams.
- Uphold the integrity of the sport and tournament.

Fig. 4.13: Officials

4.6 Pre-tournament Day

1. **Planning and Scheduling:**
   - Define the tournament type (knockout, league, round-robin, etc.).
   - Set the date, time, and venue for the tournament.
   - Prepare a detailed tournament schedule and fixture list.
2. **Venue Preparation:**
   - Confirm venue booking and inspect facilities.
   - Ensure the playing area is marked and ready (court, field, or arena).

- Set up spectator areas, registration desks, and seating arrangements.
- Arrange first aid kits and emergency protocols.

3. **Equipment and Logistics:**
    - List and secure all necessary equipment (balls, nets, scoreboards, etc.).
    - Arrange for water, refreshments, and rest areas for participants.
    - Check power supply, sound systems, and PA systems for announcements.
4. **Team Registration and Communication:**
    - Confirm team registrations and finalize the list of participants.
    - Share tournament rules, schedules, and guidelines with teams.
    - Assign referees, umpires, or judges as required.
5. **Staffing and Volunteer Management:**
    - Assign roles to volunteers (registration, scorekeeping, first aid, etc.).
    - Conduct a briefing session to ensure everyone knows their duties.
6. **Sponsorship and Branding:**
    - Finalize sponsors and ensure their branding is placed properly.
    - Prepare certificates, trophies, and prizes for winners.
7. **Safety and Security Measures:**
    - Arrange for security personnel if needed.
    - Ensure emergency contacts and medical support are on standby.
8. **Contingency Planning:**
    - Have backup plans for weather issues (if outdoor).
    - Prepare an alternate schedule for any unforeseen delays.

4.7 Post Tournament Day

1. **Cleanup and Equipment Collection:**
    - Clear the venue of any trash or leftover items.
    - Collect and safely store all equipment (balls, nets, scoreboards, etc.).
    - Ensure the venue is returned in its original condition.
2. **Prize Distribution and Appreciation:**
    - Distribute trophies, medals, and certificates to winners.
    - Acknowledge sponsors, volunteers, and staff for their support.
    - Capture photographs for memories and social media.

3. **Feedback Collection:**
   - Gather feedback from participants, officials, and spectators.
   - Use surveys or feedback forms for structured insights.

4. **Financial Reconciliation:**
   - Compile all expenses and revenue (registration fees, sponsorship).
   - Settle any pending payments with vendors or service providers.
   - Prepare a financial report for transparency.

5. **Reporting and Documentation:**
   - Document match results, player statistics, and records.
   - Create a final report summarizing the tournament's success.
   - Share a post-event summary with participants and sponsors.

6. **Social Media and Public Relations:**
   - Post highlights, photos, and results on social media.
   - Send thank-you messages to sponsors, teams, and volunteers.
   - Publish a press release if needed.

7. **Identifying Improvements:**
   - Review feedback and team observations.
   - List down what went well and areas for improvement.
   - Begin planning for the next tournament with these insights.

4.8 Tournament Day

1. **Opening Ceremony**
   - **Welcome Address:** Greeting participants, officials, and spectators.
   - **National Anthem:** Playing the national anthem(s) of participating countries or teams.
   - **Parade of Participants:** Teams or individuals march into the venue, often dressed in their respective uniforms.
   - **Guest Speeches:** Remarks from dignitaries, sponsors, or honorary guests.
   - **Ceremonial First Pitch / Kickoff / Serve:** Symbolic act to mark the beginning of the tournament.

2. **Award Ceremony**

Presentation of Awards: Distribution of trophies, medals, certificates, or prizes to winners and finalists.

- **Acknowledgments:** Thanking sponsors, officials, volunteers, and supporters.

- **Speeches:** Remarks from organisers, sponsors, or special guests.
- **Photo Opportunities:** Group photos with winners, officials, and sponsors.
- **Closing Remarks:** Concluding the ceremony and expressing gratitude to all involved.

3. Closing Ceremony

- **Review of Highlights:** Recap of memorable moments and achievements throughout the tournament.
- **Handover Ceremony:** Passing on the responsibilities or symbolic items to the next host or organising committee.

Tournament structure

A guideline for knockout tournament

A knockout tournament structure, also known as a single-elimination tournament, is where teams compete in matches, and the loser of each match is eliminated from the tournament. This continues until there is only one team left, which is declared the winner.

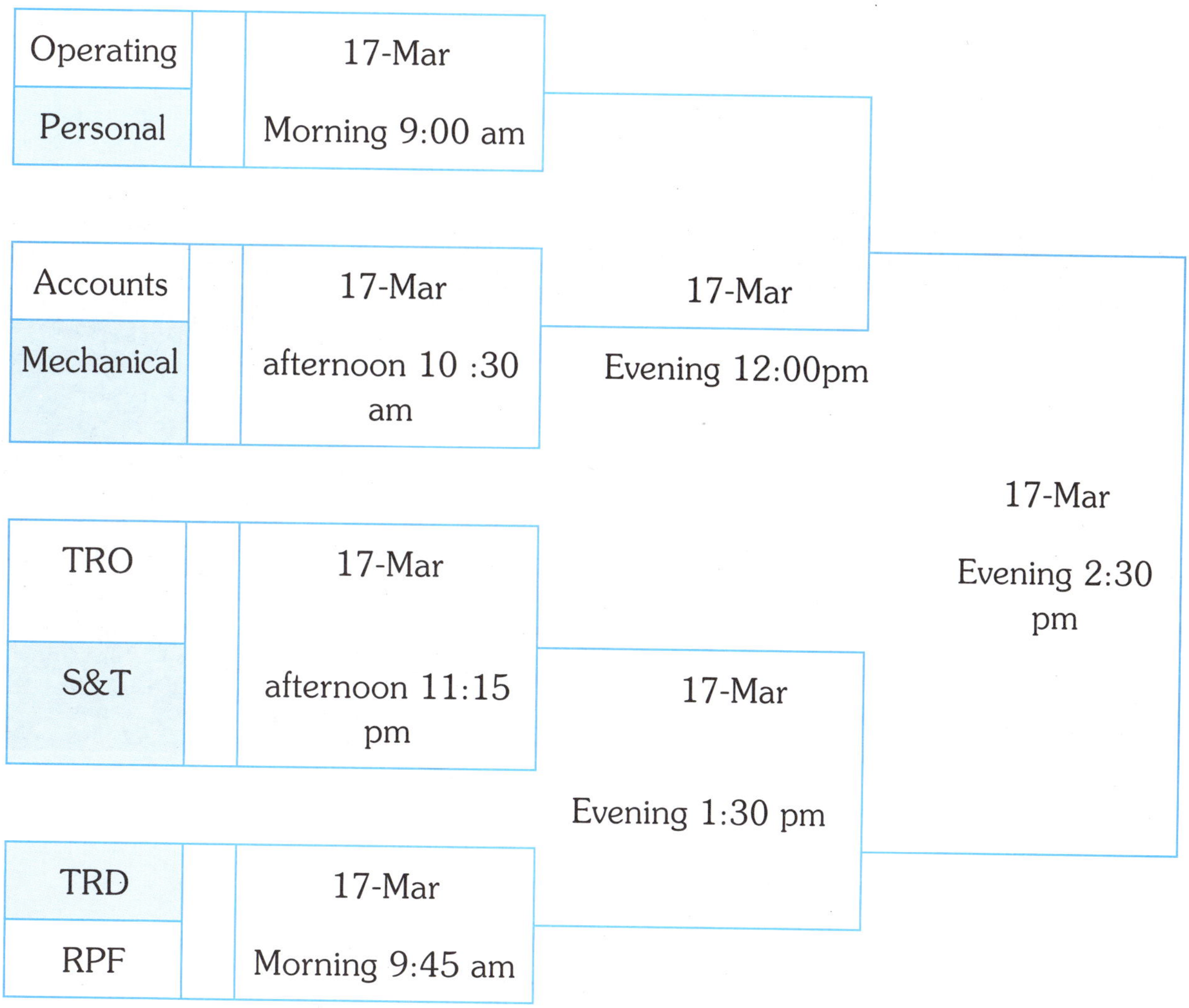

4.8.1 Mass Drill and Display

A Mass Drill and Display event typically involves a large number of participants performing synchronised movements or exercises, often for ceremonial or display purposes. This type of event requires careful planning and coordination.

Design and Choreography

1. **Formation and Movements**
   - Design formations (e.g., lines, circles, geometric shapes).
   - Plan synchronised movements and transitions between formations.
   - Incorporate elements such as flags, banners, or props, if desired.
2. **Music and Sound**
   - Select appropriate music or marching tunes.
   - Coordinate movements with the rhythm and tempo of the music.
   - Arrange for a sound system if needed.
3. **Costumes and Uniforms**
   - Decide on uniforms or costumes for participants.
   - Ensure uniformity and suitability for the movements.

Fig. 4.14: Mass Drill

Programme for parents and staff

Parents play a pivotal role in promoting their children's well-being and academic advancement, providing guidance through the intricacies of the educational system, and advocating for both their children and the efficacy of educational institutions. Parental involvement in schools is characterised by collaborative efforts between parents and the school faculty to bolster and monitor the educational, personal, and physical development of children and adolescents.

It is a mutual obligation, wherein educational establishments and various community entities are dedicated to actively involving parents in substantive ways, while parents are committed to wholeheartedly nurturing the educational and personal growth of their children and adolescents. This collaborative bond between schools and parents transcends and fortifies the well-being and academic progress of children across various spheres – encompassing the home environment, educational institutions, extracurricular activities, and the broader community.

List of Activities:

(i) Mother's Day

(ii) Father's Day

(iii) Grandparent's Day

(iv) Play date

Fig. 4.15: Parents Activity

Summer Camp

Summer camps provide an abundance of options for kids to explore and enjoy different activities. Among these options, sports camps stand out as they engage children in physical activity while simultaneously teaching them valuable lessons in teamwork, sportsmanship, and the importance of following instructions from a coach. Additionally, during the early stages of participation, kids focus on mastering essential skills and grasping fundamental movement concepts relevant to their chosen sports.

Sports Camps

1. General Sports Camps

- Activities: Multiple sports (soccer, basketball, tennis, etc.)
- Focus: Skill development, teamwork

2. Specialised Sports Camps

- Activities: Focus on one sport (soccer, basketball, swimming, etc.)
- Focus: Intensive training, skill enhancement

Winter Camp

During the winter break when schools are closed and outdoor activities may be limited, children often become less active physically. In the same way that summer camps provide kids with opportunities for exercise and fun, winter camps offer a chance for children to engage in different physical activities and games, keeping them active and entertained during the colder months.

1. Hitting the target
2. Clap and catch
3. Yoga
4. Gallop like a horse
5. Building and bulldozers

ACTIVITY

Materials Required: Props and equipment mentioned in the above session.

Conduct on-ground activities/ games with the props available and relate the use to age appropriateness.

Subjective Questions

Part A

Students could differentiate between

1. March Past and Drill
2. The requirements for organising Sports Day and Tournament

Part B

Students could answer the following questions:

1. What are the key factors to decide the format of a tournament?
2. What are the roles and responsibilities of head of the institution, sports teacher and other teachers?
3. What are the roles and responsibilities of students in planning and execution of Sports Day?

4.9 Conduct Fitness Sessions

When you play a sport, you want to do the best you can. Training improves your fitness, thereby your performance. The basic components of physical fitness such as endurance, strength, speed, and flexibility can be developed through different training methods that are briefly described here. Training is important for a number of reasons. Some of these reasons are as follows:

(i) It increases cardiovascular capacity.

(ii) It helps your body in converting more fat to energy.

(iii) It strengthens your muscles, making them more tolerant to the stresses caused by prolonged exertion.

(iv) It strengthens the connective tissue (tendons and ligaments).

(v) It can be fine-tuned to your specific sport which will help you improve your performance rapidly.

4.9.1 Aerobic and Anaerobic Capacity

Warm-Up

Duration: 5-10 minutes.

Activities: Light cardio (jogging, jumping jacks) and dynamic stretches to prepare the body.

Aerobic Segment

Duration: 20-30 minutes.

Activities:

Steady-State Cardio: Activities like running, cycling, or swimming at a consistent pace.

Interval Training: Alternating periods of high-intensity activity (e.g., sprinting) with low-intensity recovery (e.g., walking).

Instruction and Demonstration: Clearly explain and demonstrate aerobic exercises, emphasising proper form and breathing techniques.

Monitoring and Feedback: Observe participants and provide feedback to ensure safety and effectiveness.

Fig. 4.16: Aerobic

1. Anaerobic Segment

Duration: 15-20 minutes.

Strength Training: Exercises like squats, lunges, push-ups, and weightlifting.

High-Intensity Interval Training (HIIT): Short bursts of intense activity (e.g., burpees, sprints) followed by brief rest periods.

Instruction and Demonstration: Clearly explain and demonstrate anaerobic exercises, emphasising proper form to prevent injury.

Monitoring and Feedback: Observe participants and provide feedback to ensure they maintain correct form and intensity.

2. Cool-Down

Duration: 5-10 minutes.

Activities:

Light Cardio: Gradually reducing intensity (e.g., slow jogging, walking).

Static Stretching: Targeting major muscle groups to improve flexibility and aid recovery.

Fig. 4.17: Jump

Conduct the following activities to raise the fitness levels of students.

ACTIVITIES

Activity 1. Strength

Aim:

To improve cardiovascular endurance, overall stamina, and the ability to sustain prolonged physical activity.

Procedure:

Planning and Setup

Duration: 30-40 minutes.

Stations: Set up 5-6 stations with different aerobic exercises (e.g., jumping jacks, high knees, burpees, mountain climbing, skipping rope, and jogging in place).

Equipment: Mats, skipping ropes, cones for marking stations.

Warm-Up (5-10 minutes)

Light jogging or walking.

Dynamic stretches (e.g., arm circles, leg swings).

Circuit Training (20-25 minutes)

Instructions: Explain each station's exercise and demonstrate the correct form.

Activity: Students spend 1-2 minutes at each station performing the exercise at moderate to high intensity.

Rotation: After each interval, students rest for 30 seconds before moving to the next station.

Supervision: Monitor students, offering them feedback and encouragement.

Cool-Down (5-10 minutes)

Slow walking to lower heart rate.

Static stretches focusing on major muscle groups (e.g., hamstrings, quadriceps, calves).

Fig. 4.18: Crossfit

Activity 2

Muscular Strength Activity: Bodyweight Exercises

Aim:

To build muscular strength, and endurance, and improve the overall body composition.

Procedure:

Planning and Setup

Duration: 30-40 minutes.

Exercises: Select 5-6 bodyweight exercises (e.g., push-ups, squats, lunges, planks, tricep dips, and sit-ups).

Equipment: Mats for floor exercises, a stable surface for tricep dips.

Warm-Up (5-10 minutes)

Light jogging or walking.

Dynamic stretches (e.g., arm swings, hip circles).

Strength Training (20-25 minutes)

Instructions: Demonstrate each exercise, highlighting proper form and technique.

Activity: Students perform each exercise for 30-60 seconds, followed by a 30-second rest.

Sets: Complete 2-3 sets of each exercise.

Supervision: Monitor the form and provide corrections to prevent injury.

Cool-Down (5-10 minutes)

Slow walking to lower heart rate.

Static stretches focusing on the muscles used during the workout (e.g., chest stretch, quadriceps stretch).

Fig. 4.19: Muscular Activity

Procedure:

1. **Planning and Setup**
   - **Duration:** 30-40 minutes.
   - **Exercises:** Select a series of yoga poses and static stretches (e.g., downward dog, child's pose, seated forward bend, butterfly stretch).
   - **Equipment:** Mats for comfort.
2. **Warm-Up (5-10 minutes)**
   - Gentle movements (e.g., walking in place, arm circles).
   - Light dynamic stretches.
3. **Yoga and Stretching (20-25 minutes)**
   - **Instructions:** Demonstrate each pose and stretch, explaining proper alignment and breathing techniques.
   - **Activity:** Guide students through a sequence of poses and stretches, holding each for 15-30 seconds.
   - **Supervision:** Ensure that the students are performing the movements safely and comfortably.
4. **Cool-Down (5-10 minutes)**
   - Guided relaxation or meditation to promote mental relaxation.
   - Deep breathing exercises.

ACTIVITY 3

(a) Game: Capture the Flag

Aim:

To promote teamwork, strategy, physical activity, and fun among participants.

Procedure:

1. **Planning and Setup**

   Duration: 30-60 minutes.

   Participants: Ideally 10-20 players, divided into two teams.

   Equipment: Two flags (or objects to serve as flags), cones or markers to define boundaries.

   Location: Large open area, such as a field or gymnasium, with clear boundaries.

2. **Game Setup**

Define Boundaries: Mark the playing field with cones, including a centre line dividing the two territories.

Flag Placement: Place each team's flag in their territory, in a visible but strategic location.

Jail Areas: Designate an area on each side where captured players will be held (the "jail").

3. **Rules Explanation**

Objective: Each team tries to capture the other team's flag and bring it back to their own territory without getting tagged.

Tagging: Players can tag opponents who are in their territory. Tagged players go to the jail and wait to be freed by a teammate.

Freeing Teammates: A player can free a jailed team mate by tagging them, but they must return to their own territory safely.

Winning: The game is won when a team successfully captures the opponent's flag and brings it back to their own side.

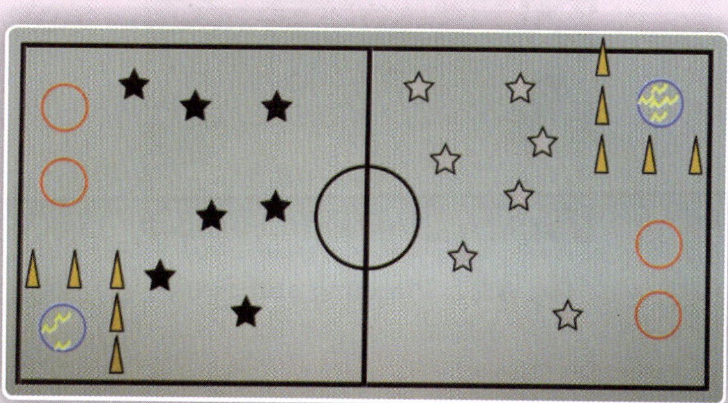

Fig. 4.20: Game Setup

(b) Game : Kickball

Aim:

To promote physical activity, teamwork, coordination, and fun among participants.

Procedure:

1. **Planning and Setup**

Duration: 30-60 minutes.

Participants: Ideally 10-20 players, divided into two teams.

Equipment: Kickball, bases (four markers or cones), and a playing field (similar to a baseball/softball field).

2. **Game Setup**

Field Layout: Set up four bases in a diamond shape, similar to a baseball field.

Team Division: Divide players into two teams. One team starts as the kickers, and the other as the fielders.

3. **Rules Explanation**

Objective: The kicking team tries to score runs by kicking the ball and running around the bases. The fielding team tries to get the kickers out.

Kicking: Players take turns kicking the ball from home plate.

Running: After kicking, the player runs to as many bases as possible without being tagged or having the ball thrown to the base they are running towards.

Getting Out: A kicker is out if the ball is caught in the air, if they are tagged with the ball, or if the ball is thrown to a base before they reach it.

Scoring: A run is scored when a player successfully runs around all bases and returns to home plate.

Fig. 4.21: Planning and Setup

(c) Game : Ultimate Frisbee

Aim:

To promote cardiovascular fitness, teamwork, coordination, and fun among participants.

Procedure:

1. **Planning and Setup**

Duration: 30-60 minutes.

Participants: Ideally 12-20 players, divided into two teams.

Equipment: Frisbee, cones to mark the field and end zones.

2. **Game Setup**

Field Layout: Set up a rectangular field with end zones at each end.

Team Division: Divide players into two teams. One team starts on offense and the other on defense.

3. **Rules Explanation**

Objective: To score points by catching the Frisbee in the opposing team's end zone.

Starting the Play: Teams line up in their end zones. The defence throws (pulls) the Frisbee to the offense to start play.

Movement: Players can't run with the Frisbee; they must pass it to team mates to move it down the field.

Turnovers: Occur if a pass is incomplete, intercepted, or goes out of bounds. The opposing team gains possession of the Frisbee.

Scoring: A point is scored when a player catches the Frisbee in the opposing team's end zone.

Fig. 4.22: Friesbee

4.10 Warm-Up

1. **General Warm-Up (5-10 minutes):**
   - **Light Cardio:** Jogging, skipping, or dynamic walking to increase heart rate.
   - **Joint Mobility:** Gentle rotations of the neck, shoulders, wrists, hips, knees, and ankles.
2. **Dynamic Stretching (5-10 minutes):**
   - **Leg Swings:** Forward and sideways for hip mobility.
   - **Arm Circles:** Small to large circles for shoulder mobility.
   - **Lunges with Twist:** To activate legs and core.
   - **High Knees and Butt Kicks:** For quick lower body activation.
3. **Sport-Specific Warm-Up (10-15 minutes):**
   - **Drills Related to the Sport:** Passing, dribbling, shooting, or basic skill drills.
   - **Partner Drills:** Light passing, rallies, or practice shots.
   - **Reaction Drills:** Quick movements and direction changes.

4. **Mental Preparation (5 minutes):**
   - **Positive Visualization:** Picture yourself performing well.
   - **Breathing Exercises:** Focus on deep, calm breaths to reduce anxiety.
   - **Team Huddle (if team sport):** Encourage, set goals, and build team spirit.

4.10.1 Benefits of Proper Warm-Up:

1. **Increases Blood Flow:**
   - Enhances oxygen supply to muscles, improving performance.
2. **Improves Muscle Flexibility:**
   - Prepares muscles and joints for a full range of motion, reducing stiffness.
3. **Reduces Risk of Injuries:**
   - Minimizes the chance of muscle strains, sprains, and joint injuries.
4. **Enhances Athletic Performance:**
   - Prepares the body for explosive movements, speed, and agility.
5. **Boosts Mental Focus:**
   - Helps athletes clear distractions and focus on the game.
6. **Prepares the Cardiovascular System:**
   - Gradually increases heart rate and breathing, preventing sudden stress.
7. **Enhances Coordination and Balance:**
   - Activates neuromuscular connections for better body control.

ACTIVITY

1. With the help of your teacher, conduct the activities to build fitness

Differentiate Between

1. Warm up and cool down
2. Upper body stretch and lower body stretch

Subjective Questions

1. What are the different types of training to improve strength?
2. Explain what happens when you stretch.